PERFORMATIVE DEMOCRACY

THE YALE CULTURAL SOCIOLOGY SERIES

Jeffrey C. Alexander and Ron Eyerman, Series Editors

PUBLISHED

Triumph and Trauma, by Bernhard Giesen (2004)

Myth, Meaning, and Performance: Toward a New Cultural Sociology of the Arts, edited by Ron Eyerman and Lisa McCormick (2006)

American Society: A Theory of Societal Community, by Talcott Parsons, edited and introduced by Giuseppe Sciortino (2007)

The Easternization of the West, by Colin Campbell (2007)

Culture, Society, and Democracy: The Interpretive Approach, edited by Isaac Reed and Jeffrey C. Alexander (2007)

Changing Men, Transforming Culture: Inside the Men's Movement, by Eric Magnuson (2007)

Do We Need Religion? On the Experience of Self-Transcendence, by Hans Joas (2007)

A Contemporary Introduction to Sociology: Culture and Society in Transition, by Jeffrey C. Alexander and Kenneth Thompson (2008)

Staging Solidarity: Truth and Reconciliation in a New South Africa, by Tanya Goodman (2008)

Inside Jihadism: Understanding Jihadi Movements Worldwide, by Farhad Khosrokhavar (2008)

Meaning and Method: The Cultural Approach to Sociology, edited by Isaac Reed and Jeffrey C. Alexander (2009)

Performative Democracy, by Elzbieta Matynia (2009)

FORTHCOMING

Injustice at Work, by François Dubet

PERFORMATIVE DEMOCRACY

Elzbieta Matynia

Paradigm Publishers

Boulder • London

Copyright © 2009 Paradigm Publishers

Published in the United States by Paradigm Publishers, 3360 Mitchell Lane, Suite E, Boulder, CO 80301 USA.

Paradigm Publishers is the trade name of Birkenkamp & Company, LLC, Dean Birkenkamp, President and Publisher.

Library of Congress Cataloging-in-Publication Data

Matynia, Elzbieta.
  Performative democracy / Elzbieta Matynia.
    p. cm. — (The Yale cultural sociology series)
  Includes bibliographical references and index.
  ISBN 978-1-59451-655-9 (hardcover : alk. paper)
  ISBN 978-1-59451-656-6 (pbk : alk. paper)
    1. Democratization. 2. Democratization—Poland. 3. Democracy. 4. Democracy—Poland. 5. Social change. 6. Social change—Poland. 7. Intercultural communication. I. Title.
  JC489.M38 2009
  306.2—dc22

                                                           2008031675

Printed and bound in the United States of America on acid-free paper that meets the standards of the American National Standard for Permanence of Paper for Printed Library Materials.

Designed and Typeset by Straight Creek Bookmakers.

13 12 11 10 09   1 2 3 4 5

Contents

Acknowledgments

I am a very fortunate person, as there are many generous and affectionate people in my life—not just parents and friends, but teachers, mentors, and colleagues both here and abroad, including Poland—and, of course, my own American/Polish family. They have all helped me to grow, and to understand—and more importantly, to engage in—the world around me, both when that world was changing and later, when I changed the place from which I was trying to understand the world. I am also very lucky to have experienced moments in my life worthy of several kitschy novels that could easily outsell any of my academic prose.

It took a long time for me to make up my mind to start writing this book. It took developments in both my old country and my new one in the first decade of the new century to get me to sit down and write. When I think about it now, I realize that the entire project is the result of a truly bicontinental nurturing, as I owe it to certain people who, though divided by space, provided me at various times with a strongly supportive virtual community: they were and are my touchstones.

They are Jerzy Szacki, my first mentor at Warsaw University, and Ira Katznelson, my first dean at the New School for Social Research, both of whom I asked to look at early bits of the manuscript and who gave me invaluable criticism and suggestions. There is Shlomo Avineri in Jerusalem and Monroe Price at the Cardozo School of Law next door to the New School—two individuals who helped me to think about the possibility of building bridges between the political imagination that had emerged in Central and Eastern Europe and developments beyond the region. There are the many women professors and colleagues dedicated to the cause of academic and political freedom, from Aldona Jawlowska, who inspired me in the 1980s, to Arien Mack, editor in chief of *Social Research,* who believed in me when I met her a decade later, and from whom I have learned so much. There was the brilliant Polish cultural critic Konstanty Puzyna, who would have loved the idea of democratic performativity, and

Jonathan Fanton, then president of the New School for Social Research, whose commitment to the idea of human rights in the region I come from brought new life to the agenda of our university and turned the idea of the university as a civil society into reality.

And, of course, there are friends, whether academics or those who call themselves "practitioners of ideas," who combine both vocations, like my first American friends, Jeffrey Goldfarb and his family, who helped me become a dedicated New Yorker and an American academic—Jeff having instigated my first fellowship at the New School, a trusted colleague with whom I can always share my projects and aspirations. Like Jonathan Schell, whose own writing and the attention he paid to my manuscript gave me courage when I needed it. And Judith Friedlander, whose continuous encouragement and the offer of a secluded office space helped me to sit down and write the main body of the text.

There are my South African friends and colleagues from whom I learned to transcend my parochial—whether American or Polish—attachments: above all, the feminist scholar Shireen Hassim and economist Stephen Gelb. At the New School, Richard Bernstein and Agnes Heller, two philosophers who have kept the New School's legacy of Hannah Arendt very much alive, have afforded fertile ground for people like me. And those New School colleagues without whom it would not be possible to imagine, much less implement, the summer institutes we conduct in Krakow and Cape Town, where we learn about local performative strategies, and how it is to "walk in other people's shoes": Ari Zolberg, Vera Zolberg, Ann Snitow, Jan Gross, Jonathan Veitch, David Plotke, Will Millberg, Jim Miller, Jose Casanova, Andrew Arato, and, of course, Jeff Goldfarb.

My friends and colleagues from the so-called region helped me to understand the early processes of democratic transformation taking place there: Martin and Zora Butora, Jan Urban, Alena Miltova, Ivan Vejvoda, Sonja Licht, Renata Salecl, Martin Palous, Janos Kis, Miklos Haraszti, Gyorgii Csepeli, Vladimir Tismaneanu, Andrei Marga, Anatolii Tikholaz, Yaroslav Hrytsak, Alex Grigorievs, Rumiana Kolarova, Dobrin Kanev, Dimitrina Petrova, Claus Offe, Ulrich Preuss, Gesine Schwan, Sigrid Meuschel, Adam Michnik, Marcin Krol, Edmund Mokrzycki, Jerzy Axer, Pawel Spiewak, Ewa Letowska, Jerzy Warman, Jacek Purchla, Tomasz Kitlinski, Pawel Leszkowicz, Agnieszka Graff, Jan Jozef Szczepanski, Jacek Wozniakowski, and the late Galina Starovoitova.

There are workers, dissidents, poets, printers, theater people, women activists, women artists—and many, many students to thank. Some I have inevitably overlooked but treasure nonetheless.

And finally, I want to give credit to some people who helped me in very special ways throughout the process of writing this book: an amazing person and scholar who has inspired many, an intellectual leader, a true performativist, and a person who makes things happen, Irena Grudzinska

Gross; my lifelong friend, Romek Stachyra; and my long-suffering husband, Dick Adams, whose ear for English is as well-honed as his patience.
I thank you all.

Elzbieta Matynia

I

Invitation to Performative Democracy

Quintus Ennius tria corda habere sese dicebat, quod loqui Graece et Osce et Latine sciret.

—*Gellius (17.17.1)*

"Where are you from? Holland? ... Oh, you're from Poland. So how do you like it here?"

It was late summer in 1981. I had just arrived in New York on a scholarship at the New School for Social Research, with the precious passport I had received thanks to the recently liberalized policies during Poland's Solidarity period. From the tone of that last question I could sense what kind of answer was anticipated. And I quickly began to feel a bit guilty that the city did not put me, a poor visitor from behind the Iron Curtain, into a state of awe, that my initial experiences were not as breathtaking as one would have expected, and that—perhaps—I was not appreciative enough of this amazing opportunity I had been given. Perhaps it was the late August torpor of a half-empty city and the fact that my English was minimal at best. Or perhaps I was still so absorbed in my life in Poland that I could not fully appreciate the cosmopolitan energy of New York, which would later turn me into an utter devotee.

Still, although I had arrived from a land of eerily empty shops, I could not avoid the feeling that I had just left the most exciting place on earth. Leaving Poland in order to broaden my scholarly understanding of sociology, I had reluctantly left behind the most marvelous dream come true, more thrilling even than a ticket to the U.S.A. New York's soaring buildings, magnificent museums, stores with everything you could imagine—none of

1

this could impress me at that time. For I had come from a place in which a once-excluded and silenced people had found the courage to talk to each other, through what sometimes felt like endless discussion, and had begun to rebuild their lives together on the principles of self-respect, dialogue, and the shared responsibility of all.

How in the world to convey to Americans—lucidly and without sounding naïve—the extraordinary kind of happiness that I had experienced day after day, and that I saw everywhere in Poland, and now missed? Is it even possible at all to communicate what that kind of *public happiness* is? Somehow the whole experience would not fit into existing molds. It eluded our own ways of knowing things. How to convey the minute discoveries, the details of otherwise big and tense events, the moments of transformative power not easily grasped when one is reporting events, facts, numbers? How to convey the overwhelming sense of friendliness, and the larger than ever context of friendship that one began to live in?

Imagine long late-night meetings, in a factory or at the university, often night after night, and picture everyone exhilarated. So exhilarated that we kept on talking at home, once those meetings were over, comparing notes on our discussions and on extraordinary people whom we would otherwise never have met, since we hadn't even known such people existed. It still surprises outsiders to learn that beneath the veneer of socialist equality, and apart from the better-known division between those who belonged to the Party and those who did not, the Communist state had carefully maintained mechanisms that further divided and separated people. So that in these late-night meetings, still incredulous and a little anxious, we were reintroducing ourselves to each other—and on our own terms. This was a huge discovery: that we could do it without any powerful facilitator, on our own; and, most startling of all, that even while speaking publicly we were still in charge of our own speech.

I was at one meeting where workers invited poets because they wanted to hear the forbidden poems and to discuss with them how censorship worked, and how one could circumvent it. I attended discussions in which students and workers tried to figure out why twelve years earlier the workers—marshaled by the state—had condemned the students' demands for freedom of speech.

So we were all there together, and we asked questions, and we learned from each other and began to think on our own, form our own organizations, and write our own statutes. We took pains to make sure that the procedures we were planning would be transparent and thus would make Poland more like any other "normal country." And the next day we read in our homemade bulletins and newsletters about the arrangements we had just agreed upon, and what others had agreed upon in other parts of the country. What a perfect mechanism for disseminating reliable information—and getting almost instant feedback! We argued for hours, and then we voted and elected people whom we recognized as the best among us. This really was self-governance, we realized. But we still could not believe that we were actually able to talk about things in public, and to publish it, and that all of this was really happening. Yet it really was. We felt that we had begun to count—in fact, to be. It was an amazing feeling.

"And the most fascinating thing," observed Seweryn Blumsztajn, one of the leaders of the Solidarity movement—recalling this extraordinary reemergence of self-respect and dignity during the sixteen months of the union's legal existence—*"was to see how people's backs straightened up."*[1]

I believe now that the reappropriation of language by the people and exercising freely the new nonmandatory speech were at the very heart of what was happening in 1980–1981. But in the rush by outside observers to cover the news—the protest strikes, marches, negotiations, Soviet troop movements—this verbal dimension of our experience was simply too subtle, too personal, too invisible, to be captured by the press, much less by television. The foreign language media especially were not a good vehicle for conveying or even grasping processes that were so deeply anchored in language, speech, and words. When translated, the impact of their native freshness was lost, and the subtle but significant differences between the old and the new use of language eluded reporters and political analysts. I myself realized only much later that this was a major reason for the difficulty in describing and explaining those times.

And so there I was in New York, wondering how to get across to friendly Americans the things that had been taking place back home for more than a year, things that were not part of the picture painted by American newspapers and television. It was not easy to miss the assumption, present in the voices of almost everyone I met during my first months here, that most of us arriving at JFK Airport had come with the intention of staying here forever. Why wouldn't we? Well (and I tried not to sound arrogant), because some of us, no matter how desolate our home might seem to any Westerner, felt we had just left a time and place of truly tangible hope.

Four months later martial law was declared in Poland ("in the vital interest of the state and the nation"), Solidarity was outlawed, thousands of people were arrested and sent to internment camps, tanks entered the streets, and I was stranded in New York—temporarily, I hoped.

In Poland all the energies of the military regime went into tearing down the newly created independent public sphere—into destroying above all the very channels of social communication that had been the greatest source of society's power. No mail, no phone connections within or out of the country, no intercity travel, no public gatherings.... Armored vehicles controlled the streets, emptied by an early curfew. For the people there, the declaration of "a state of war" (as the decree introducing the state of exception, or martial law, was officially called by the government), the use of sheer force against its own citizens, utterly exposed and delegitimized the system. But for the outside world, it only further obscured from view the creative ways in which the democratic project had been pursued there.

Before there was even time for the West to absorb what had been happening, the imposition of martial law prompted a quick paint job: the new language that had entered public life in Poland, so meticulously stripped by the people of any ideological coloring, was painted over with the familiar thick layer of cold war rhetoric. Now the Polish movement conveniently remained in the familiar mold, easily explained as just another anti-Soviet uprising crushed by force. Though books were written and films were made, the images of tanks and militarized police supplanted those of backs straightening up, and soon the attention of a sympathetic American public moved on. An opportunity was lost.

Still, a number of Western scholars continued to struggle with what had happened in Central Europe, and it was they who were the first to give it the name "civil society." This phrase promptly moved beyond academia, entered the larger public discourse, and soon, embraced by American policymakers, assumed a conveniently generic life of its own, as if it represented a universally democracy-enhancing tool. Though not exactly a "paint job," vague references to "civil society" paradoxically obscured the more specific, vital stories of real people and their distinctive ways of changing an oppressive state.

Most people in the United States also failed to appreciate that, although forced underground by the military coup, these very determined and committed people refused to resort to violence, focusing instead on ingenious ways of sustaining the banned media, the flying universities, semiclandestine cultural initiatives, underground publishing houses, and unofficial associations of all kinds. Through the accumulation of such seemingly "small things,"[2] sites where speech could be exercised, the people were able a few years later to make the regime talk with them after all and to agree to a peaceful dismantling of authoritarian rule: without a single tank on the street, without one bullet, without insurgents, and without prisoners.[3]

And yet again, mesmerized by the carnival taking place atop the Berlin wall, most people in America failed to notice that the birth of democracy in the region had been brought about half a year earlier through *talk*—specifically, the Round Table Talks between the regime and civil society. It was neither a miracle nor an accomplishment of foreign powers (no matter how important the influence of Ronald Reagan, Mikhail Gorbachev, or Pope John Paul II) but the gradual, persistent, and inventive work of citizens that led to that giant round table in Warsaw.

Blumsztajn's poetic image of people's backs unbending, the self-propelled movement that revealed how subjects had been transforming themselves into citizens, with heads held high, is one of the most compelling—even literal—expressions of an *uplifting* social experience that we have seen in the recent past.

But is it so compelling to Americans, I wonder, whose very history has evolved as a narrative of *uplifting*, entailing a kind of *Yankee ingenuity* in civic matters? Or is it that we Americans (speaking now as a devoted American citizen) have simply become so brashly complacent that we really do not need to know about the ways of others? Are we so impatient—since not all experiences are translatable into our own—that we do not want to bother to understand them on terms that are not ours? And how do we reconcile this with the fact that today's America is increasingly made of people who, like the Roman poet Quintus Ennius, feel at home with two or more languages, have more than one heart, and therefore have at their disposal more than one way of comprehending the world?

As a person who over the past quarter of a century has grown a strong second heart—an American one—I would like to try to bridge the experiences of my two worlds, translating and contextualizing an unfamiliar stock of terms and experiences and thus helping to expand our ways of knowing.

When I ask, "What does it take for people's backs to straighten up?" I am really asking about alternatives to violent solutions and to despair. What—in today's world—are the conditions that generate dignity rather than humiliation, trust rather than suspicion? What are the hopeful alternatives? And what does it take for hopeful alternatives to spring up and take root?

*   *   *

I would like to invite you to visit with me some recent sites and narratives of what I consider this tangible hope, which I feel many in the West failed to fully comprehend at the time. I would like us to look closely at the self-making of democracy, a locally inspired—perhaps for some, even parochial—project, that I call here *performative democracy.* In this project local people talking to each other in public illuminate the reality around them and help to find ways of changing it. Activated by a newly arisen public realm, performative democracy creates the conditions for engaged conversation, negotiation, and ways of finding the middle ground—often startlingly new experiences in the lives of those involved. Though it is not just another name for *direct democracy,* it does indeed reduce the distance between elected representatives and the people, and brings the people themselves closer together, thriving as it does on a rich practice of face-to-face meetings and ceaseless discussions. These launch a process of learning, forming opinions, reasoning, and appreciating the value of compromise, and this is indeed transformative for those who take part.

Although performative democracy is hard to operationalize, one can observe instances of it in concrete situations and processes having to do with the forms and genres of speech, broadly understood, that constitute public action and bring about change. I must emphasize that I see it as a practice arising from a strong sense of being *born free and equal in dignity and rights* and of acting *toward one another in a spirit of brotherhood*—a sense that is so well captured in the first article of the Universal Declaration of Human Rights. At the same time, it is a dimension of democratic practice that—although exercised through the conduct of reasonable citizens—is not alien to emotions, as it can be surprisingly warm-spirited, which it certainly was in the case of the Poles in 1980. With its eye on *publicness,* dialogue, and compromise, performative democracy is not a realm in which insular groups that exploit fear can feel comfortable—or generally those advocating illiberal arrangements. As I hope to show, despite its inherent drama, performative democracy can actually be a joyous and affirmative dimension of the political, yet one that self-limits its passions by necessarily framing them into agreed-upon forms, genres, and conventions.

But this emotional aspect of democratic life is naturally transient, and that is perhaps another reason why it has been overlooked by theorists and critics. A healthy well-functioning democracy may, after all, appear humdrum, colorless, and gray. Yet performative democracy represents a kind of political engagement—critical for any democracy—in which the key identity of its actors is that of citizens, and in which the good of society at large, and not that of a narrow interest group, is at stake. Such an engagement clearly resists the minimal view of democracy as an institutional arrangement for competing interest groups with their eye on the people's votes.

Nevertheless, I would like to emphasize that what I call performative democracy captures only one dimension of democracy and is not in itself "qualified" to substitute for a well-functioning representative democracy with established mechanisms and procedures. Yet it brings out the richer texture of liberal democracy and makes it easier to see the prospects for democratic action in times of crisis: reviving the spirit of democratic polity when the system has become weakened by complacency, for example, or preparing the ground for a democratic order to emerge where there was none before. Exploring the possibilities both for peacefully establishing democracy and for reinfusing a jaded democracy with a heightened sense of public life is my main interest here.

I would like us to see how building democracy depends on prior societal initiatives, ones that are grounded in, and empowered by, local ways of knowing, and performed in the vernacular by local actors. I should add that in our journey there will be an unlikely couple hovering over my shoulder, two philosophers of dialogue, emancipation, and carnival, people with more than one heart, magnificent bridge-builders who experienced the darkest of times and who have helped me in thinking about this project— Hannah Arendt and Mikhail Bakhtin.

WHAT IS PERFORMATIVITY?

The concept of performativity is usually associated with J. L. Austin's set of lectures on language, in which he discusses sentences that do not just describe reality or state facts but have the quality of enacting what they actually say. "There is something which is at the moment of uttering being done by the person uttering," and such a "speech act" has more than just a meaning, as it has, above all, an effect, as Austin explains.[4] Recognizing the importance of speech in the constitution of democracy, and the prerequisite of freedom of speech in the functioning of democracy, I would like to extend this narrow if not technical understanding of performativity beyond linguistics[5] and insert into it the more textured social dimension of speech.

In the case of societies living under dictatorship, the conditions for performativity first occur when the long unused, action-oriented word transcends the private realm, when it comes out from hiding, squeezing itself out through the cracks into the open. And when it is first heard, it instigates the emergence of an undeniably *public* realm. Hannah Arendt most eloquently evoked what I mean by performativity when she said, "No other human performance requires speech to the same extent as action does."[6]

Her key condition for the constitution of a public sphere is a "space of appearance," that is, any public setting where people can come together and interact through speech. Such space was furnished for the early Solidarity gatherings by factories, universities, churches, and even state enterprises. It was there that the anonymous, impersonal, and "institutional" way of speaking was replaced by concrete, individual, and distinctive voices. Such voices, or speech acts, are the opposite of violence, "which is to act without argument or speech and without reckoning with consequences."[7]

Such was the voice of Nelson Mandela, newly released from prison, who after the assassination of his younger friend, Chris Hani, the popular antiapartheid leader, spoke to thousands of enraged people at a football stadium, stopping the imminent violence and salvaging the talks on the dismantling of apartheid: "We are a nation in mourning. Our pain and anger are real. Yet we must not permit ourselves to be provoked by those who seek to deny us the very freedom Chris Hani gave his life for."[8]

Such was the voice of Adam Michnik, Polish dissident and frequent political prisoner, who stopped an angry mob from burning a police station in which a pair of policemen known for their brutality were locked inside. With only his name—not his face—known to the larger audience, he said: "My name is Adam Michnik, and I am an enemy of the system." The crowd calmed down almost immediately. Confrontation with a regime that was looking for any good excuse to outlaw Solidarity was again avoided. Performative speech, filled with a sense of caring responsibility—what a genre of hope!

This performative dimension of democracy had already manifested itself earlier, in Spain in the 1970s; it came to Poland in the 1980s and to South Africa in the 1990s. The three authoritarian regimes were very different from each other, as were their respective histories and the strategies with which they were resisted by the citizenry. What they had in common was that their citizens challenged and peacefully changed their oppressive regimes, disassembled the immensely concentrated power structures, and launched a process of democratization. Deeply rooted in distinct and diverse sociocultural sites, performative democracy is thus neither a theoretical model, a political ideal, nor a tested system of governance, but a locally conditioned process of enacting democracy in politically varied contexts. And though it assumes an array of forms and is expressed through various idioms, when it occurs under the conditions of authoritarian rule, it usually reflects its actors' basic sense of democratic ideals and of their belief that there are indeed places—"normal countries"—where civil rights are observed, and where democracy is actually implemented and practiced. And one should not dismiss the power for such people of the image of a normal country.

The foundations for hope and a democracy-oriented performative strategy for the societies of Central Europe had already been laid out in the 1970s in three key essays written by authors from the region only a few years apart from each other: *Hope and Hopelessness,* by a Polish philosopher living in exile, Leszek Kolakowski; *The New Evolutionism,* by a young unemployed historian from Warsaw, Adam Michnik; and *The Power of the Powerless,* by a playwright from Prague whose plays were not allowed to be produced there, Vaclav Havel.[9] Their program for change abandoned the path of revolution that had been cherished by progressive thinkers for more than a century. That universal path—the violent overthrow of the power structure—though costly, was still an attractive one in many corners of the world, as it promised swift, fundamental change, a cleansing of the past, and a fresh start. That was not true in my part of the world, in which revolutions had brought the experience of civil wars, loss of lives, loss of cultural capital, and for many not just loss of the past but also the loss of the future. The insights of our three performativists were all well grounded in a domestic canon of cultural references, informed by local conditions, microhistories, and political experiences. Exposing the contradictions of the existing system at the level of language—with its broken contracts and promises, and overt and hidden discourses—the dissident authors showed that those could be exploited in the contest with the regime without recourse to violence.

Kolakowski, Michnik, and Havel asked not to expect miracles, quick fixes, help from outside, or any automatic self-correction of the authoritarian system. Instead they made a case for small, incremental changes. These could be advanced in two ways: by revealing—if possible, to the larger public—the contradictions, ambiguities, ineptness, and absurdities within the system itself; and by bringing into play the human rights instruments provided by the international agreements that had already been signed in the mid-1970s in Helsinki by most of the Communist states. Kolakowski's argument that the rigidity of the system depends partly on the degree to which people living under it are convinced of its rigidity and Michnik's well-known advisory that one should behave as though one lives in a "normal" country were brilliantly elaborated six years later by Havel in his tale of the greengrocer as an unaware accessory of a dominant power built on a combination of conformity and deception. When living with truth is repressed—as Havel might have said—*performativity* is repressed. A careful reading of the three thinkers reveals that the instruments for change are anchored in public *speech acts,* whether they turn out to be a theater performance, an open letter by a group of citizens like Charter 77, a poem circulated outside of state censorship, or the demands written on cardboard and displayed by the striking workers at the gate of the Gdansk shipyard.

Although any democratic process, in order to be called democratic, has to observe certain minimal procedures, at the core of performative democracy are, above all, people whose backs have straightened up, the local citizen/actors,[10] whose main role—importantly—neither begins nor ends in the election booth. Their ever more public interplay with the ruling bodies—testing the latter's legitimacy and performance, inventing new institutions and practices, and introducing alternatives—provides the processes with content and meaning, and endows the actors with agency.

Performative democracy, very much like the carnival studied by Mikhail Bakhtin, is a temporary phenomenon. And even though it evolves in real time, not in the a priori carnival-restricted time frame of an annual ritual, necessarily followed by a time of lent, it does not last. In its most glorious instances it constitutes a site of both joyous and subversive experience in the carnivalesque public square where fear and suffering are, as Bakhtin would have said, degraded. Although performative democracy cannot be easily institutionalized, it leaves behind a vital legacy: just like carnival, it happens, and when it happens, it releases a robust civic creativity, prepares conditions for backs to straighten up—and this is an achievement of lasting value. I would like to argue that this particular dimension of political life can occur in both nondemocratic and democratic contexts. In the case of the former, it usually constitutes the early stages of a democratic project; in the case of the latter, it supplies strategies to keep democracy vibrant and helps it to survive a season of democratic lent.

The terms *carnival* and *lent* are not introduced here for their religious connotation, nor are they meant to suggest any chronological regularity in the life of a democracy. Rather, they are used as metaphors that capture both democracy's potential and its vulnerability—fertility, imagination, and generosity on the one hand, intellectual poverty, complacency, and abuse on the other. And what I call lent does not necessarily follow on the heels of the carnival. What makes the two categories interesting for us is their opposite relationships to human agency. Whereas carnival, as discussed by Bakhtin, is the explosion of human ingenuity, "a time for working new interrelations between individuals" and a place "where new social forms are created,"[11] lent works toward reducing or eradicating this aspect altogether. Carnival is a time when human agency is being encouraged and rewarded; in contrast, the time of lent, with its reminder that "you are nothing but dust, and to dust shall you return," is encouraging and rewarding the opposite.

* * *

The instances of performative democracy that we are about to visit are the perfect reverse of the kinds of oxymoronic democracy that we have been seeing recently—imported or imposed from the outside, along with their key benchmark, free and fair elections that could legitimately bring to power nondemocratic regimes. These instances—if reflected upon—should serve as a cautionary reminder for democratic missionaries, but also for the citizens of any democracy that has become taken for granted and relies increasingly on experts, electoral campaign managers, bureaucrats, and money. The performative democracy that I shall discuss here is the life experience and imagination that local people bring to the system.[12] And this micropolitical facet of modern politics, especially critical for the birth of democracy but also important for an established democracy to thrive, should not be ignored by political thinkers or policymakers, whether domestically or in their foreign agendas. The transition to a meaningful and enduring democracy, never an easy project, has the best chance to succeed if it is initiated and owned by the local people and takes into account their voices, imbued as they are with their respective histories, cultures, and economies.

The invitation I am extending here is to revisit this elusive dimension of democracy with all its humanity, its drama, its brilliant inspiring moments, its indispensable improvisational mode, and its imaginative solutions. As I describe manifestations of performative democracy I would like to convince the reader that it ought to assume its legitimate place in our thinking about democracy today. There is a readily discernible trajectory in my narrative of various instances of this dimension of democracy, as I discuss its gradual emergence. At its hub is the development of civic *publicness* and agency in various forms, idioms, and occurrences.

I thus begin by discussing the *performative* potential of theater—though not conventional professional theater, as I am focusing on the successful but inadequately studied community of experimental theaters, or the Young Theater movement in the Poland of the early 1970s, still under Communist rule. In Chapter 2 ("Staging Freedom") I show the initial recovery of an embryonic public sphere as it occurred in this Young Theater movement, where private voices appeared in public and became social ones. I show how this contributed to a gradual loosening of the constraints of the system and how it initiated into democratic thinking a whole generation of young intelligentsia.

The systemic constraints were finally broken down by the Gdansk workers, and a fully public sphere opened up, facilitating an unprecedented degree of citizen participation and providing a forum for responsible discourse devoted to public causes. The emergence of Solidarity, a masterwork of performative democracy, that peculiar nationwide union of trade unions whose legal existence was negotiated between the Gdansk shipyard workers and the Communist government in Poland, is presented in Chapter 3, "The Public Matter." I bring in numerous voices demonstrating the new civic competence acquired and brilliantly promulgated by the workers, and I argue that in order for the word to acquire performative qualities, it has to be permeated with a sense of authenticity that reflects the vital experience of the public. Such was a famous speech delivered by the strike leader, Lech Walesa, at the gate of the Gdansk shipyards announcing the signing of accords with the regime, a speech that is one of the century's most emblematic displays of performative democracy.

My next step in exploring the performative dimension of democracy is to turn in Chapter 4 to the work of a consummate thinker of action, an activist of thought, and above all a mastermind of performative democracy, Adam Michnik. But Citizen Michnik the strategist and thinker is also a seductive performer, a dream come true for any carnival, the perfect jester-king, spontaneous, moving, courageous, controversial, and bold. The performativity of his writings (many of them not translated into English) and his actions is that of both an instigator of new civic knowledge and a *spiritus movens* of a democracy in the making. His essays, geared to producing results, are examples of what Austin, the theorist of performativity, would call *classic perlocutionary acts*. And indeed they became key to the preparing, staging, and producing of the momentous actions that brought about sweeping political change, a peaceful transformation of dictatorship into democracy.

As with any speech act, the prerequisite for any performative act is that it be a rule-governed, agreed-upon conventional act. Its conventionality has to be carefully balanced with its inventiveness and novelty. I am proposing to illuminate the process of constructing what paradoxically could be called a *new convention* and examine the *round table* as a political genre that, by taking dialogue seriously, facilitates peaceful political change. In Chapter 5, "Furnishing Democracy," I reconstruct the theatrics of negotiated settlements at the two separate round tables that brought an end to communism in Poland and to apartheid in South Africa. I show how in both cases this was accomplished by providing a space of appearance, by authorizing and legitimizing the actors, by necessitating the drafting of a script, by establishing the rules of negotiations, and by foreseeing the need for a contingency infrastructure in which any lack of agreement could be dealt with. In such a situation the agreement expected to be produced at the round table represents far more than what it actually states. The round table itself, as a conventional act, becomes a political genre, an idiom of political compromise, which is both a site of, and a powerful instrument for, the release of performativity. In both places, Poland and South Africa, it established the grounds for the new order and marked the beginning of the long, tedious, and less thrilling process of building the new—in Michnik's words—"gray democracy." This is everyday democracy, neither from the time of carnival nor from that of lent—an ideal that is daily translated into practice through those mechanisms for settling preferences in public matters that are furnished by the procedures of representative democracy.

Yet even gray, well-established democracies, with all their infra-structure, tools, well-weathered practices, and widespread democratic dispositions, are often put to the test. A season of democratic lent, with its vulnerability to illiberal arrangements, does not come along only in recently consolidated democracies but periodically reappears in the old democracies as well. Even though democratic institutions may still be in place and democratic procedures are still observed, when civic agency is ignored, public scrutiny resisted, imagination postponed, dialogicality marginalized, and diversity abhorred—that means a season of lent has set in. Americans experienced such an anxious time of lent—to mention only one—during the McCarthy period in the middle of the twentieth century. It is in such times that the status of speech is altered: what was protected speech becomes unprotected action, and what was protected silence becomes mandatory speech.[13] The word loses its dialogical and discursive dimension, the space of its potential appearance is shrunken or gone, and the conditions for democratic performativity, with its eye on public debate and on reaching a consensus, are destroyed. The hegemonic—or what Bakhtin calls authoritative—word, as found in a demagogic and uncontested speech, seems to retain its performative qualities, as it is often used with a back-drop of fear, the legislative power granted to the executive (e.g., martial law decree), and embellished by the regalia of military/police might. It is also in such times that the noninstitutionalized, performative dimension of democracy, with its citizen-actors, may be most urgently needed to "reset" the system by injecting fresh voices, bringing a pluralism of opinion back to center stage, restoring the system's lively dialogical potential, and opening up space for democratic debate.

My final considerations of performativity are set in a period of lent that coincided with the new democratic Poland's admission to the European Union. Though the main roles in the theater of political life, whether democratic or not, are typically played by men, it is striking how womanless the newly established democratic order in Central Europe is. I discuss here the important legacy of performative democracy employed by feminists in Poland's second decade of democracy. In the two final chapters, I consider women in their leading roles, whether the newly emerged drama is focused on women's issues—more specifically on reclaiming their public position in the newly established democratic polity (Chapter 6, "Provincializing Global Feminism")—or on political culture in general, as in the astonishing battle fought by women artists to save and sustain a barely reestablished pluralistic public sphere (Chapter 7, "EnGendering Democracy"). In a period of lent this is hardly a spontaneous or carnivalistic mode of politics, but one that reveals a lesson learned, with a reasoned, strategic performativity aimed at reaching concrete goals. This last instance investigates the "enGendering" (in both senses of that word) of public discourse—the key principle of democratic politics. I argue that the very language of installations—the language employed by many of the local conceptual artists—displays performative features and facilitates direct engagement and dialogue with the public, the media, political and cultural organizations, and finally with the past.

Just like the Young Theater movement that created the conditions, even if limited, for public discourse in predemocratic Poland, conceptual art now watches over institutionalized democracy, making sure that the societal drama over rights and priorities is actually being performed in public and not just being controlled and operated from backstage. Speech and action are not only attributes of freedom, as Arendt says, but key sources of individual dignity and of societal hope, as they contribute to the sense of a polity in which people and their different voices matter in both making and maintaining it.

Those sites and junctures of performativity that we are about to explore demonstrate the realistic prospects for those of us who are interested in infusing an undemocratic environment with some democratic qualities; in transforming an authoritarian context into a democratic one; or in enhancing—or even just sustaining—an established democratic culture. I would like to think that this is not only a real alternative to tanks and bullets but also a kind of force that can help people's backs straighten up.

In the brief "Postscriptum on an Old Bridge," I shift attention from *speech*—as facilitator of democratic performativity—to a certain kind of *space* that could prepare the ground for such speech. It is in such a space, I believe, that anxiety, fear, and distrust in facing "the other" can be negotiated, tensions eased, fences mended, and perhaps even friendships launched. I have often wondered—as someone trying to create such spaces through various "transregional" projects I designed at my university—why it is that contemporary thought is so surprisingly lacking in reflection on how diverse peoples, cultures, or civilizations could actually get along with each other and learn how to grow together. Why is it that in these times visions and patterns of destruction are always given more consideration than visions and patterns of construction? Although understandable—though not easily defensible—in the world of politics and politicians, this absence in the works of philosophers, or intellectuals in general, is disturbing. There are, of course, some exceptions, Michnik and Havel being very eminent ones; but more often than not, we are left with anecdotal evidence, or partial narratives that do not necessarily add up to a lesson, or a model. In a time of such a drought one may turn for help to the arts or to literature. Some time ago I was struck by the image of a bridge in Ivo Andric's novel *The Bridge on the Drina*. This very special bridge was envisioned by a fourteenth-century builder not just as a span for crossing the river but also—with his addition of an extra space in the middle—as a place for meeting the other. This bridge's social, cultural, and political power lies in that extra space, the *kapia,* with its terraces and "sofas" on either side that can accommodate conversations, get-togethers, or the savoring of Turkish coffee by those who most frequently used the bridge: Muslim Bosnians and Turks, Orthodox Christian Serbs, and, later on, Catholic Croats and Jews.

I am suggesting that we be alert to such *kapias,* locally conceived spaces and practices in the world around us; that we try to identify them and learn from them, for these spaces and practices make it possible for people to build trust and disarm resentments. They can be found in many different parts of the world, from Ireland, India, and Iran to Burma, Cuba, and Rwanda.

Finally, I hope that we can start putting greater stock in local knowledge as a source for new arrangements and practices that can address matters that so sharply divide communities and societies today.

2

Staging Freedom

> Theatre is the only art whose sole subject is man in his relations to others.... This is why theatre is political art par excellence.
>
> —*Hannah Arendt*

Two years before the expression *Velvet Revolution* captured the imagination of the world as it watched the peaceful dismantling of communism in the Soviet bloc, Miklos Haraszti, a young Hungarian dissident, published in English a book called *The Velvet Prison*.[1] Published more than three decades after the classic *Captive Mind,* by Czeslaw Milosz, Haraszti's book discussed some of the new, more sophisticated, and—since they appeared more subject to negotiation—less absolute forms of control over art and artists under real socialism.

By the time Haraszti was writing his book, in the mid-1980s, every society in Communist Central Europe had endured—at least once—a traumatic onslaught on its prodemocratic aspirations or valiant efforts to reform the system.[2] And although from the late 1970s on there had already been no artists in the region or even hardly a Party leader who still had confidence in the merits of the Communist project, the party-state was still very much there, with its complete monopoly over all aspects of economic and social life, including all forms of media, and all means of communication, education, dissemination of information, and artistic expression.

Still, as Haraszti convincingly argued, the state's efforts to be more "accommodating" to the artists' need for "aesthetic freedom" led to a situation of "mutual embrace" between artists and censors that became a key principle of how to function in the velvet prison. Haraszti observed that artists had been persuaded that some minor "creative compromises" and "self-corrections" that they themselves introduced to their works would make the censor's intervention virtually unnecessary. "The perfidy of modern totalitarianism lies precisely in the fact that it imperceptibly blurs the difference between the oppressed and the oppressor, by involving the victim in the process of victimization,"[3] wrote the Polish poet and dissident intellectual Stanislaw Baranczak in his review of *The Velvet Prison*. The credibility of his observations is beyond question, as he had himself experienced firsthand the work of the censorship office, his poetry, not allowed in the mid-1970s to be published by any state-run publishing house, appearing only in the form of illegal *samizdat*.

Although I accept Haraszti's analysis and Baranczak's observation, which focus on the state's control over literature and the visual arts, I would like to consider some of the largely overlooked and clearly unanticipated outcomes of the "velvet prison" policy of late communism. I shall examine a specific field of artistic activity, namely theater, which, I believe, took advantage of that cultural policy, and by wrestling with it rather than embracing it, under very tricky circumstances devised a framework that was conducive to expressing, practicing, and disseminating elements of democratic culture. In the absence of any democratic institutions, some small theaters in Prague, Budapest, Krakow, or Warsaw—unlike any other artistic institutions under communism—managed to transcend their own aesthetic and institutional confines and turn themselves into centers of critical thinking, imbued with a spirit of civic responsibility, practicing self-governance, and committed to engagement with the public.

Theater has always been an important social institution in Central Europe, as it was a leading site of the public debates on art and politics that were especially fervent in the 1920s and 1930s. The kind of theater I have in mind, which I will call *Young Theater*[4]—known at times as "experimental theater," "avant-garde theater," "student theater," or "open theater"—emerged across the Soviet Bloc soon after Joseph Stalin's death and sprouted luxuriantly under the benign tag of an "artistic" movement with every political thaw behind the Iron Curtain. In the decade 1970–1980, for the generation of people in their twenties and thirties, born and educated under communism, it was this theater that—in a world of very limited choices—provided space for discussion and for a sense of having a community of one's own choosing. I believe that a closer examination of the activities of the Young Theater movement of the 1970s and 1980s may help us to understand how—under the impossible constraints of a hegemonic rule in which the Party proclaimed that it knew best what was good for the people—the establishment of a public space could nevertheless take root, preparing the way for a breakdown of the structures of domination. Incidentally, my argument may also contribute to the discussion among some Western scholars that assumes the validity of the liberal concept of a division between private and public under communism.

SOCIAL TRANSACTIONS OF LATE COMMUNISM

When Antonin Liehm[5] offered reasons for the relative stability of Communist rule in Eastern Europe, he spoke of a "new social contract" between the Communist power and its subjects: the state was to assure some elementary level of security and welfare while society was to keep quiet and give up any attempts to reform the system of power or to protest against its abuses.

But that contract, above all, was an agreement about command over what Hannah Arendt calls the "spaces of appearance"[6]—that is, an agreement over maintaining control of any potential public realm. Anyone who attempts to account for the presence of what could become a public realm—or to find evidence that bears out the liberal concept of a separation between the public and the private—under real socialism has to come up with many qualifications, amendments, and fine-tuning to make the effort work at all.[7] On the one hand, everything that was state-run—which meant nearly everything, including the economy—was called "public." On the other hand, what is known as the liberal public sphere, the sphere of associational life, of communication, debate, and mediation, was preempted by state institutions designed to eliminate any alternative voices, discussion, or debate. The *public,* then, was replaced by what was a monological *official,* a huge realm of false facades carefully choreographed by the state (a kind of Potemkin village of NGOs). The real distinction that emerged, therefore, was not between public and private but between *official* and *unofficial.* And since the official sphere, with the entire economic sector, was supersized, the unofficial appeared vastly reduced.

But tucked under the wraps of this unofficial realm were elements of both the *private* and the *public* as conceived under the liberal definition—that is, anything from dissident and antiofficial (and therefore necessarily underground) activities that were illegal, to those that were borderline and that, though not official, were marginally tolerated and could, in a limited way, emerge into the open. In Poland, the peculiarity of this "unofficial" world was that in fact it gradually became an enormously swollen private sphere that the state could not, or did not want to, penetrate.

The only *public* that existed under "real socialism" was thus heavily blurred with the *private,* and only with great difficulty and many qualifications, as I suggested, could one recognize in it some elements of Arendt's concept of the public as a "space of appearance" and as "world," that is, something that is not private. But this was exactly the project that the Young Theaters—places, after all, where one speaks and acts—took upon themselves: to reinstate the public sphere, to insert it next to the official, to turn it into a world that is of "persons" rather than just purely personal or private. The intense symbiosis between the actors and their potential public, who were all forced to hide in the private, influenced the emergence of a certain model of engaged personhood, made particularly visible through the activities of the Young Theater.

In the Poland of the 1970s, the timing for those borderline activities seemed to be favorable. Though nobody expected then that the party-state would wither in the foreseeable future, the Polish regime in the midst of an escalating economic crisis began to have serious problems with keeping up its end of the contract.[8] (The ostentatious consumption and blatant privileges of the Party apparatus helped in its further erosion and ultimately led to a renunciation of the contract by the people in August 1980.) Unable to perform by fulfilling the basic material needs of the population and trying to maintain the contractual mode, the regime initiated separate *velvet transactions* with selected social groups involved in the production of symbolic goods, images, narratives, and knowledge.

The basis for the transactions was provided by a simple arithmetic worked out by cultural policy makers at the Central Committee of the Party. The bigger the audience and access to a given form of expression, the tighter the state control over its products; the smaller the public, the bigger the chances for some degree of freedom. One could imagine total cultural production as a large iceberg, its broad bottom being totally submerged, with only its tip sticking out into open air. The extensive bottom of the iceberg that had the biggest audience was radio, TV, and daily newspapers, all under strictest control. Film—as it had a smaller audience—was a bit above it, along with theater and monthly journals. The specialized academic journals, which were published in small numbers of copies, and some small experimental productions, done, for example, by student theater groups and intended for a very limited audience, were near the tip of the iceberg, often reaching the air. The assumption—initially correct—was that the society at large did not have access to it, and that those who did, students and the critical intelligentsia, were not learning anything that they didn't already know. Hence students, along with the extensive layer of recent graduates known as the young intelligentsia, were one of the groups that became a party to this transaction.

Cemented by the traumatic experience of repressions following the student protests in March 1968, and distraught over the massacre and imprisonment of protesting workers in the 1970s, the performers, poets, musicians, visual artists, and cultural critics who articulated the aspirations of their generation found the language of performance and the strategies of theater to be the most pertinent medium of expression for a homegrown counterculture. But to do theater they needed some authorized physical space, and since the only spaces at that time were owned and controlled by the state, state patronage was a prerequisite.

From the point of view of the state, the transaction highlighted a declared principle of cultural pluralism, "inviting" students to develop more freely their creative potential. As the party-state promised to increase financial support for students' cultural initiatives, it was also clear that it reserved the right to keep watch over their expressive productions. The manifestly liberalized policies were intended to mend the growing legitimization gap at home, and it was also hoped—since the best theater groups were traveling to major international festivals with great success— that such policies would have a favorable reception in the West.[9] The legitimization crisis then forced the party-state to develop new strategies of softer control over cultural and especially countercultural production. And it is my belief that in the absence of a real public sphere and of reliable institutional channels through which to learn about more than the economic interests of society, some within the ruling party began to see the young theater and its milieu as a very sensitive social seismograph, or barometric gauge, indicating the social mood and spotting changes in social attitudes and preferences—and thus as a real asset, in fact, for the ailing and alienated regime.

For both parties—the state and the young theater—the transaction involved financial support, but its most crucial benefit was physical space. There cannot be theater without a space in which to perform for the audience, and under state socialism all public buildings, halls, rooms, plazas, and streets—the entire infrastructure—belonged to the state. Most important, any gathering of people—and theater by definition is a gathering of people—had to be authorized by the state, and the space permit was a part of such authorization. The transaction was unwritten, and it was arranged through the natural surrogate of the state, the Students Association, an organization that had a line in the state budget and that was in charge of students' clubs with their basements, cafes, and disco floors; it became the initial and generous patron and home for the young theaters. Theatrical productions—costumes, props, instruments, travel, per diems—were then subsidized by the Students Association, which was subsidized by the state.

Thus, with the assistance of the Students Association,[10] a remarkable theatrical movement was unfurled. This young theater, far from resembling any official or traditional theatrical institutions, became a way of life and of action, with both actors and audience pushing the limits of what was permissible under state socialism, and testing the possibility of a relative communicative autonomy. Theater became an opportunity for expressing matters that were on people's minds but could never be discussed in public, matters to which professional theater remained indifferent. Some matters of that kind were referred to euphemistically as "events": the "March events," for example, were the 1968 student demonstrations for free speech, and the "December events" referred to the 1970 workers' demonstrations in Gdansk over drastic preholiday food price increases.

But the regime, while engaging in this velvet transaction, had not taken into account the peculiar political power of the theater as an art form that brings people together and that does not exist without their interactions. Arendt's appreciation of theater as political art comes from her reflections on power, which "springs up whenever people get together and act in concert."[11] Theater deals with a live audience, and—though limited in time and space, like a carnival—may quietly challenge the existing order.

SPACES OF APPEARANCE

The old industrial city of Lodz in central Poland, known as the Polish Manchester, is not an attractive place to visit in December. It is cold, damp, and gets dark very early. Even if it is snowing, the streets quickly turn into dirty, soggy trails. But it is here that, since the 1970s, large numbers of people stream out from the railroad station and head through the main thoroughfare, Piotrowska Street, for the Students' Theatrical Encounters. The heart of the festival, the local Max Yasgoor farm (I refer here to Woodstock), is the Student Club at Piotrowska 77, in an old Art Deco brownstone once owned by a wealthy bourgeois family. Some performances will be shown here, but above all, in this decadently decaying space, with mahogany-paneled halls, tiled stoves, and a long bar, everybody congregates: the audience, the artists, and the critics, talking and drinking until late into the night.

In December 1971, a crowd of mixed age is excitedly debating three performances that in years to come will be known as the emblematic expression of the generation, setting up high expectations concerning both the aesthetic and the discursive-political dimensions of the theatrical message. Exactly one year before, the then first party secretary had given an order to shoot at the workers arriving for the morning shift at the Gdansk shipyard. The tragedy had led to a shakeup of the regime, and a newly appointed party leader, enlightened and eager to improve the state's relationship with the West, extended to society a promise of prosperity and political liberalization.

Now one year later, at this 1971 Lodz festival, three theater groups that had taken that promise seriously stood out from the rest, presenting performances constructed in such a way that the audience had to have as active a relationship with the presented content as the creators, the theater group itself. Though the theater groups used different strategies to involve the audience, the outcome was the same: those who saw these performances could not say, "This does not concern me." The festival events taking place on this first anniversary of the Gdansk carnage generated an articulation, and prompted recognition, of the special role of the Young Theater in the society of its time. It was not only the message, but above all the structure of the presented content itself, its built-in dialogicality,[12] that brought about a major shift in the way theater began to function in Polish society.

The Eighth Day Theater was a relatively new group from Poznan that a decade later would be known as "the conscience of the 1970s." In one of its early declarations its members described their mission thus: *to be distrustful vis-à-vis what's in us and what's outside of us, and to awaken this distrust in others.* In December 1971 it had brought to Lodz a performance based on a recent volume of poetry by Stanislaw Baranczak, *Without Stopping for Breath,*[13] which was set in a blood donation facility.

The story line was fragmented at best, as the images evoking a hectic emergency room were not logically connected and ran mostly parallel to the poetic text about "an average day in the life of an average citizen." The ordinariness and predictability of people's lives under socialism (a worker donating blood, a manipulative TV journalist preparing a constructive portrait of an "average" donor) collided here with the subtle irony of a poetic text restlessly shouted out by the actors, and with the feverish activity of blood-giving, blood-taking, and finally blood-letting. The setting is simple, with bloodstained robes and the poster of a superquota worker juxtaposed with dignified national and religious symbols. In this anxious and jittery space the audience sat mostly on the floor, close to the actors who were in a constant rush with the procedures of blood donation.

After a while it becomes clear to the characters in the play—the nurse, the average man, the journalist, the petty bureaucrat—that they are all simply acting according to a script written for them by somebody else, somebody they do not have access to. When the incessant and clearly physically exhausting routine provokes resistance among the "average" blood donors, the rubber pipes meant for donating blood become the tools of punishment and incarceration. The actors wash their faces in a bucket of red paint as though it is water. The protest in the blood donation center ends up in bloodshed. An innocent person is killed. Full of passion and desperation, the performance ended with a song: "It's only the word, 'no,' have it in your blood/That runs down the wall, drop by drop at dawn." At the play's end, the audience did not move, for it could hardly believe what it had just seen. No one wanted to leave a room where one could speak the unspeakable.

Without Stopping for Breath launched a series of performances, or "theatrical statements" as they were called, by the Eighth Day Theater, that all dealt with problems of power and captivity, truth and lying, fear and courage, and that were always high-strung, emotionally charged, and painful. With its many contradictory voices, shifting tones, simmering passions, and double meanings, the thickly textured, polyphonic performance needed a very attentive audience rather than an enthusiastic one. And it demanded from the group itself—as it was the ensemble as a whole that was responsible for the final product[14]—not only major intellectual and literary curiosity and preparation, but also advanced vocal skills and extreme physical fitness. Still, we in the audience had a sense that as good as the actors were while performing, they were not common theater actors; that the theater they were doing was not really just theater. The pain was theirs, the anxiety was theirs, the passion was theirs, the commitment to shout out the truth was theirs. They seemed to burn before our eyes—their tired bodies, their expressive faces, while "playing," or while not playing.

Their theater was their own struggle. They had chosen theater as a vehicle through which to live and act—not as theater actors, but as actors in society, as citizens.[15]

That same year Krakow's Theater STU brought to Lodz *The Polish Dreambook,* one of the most spectacular performances of the time, a real "show," with captivating music, vibrating lights, and impressive acting. Far from examining current events, the performance posed chilling questions concerning the condition of the Polish nation as both a historic and a political construct. Why are we always deep in national tragedy? Where do all those dreams of ours about national glory come from? Why has everything here always been extreme, extraordinary, specific, peculiar? And finally: what's wrong with us, always intensely suffering, Poles? Is it our history? Is it the geography? Can't we be normal, as others are?

Trying to pose these questions, STU reached beneath the skin of present-day life and turned to the country's most potent cultural tradition— the narratives, imagery, and tunes developed by the nineteenth-century romantics and their followers, celebrating the glory and sacred suffering of the Polish nation under almost 150 years of foreign domination. Dignified passages lifted from the Polish classics, blended with a tone of mockery and farce, were to examine the native preoccupation with parochial and paralyzing myths, however grand.

The audience was seated along four sides of a massive but simple rectangular table, with its surface used as a stage or ramp for a puppet theater, and the space beneath representing a bunker and a basement. The table also was an object that would be dismantled by the artists in a fury, only to be reassembled later in a positive spirit of rebuilding the future. On the table, under the table, or next to it, fifteen theatrical scenes—dream images—appeared in a spiritualistic national séance.

Bits of poetry and prose tailored into a new dramatic dialogue had a decidedly familiar ring for the audience, as their sources were the great works of romantic authors that are required reading in school. The figures also were easily identifiable: Jesus, who was also at times a romantic poet— Konrad—the patriotic savior of a tortured nation; Jasiek, a simple young peasant dressed in colorful Cracovian garb who fought under his masters in national insurrections against the tsar, and who also fought against the Polish masters that oppressed him; the emblematic figure of Mother Pole begging the tsar to free her son from prison; a nameless, pathetic member of the intelligentsia, always on a mission, lecturing the nation in his talk entitled "My Nation and I"; and a colorful, mixed entourage, dancing in a blind stupor—as in a bad dream—the national dance, the polonaise.

Although, unlike the performance by the Eighth Day Theater, the STU did not refer to any current events, the performance evoked tangentially both the initial reasons and the political outcomes of the key experience of the generation, the student protests of March 1968. The students that year had gone on strike over the termination—at the request of the

Soviet ambassador in Warsaw—of the admired theatrical production at the National Theater of *Forefathers' Eve,* a nineteenth-century patriotic drama, taught in every school, whose main character, a poet named Konrad, engages in a long antitsarist soliloquy. The enthusiastic reception of the play prompted the Soviet Embassy to realize that under the cover of a romantic antitsarist play, real anti-Soviet resentment was being expressed and encouraged.

The news of the closing of a classic play by Poland's biggest poet-prophet, Adam Mickiewicz, instigated a weeklong student protest over freedom of speech. Though the immediate reason for the eruption at the universities was the censoring of a national literary treasure, the Communist government framed the protests as having been instigated by "cosmopolitan elements" among the students and faculty, and using sharp nationalistic rhetoric, launched a major anti-Semitic campaign.

The *Polish Dreambook* was the first post-1968 reexamination of romantic national dreams and their juxtaposition with the nauseatingly petty reality that had always accompanied those dreams; it opened a discourse on the traps and pitfalls of the Polish national tradition. The debate was nothing new, having reappeared throughout history, but could recently be conducted only by those who lived and published in exile, like Gombrowicz, Milosz, or the other writers of *Kultura,* an émigré monthly published in Paris. Performances by the STU Theater over the next four years filled that vacuum in Poland by bringing this debate—uncomfortable for the public and unwelcomed by the authorities—home again.

(Ironically, though the *Polish Dreambook* was centered on national tragedies and the never-ending aspiration for freedom, the performance's main message seems to be relevant thirty years later in a free democratic Poland. As in a bad dream, the rhetoric of nationalism and the cultivation of gratifying stereotypes, as we shall see in the last two chapters, remain powerful tools of persuasion and populist mobilization.)

The third standout performance of that memorable Lodz festival was *Circle, or Triptych,* by Theater 77 from Lodz, a group named after the Student Club at Piotrowska 77. If the presentation by the Eighth Day Theater was almost stripped of theatrics, following Artaud's concept of performance, and designed to be painfully close to life, to everyone's senses, to everyone's body; and if the production by the STU Theater was ostentatiously theatrical, creational, full of dazzling scenes, and with an emphasis on acting, clowning, and the playing of roles—the performance of Theater 77 was almost like a newspaper, intentionally nontheatrical, a discursive presentation on present-day events.[16]

The audience was led into the upstairs offices at Club 77. There were no chairs; the place soon became very crowded, with no place to sit. With the audience settled in, a man sitting next to the desk and smoking a cigarette announces: "I am opening a press conference on the events in Gdansk." He turns on a tape recorder to play an official statement by a party official, only to realize, along with the audience, that the speech comments on a similar workers' protest that took place twelve years earlier in 1956 in the city of Poznan. He promptly changes the tape, and now a new, but almost identical (though authentic) statement is played.

The man opens a discussion. The audience is silent and feels uncomfortable. Finally somebody speaks: "In our factory we produce lightbulbs, and perhaps we could improve their quality. And our sausages could be better too," says another person. Soon it is not clear who is speaking, the actors or the audience. The problems raised are usually petty, as those are the only matters people feel are within their reach. It becomes clear that people are not used to thinking about themselves as being capable of influencing policies and decisions of the state. The discussion is getting out of hand when suddenly a large door opens to the adjacent room, and the audience is invited to enter a large banquet hall.

Tables arranged in a horseshoe shape are laden with food; the public—with some hesitation—takes seats behind them. Waiters pass around finger bowls. Several pairs of dancers dressed in colorful folk costumes wait for everyone to sit down, then dance the polonaise. Somebody gets up, gives a speech, and others follow him. They all speak about a bright future for Poland in the next fifteen years, offer toasts, and since the food and vodka are real, it is soon getting noisy; somebody tries a striptease, and things start getting out of hand. A glass is broken, the tablecloth is pulled off the table, and somebody screams: "And we, all of us, where have we been?" A sense of uneasiness: after all, it is not just THEM; it is also US, all of us in this room who took part in the senseless ritual and did nothing about it.

Another door opens. This third room is dark, and from the loudspeakers a raspy voice reads a poem by a romantic author, Norwid; the only source of light are six glasses with flaming alcohol, a visual citation from Wajda's film *Ashes and Diamonds,* easily recognized by any Pole. Everybody is quiet.[17] A Polish sociologist writing about the performance fifteen years later said: "The message is clear: Are we to join this erroneous circular movement, or are we to bring back a meaning to reality by building a third part: a triptych."[18] One could also read the performance as an invitation to action, supported by the conviction that we can change reality, if we only take responsibility for our actions. It is less clear whether the socialist reality is to be changed or replaced by an alternative one, or whether it is simply to be improved, perfected.

These three early performances of the Young Theater, first shown in Lodz, received the main festival awards, were highly acclaimed in both the student and professional press, and traveled to university campuses, where they quickly became the hottest ticket in town. They were not seen merely as artistic productions, since the reality in these theaters was not an illusion but an argument, an investigation, or a diagnosis. Thus they became institutions that initiated discussion in a space that seemed to be safe, a process that stimulated the emergence of increasingly informed and concerned social actors, a process that turned both creators and audience into aspiring citizens.

CITIZENS THROUGH THEATER

One could look at the Young Theaters in terms of today's nongovernmental organizations (NGOs), except that those NGOs functioned in a state where everything was governmental, and where the state was to be the only source of civic action. Yet those early governmental "NGOs" displayed distinctive and authentic civic features through their commitment to work on behalf of a larger community and their efforts to build communities through their work; through their knowledge-oriented and critical approach to reality, and their aim of making such an approach appear to the public neither deviant nor incorrect; through their already mentioned contribution to the creation of a space in which people could communicate without major constraints imposed on them; through their work on developing and perfecting new forms of communication unmediated by the state; and finally, through their work on the development of the individual as a self, as a subject endowed with dignity, and therefore with agency.

Most of the theaters subscribed to, and implemented in their work, a method then popular in the West called collective creation. All members of the group took part in thinking about the message they wanted to convey; they all searched for the best pieces of literature to deliver that message, wrote their own texts, and not only performed but usually prepared the scenery, props, and costumes as well. Yearning for a community in which authentic contact with other people could be possible, beyond the private—a community of minds and souls—was a very important motivation for establishing these theaters. A sociological study done in the late 1970s discovered that Poles did not identify themselves with any state institutions or organizations, but rather with their family, friends, and the nation (as opposed to the state). An intermediate layer of authentic associational belonging was not referred to, as it did not exist.[19] The utterly fantastic project—given the political context—of living in small, self-organized groups of people, who nevertheless neither isolate themselves nor are isolated from society as such, would have been, for all practical purposes, impossible if it had not been for the available institutional shell of a student theater. The vision of a community replaced the theater of stars, and various strategies were developed to make the audience a part of this community.

Theater 77, on the premise that "theater does not end in the theater," issued an invitation to its dedicated audience:

> If you share with us the belief that the conclusions we arrive at in the theater ought to serve us in creatively shaping our reality, we would like to invite you to collaborate with us. We do not presume that our col-

laboration has to lead, as an end result, to a performance. In any case, we would like to decide with you what will be the forms of publicizing our eventual conclusions.[20]

The "collective creation" yielded an added payback in societies under one-party rule: it dissolved a crucial divide enforced in the socialist-paternalistic state, the one between thinker and doer, decision maker and average member of society, performer and spectator—those who know and those who are not meant to know. It facilitated the surfacing of civic friendships, a bond of affection bringing together those who pursued the civic good, a bond that would fully flourish during the early years of Solidarity.[21]

The general problem of knowledge, of getting to know, and the attitude of critical inquiry toward reality, though not generally the most crucial for the theatrical genre as such, was key for the activities of the Young Theater in Poland. In the late 1970s, new groups often did not call themselves theaters anymore, but chose names that emphasized, more boldly than before, the analytical, investigative, critical, exploratory character of their undertakings. They were known as academies, workshops, and laboratories, and, indeed, in preparation for their performances they conducted often elaborate research. They took care to document their activities on film, they published descriptions, programs, statements, commentaries, poetry, manifestos, and even tried to theorize about their own work. Those materials were also sought after by the audience. (Perhaps the most popular of these were radical pamphlets—mimeographed by the Eighth Day Theater—which in the late 1970s were disseminated along with *samizdat* literature.)

The actors of the Academy of Movement, a Warsaw-based theater company concerned with urban life and emphasizing visual expression, were simultaneously artists, researchers, social workers, and organizers. Their weeklong action called *House* aimed at transforming the residents of a housing bloc into copartners and cocreators of the event. It involved a prior study of a concrete neighborhood, elaborate conversations and arrangements with the residents of a given housing project, and then a joint production, each time different, reflecting the life of the community and featuring its residents and architecture.[22]

The Academy of Movement became known for arranging longer or shorter theatricalized encounters and for creating situations that facilitated expression, and an emergence of real bonds, even if momentary, among the public. The group explored the urban landscape and routine activities of city residents and selected some to provoke their encounters. Their actions addressed a broad and accidental audience and transformed them into subjects, reflective actors of daily reality. One of the most memorable was a queue going not into but out of the meat shop. Actors stood in it, often with their kids, before the store opened, until late evening. This sardonic "happening," the "queue from the shop," was conducted in various cities in the late 1970s, at a time of dramatic food shortages, when family members took turns standing in line to secure rationed bread, sugar, or meat.

The conclusions the Academy of Movement drew from its observations of city life under socialism, and the critical thinking it employed in conceiving of its encounters as a way to ameliorate the prevailing social atomization, were at times more revealing than those drawn by the findings of the social sciences. "Artists preoccupy themselves by studying reality, and they even try to transform it. . . . They are not producers of beauty, because this would mean to narcotize society through art," observed Krzysztof Wodiczko in an interview from this period (he is today a New York–based artist known internationally for his public urban art).[23] The urban analysis undertaken by the Academy of Movement produced *Everyday Life After the French Revolution,* an almost silent performance that was a study in bleakness, shortages, the hidden aggression of tired cookie-cutter citizens, and the alienating life of the socialist housing projects.

The Gardzienice Center for Theater Practices, a group named after a village in eastern Poland where it is based, first set out in 1978 in search of alternatives to the official culture in remote areas of Poland's eastern borderlands. Its work would start with an expedition, a journey, as its members called it, to the isolated countryside, where closely knit communities, hard to reach by car, lived without electricity, with virtually no exposure to popular culture or the language and calendar of socialist rituals reinforced by the state media. Like the urban encounters of the Academy of Movement, the Gardzienice Center expeditions required prior study and thorough preparation. Members of the group, which included several graduates of anthropology who had resigned their positions at the university, made trips to the area; recorded local songs; interviewed older people; familiarized themselves with local history, tales, and ceremonies; and then jointly decided which tiny village to go to.

The expedition took several days, and its task was both to get to know the local people and, in turn, to make the theater members familiar to the villagers. Gardzienice Center members stayed with families, ate with them, helped with some of the work, and then invited them to prepare together what they called an Evening Assembly. This joint performance, placed in a natural setting of the village, often outdoors, did not have a stage, actors, or a separate audience. It featured familiar folk songs, local characters, and sometimes even domestic animals. In its country-fair-cum-circus structure, both comic and dramatic situations appeared, highlighting characters and imagery taken from local stories. Long-forgotten and -neglected gestures, movements, and sounds were recalled and shared with the visitors.

For the Gardzienice Center itself, the Evening Assembly was not a performance but rather an evening animated by familiar facts of village life, by humor and imagination—a lesson in a disappearing village culture conducted by this close-knit community of locals. This culture of the peripheries, regulated by the daily work in tiny farms, shaped by a close interaction with nature, and inhabited by various local spirits, revealed not just the self-sufficiency of the community but also the striking personal autonomy of its members. And it was this culture that became the basis and source for the next stage of the Gardzienice Center's work. Once the group had returned from the journey, their work on the actual performance began. It involved not just further voice and endurance training but also follow-up research; study of the interviews, notes, and recordings from the expedition; and, finally, preparation of a script. The results—performances like *Sorcery,* or *The Life of Archpriest Awwakum*—have been shown in Poland and around the world, but for Poles it was far more than a brilliant theatrical performance. The Gardzienice Center's work, which questioned the prevailing cultural uniformity, was reintroducing the marginalized culture of the peripheries, recovering lost voices and a diversity that had once been commonplace. In the prevailing monological culture of the one-party state, its performances were not just a celebration of difference but also an argument for the feasibility of a degree of independence and self-determination within existing conditions. Incidentally, the group's work coincided—though it would be difficult to say which came first—with the growing popularity among the young urban intelligentsia of moving to rural out-of-the-way places, where one could be more the master of one's own life.

Theater has always been a place to act, and acting is something to be expected, something in fact indispensable. Furthermore, unlike other forms of art, it does require personal, live appearance and the presence of both actor and audience. Although the theatrical actions discussed here, and the portable town meetings they set up and furnished, were indeed limited in time and space, they provided a temporary residence for action and speech, an embryonic public realm.[24]

The ambiguity of theater as a genre, operating on the borders of art and reality, art and social life, art and social cognition, makes it a particularly apt system for supporting, facilitating, and channeling communication. The confines of the theater have been providing over time a frame within which—even at times of limited freedom—one can still speak, and act, with others. Theater is a place where the subjective, private voices of group experience, once "enacted," become objectified, enter public discourse, and engender new social bonds. The effort to build a community of communication was particularly palpable in the case of the Young Theater movement. By bringing people together, and by employing both representational and discursive techniques of communication, theater in general can give a powerful assist in instigating the emergence of a public sphere, even under conditions that rule out such a sphere. For Hannah Arendt such a coming into being of a *space of appearance* is a prerequisite for the formal constitution of a public realm.[25]

The ambiguity of theater's status had already been underscored in Poland by the Laboratory Theater of Jerzy Grotowski, who in the mid-1970s officially announced a transcending of the boundaries of theater and a turn toward "active culture" projects. Theater does not have to deliver a product; its work is fleeting; it is above all a space for meeting the other, a process that does not have a clear end. The Gardzienice Center was—and in many ways still is—such a project. Though Grotowski's work was never directly political, his case of a "transaction with the regime" had served as an important guide for those who formed the Young Theater movement. The lesson taken from this local knowledge was clear: one should try to test inflexible institutional structures claiming to have an "exclusive" on the organizing of social experience. One should exploit and reproduce every possible niche and exemption, thus widening the margin of alternatives that the state finds tolerable.

Perhaps one of the most consequential decisions made by these theaters, one that helped them to evolve from an artistic into a cultural and civic movement concerned with a broadening of societal autonomy, was to depart from literature. In traditional theater, it is literature, more specifically a play written for the stage, that mediates the interaction between the actors and the audience. By refusing to use ready-made, state-approved plays, and by working out their own message, members of the Young Theater insisted that theater is not a vehicle for literature to come alive, but for society to come alive.

As for the milieu of the young theaters, the theater was—though perhaps the Party's cultural policy makers did not want to notice it— neither literature, nor art, but society. Performance, as they understood it, was not a fictitious tale, or imitation of reality; rather, it was an argument, and it was an argument advanced by a specific theater group. Actors here were also authors; they created and then enacted their ideas. And it was through theater that they were able to have an active relationship to reality. The egalitarian, inclusive character of the theatrical world they constituted, and the way they as persons existed in that world, encouraged the engagement of the audience, the society. That audience was not just a group of mesmerized spectators, but rather—as was clear in the performances of the Academy of Movement or Theater 77—an extension of the actors: the audience members were their equals. Speaking their words, and acting their deeds, the Young Theater, an interaction of social actors, engendered a public space, a civic site where concerned individuals came together to articulate and discuss things they had in common.

Still—many would argue—these activities, framed as theater, being limited in space and time, are no different from carnival, the world temporarily upside-down, a pause in reality, a safety valve provided by the power holders to maintain an otherwise repressive system. But after all, a carnival—a time when the unofficial becomes official—reveals and nominates unsuspected leaders, fosters agency, and endows people with performative capacities. Carnival reveals a potential power while the prevailing power is suspended.

The performative potential of the Young Theater was grounded in its resolute repudiation of theater as a provider of fiction or entertainment, replacing it with the idea of theater as a space in which a private experience could appear in public and become a social one. As in the productions of the Eighth Day Theater, performance became an intense site for the translation of private experience (intellectual, political, ethical) into both public and social, and a site where interpretation of that experience could also occur. Thus the work of those theaters, by widening the choice of officially available interpretative keys, provided space, language, and questions, enabling a public discourse to emerge. By using theatrical means to explore a pressing reality, with the aim of transforming it, the Young Theater was testing its own performative capacities.

PUBLICIZING A PRIVATE PUBLIC

What were those semiofficial spaces that hosted the appearance of speech and action on matters brought out of the *private* and concerning society at large?

The current debates and theories about the "public" developed in the West are not very useful when applied to the reality of real socialism in the 1970s. The attractive possibility of using Nancy Fraser's concept, and calling it *subaltern public* or *counterpublic,* is problematic, as those categories imply the existence of a dominant public, and therefore a multiplicity of publics forming a real public sphere.[26]

Perhaps it would be useful to go back briefly to the time of the eradication of the public sphere in the Soviet Bloc. The process was completed in 1948 by the formal elimination of socialist parties in the countries of the region, a remnant of political pluralism, followed by the standardization of information and preventive censorship across the bloc.[27] Along with the economy, private property, land, and infrastructure that became the property of the state, so did "the public." But unlike the other objects of statization that were still there, visible, though under different ownership, the public sphere was completely replaced by the monological *official,* and so its genuinely public-spirited impulses were forced to hide in the private realm and remake themselves there. That relocation of the public into the private resulted in the occurrence of a peculiar species: the *privatized public.* The case of the Young Theater constitutes an instance of a gradual reversal of that occurrence. It demonstrated ways in which it was possible to bring some pieces of the public realm back and to reassemble them into a *publicized private,* a nascent public sphere. The *publicized private* meant here an objectified, embryonic, discursive sphere open to a limited public.

The endeavors of the Young Theater movement to publicize the private and contribute to the emergence of a public sphere were to be gradually superseded from the late 1970s on by more far-reaching projects to create a full-fledged, unambiguous sphere of social self-organization autonomous from the state. Empowered by the 1975 Helsinki Agreement on Human Rights, the emerging public sphere became a sphere of social self-defense, furnished by an array of publishing, research, educational, and philanthropic initiatives. Despite being under constant harassment, it came out into the open and established an autonomous realm for public expression and—increasingly—for effective civic action.

3

The Public Matter

The chief difference between slave labor and the modern free laborer is not that the laborer possesses personal freedom—freedom of movement, economic activity, and personal inviolability—but that he is admitted to the political realm and fully emancipated as a citizen.
—*Hannah Arendt*

HOPE IS WHERE VIOLENCE IS NOT

"Don't burn down Party Committees, create your own!" This compelling admonition by Jacek Kuron,[1] one of the founders of the Committee in Defense of the Workers (KOR), was a direct reference to the tragic events that had taken place in Gdansk in December 1970, when the police and the army massacred protesting workers, and demonstrators set fire to the Party's committee headquarters.[2]

J. L. Austin would say that Kuron's was a perlocutionary speech act, with a delayed performativity, as it found its almost literal implementation ten years later, during another protest at the Gdansk shipyards in August 1980. The workers indeed did not go to the streets, where they would be vulnerable to the police or the army, but stayed at their workplace and organized themselves into a peaceful, self-governing republic within the fenced-in space of the Lenin Shipyard. Their demands were few and straightforward: a wage increase, the rehiring of two unjustly fired shipyard workers, and construction of a monument to commemorate the victims of the December 1970 massacre.

As other major factories on the Baltic Coast joined the strike and sent their representatives to the quickly growing Interfactory Strike Committee at the shipyard, the government—in a desperate effort to maintain its monopoly on the media—tried to prevent the spread of information about the events in northern Poland to the rest of the country. There was no information about it in the media, the phone lines to the coastal cities were cut, and the roads and railroads were under thorough surveillance. People returning from their summer vacations at the seashore and the truck drivers transporting goods from the harbor cities to the rest of the country were the first carriers of the news, as traffic in the opposite direction was heavily restricted. Although the international community learned about the strike fairly promptly and saw its images in their media, the Polish population was kept in the dark for the whole two weeks. The key witness to the shipyard strike was the local population, who kept an around-the-clock vigil in front of the main shipyard gate, providing food, medicine, and psychological support.

The shipyard, though fenced in and guarded by the workers, was precariously exposed to the sea, and the two weeks of the occupation strike unfolded under continuous fear of infiltration by the secret service or attack by the navy, army, or police forces. The strike leaders learned quickly that the Soviet army stationed in Poland had been put on emergency alert. The governor of the region admitted later, "On the third day, all of Gdansk and the entire region were on strike. The strike was organized in perfect peace, and the organizers appeared to be in total charge of the city. As a representative of the authorities—I am sorry to say it—we noticed that we were actually not governing the region any more."[3]

On the fourth day of the strike, the workers formulated a longer list of twenty-one demands, printed at the shipyard and distributed as leaflets and eventually in a newsletter called *Solidarity*. This four-page publication, smuggled to other parts of the country, conveyed the unusual climate of dignity and responsibility within the shipyard along with news from the negotiations, responses of the strike committee to governmental statements, interviews with the workers and with visitors from other factories, and a lot of strike poetry.[4] After one week, when the strikes spread to the key factories and mines in southern Poland, the Communist government agreed to come to talk to the workers. The negotiations were broadcast through loudspeakers throughout the shipyard and could be heard in front of the gates.

The final agreement, signed at the Gdansk shipyards by the workers and the regime, created the formal conditions for the emergence of an authentic public sphere and launched an astonishingly speedy shift—still within the context of "really existing socialism"—from *private* to *public*. As demanded by the workers, the act of signing the agreement was broadcast by national television all over the country. As shocking as it was for many Poles—until that day the media had been silent about the strikes—it was this moment of collective participation in hitherto unthinkable agreements that opened up a space for the new spectacular forms of engagement that followed.

REALMS OF ENGAGEMENT—REALMS OF HOPE

The long-deepening legitimacy crisis, a result of the inability of the party-state to fulfill its promises vis-à-vis society, had already reached a peak in 1976, when the so-called workers' state imprisoned hundreds of protesting workers. In the face of drastic human rights abuses, the signing of the Helsinki agreements one year earlier encouraged new initiatives and inspired new forms of engagement outside the domain of the state.

Already prior to the 1980 shipyard strike one could identify the existence of separate, though most probably unwritten, policies applied by the party-state to four possible kinds of citizens' engagement. From the point of view of the authorities, the first and most desirable were those that I call here *preferred and rewarded*; the second were engagements that were *permitted, but limited*; the third were activities that, because of the unclear status of those "in between" or borderline, I shall refer to as *unofficial*; and the fourth were those that were strictly *forbidden*.

From the point of view of society, these four kinds of engagement represented four ways of coping with the system, and thus constituted four realms of possible activity for an individual. The *preferred and rewarded* was the authorized, or state-organized and sponsored, official sphere. It included a spectrum of centralized, vertically structured organizations, from the Socialist Youth through the labor unions to the Women's League, periodically orchestrated "actions of social work" (the name for supposedly voluntary work on behalf of the community), and participation in the celebration of state holidays, the most touchy being the May Day parade.

The publicness of this realm, as Habermas would have said, was staged for manipulative purposes.[5] Membership in some of these associations was obligatory, or at least not purely voluntary, as people felt compelled to join in order to gain access to the redistribution of otherwise limited goods and services. Participation—whether forced, passive, or truly voluntary—was frequently based on the conviction that there was no realistic alternative, and it reflected what a Polish sociologist called the "general theory of unfeasibility."[6] Victor Perez-Diaz talks about a similar effect that the state-sponsored "civil society" in Spain had in making Spaniards feel overorganized and apathetic toward such organizations.[7] This realm of the "preferred and rewarded" was the status quo that the Stalinist regime established at the outset and did everything it could to maintain.

The second realm, consisting of initiatives that I call *permitted but limited,* emerged after Stalin's death as a result of the 1956 thaw: a "transactional" space that seemed to depend on the good will of the regime. It included activities of the Catholic Church and the so-called Clubs of the Catholic Intelligentsia; the limited circulation of intellectually independent journals, often associated with the Church (*Znak, Wiez, Tygodnik Powszechny*); and certain initiatives within the framework of the Polish scouting organization, which was relaunched by imaginative individuals and helped to preserve the pre-Communist ethos of individual achievement, courage, self-help initiatives, the memory of the heroic participation of scouts in the Warsaw Uprising in 1944, and discussions of the underground strategies in Nazi-occupied Poland.

This realm, the "velvet transactions," also accommodated the student cultural movement, powerfully expressive through its avant-garde and critical forms of Young Theater, as we have seen, as well as visual arts, poetry, and music. And, finally, this second realm included the scholarly activities of some academic associations, mostly limited publications and conferences in the humanities and social sciences, organized outside of the big cities for a fairly select audience, and often—what was very important for scholarly life in Poland—with foreign participants.

The realm of the *permitted but limited* allowed creative citizens to take advantage of small openings in the system. It was a realm that facilitated an encounter with thoughts and ideas that had not been issued by the state, and its audience was a relatively narrow slice of the urban intelligentsia. Its relatively long existence (since 1956), reinforced by the ideals of the 1968 student protests and by Poland's version of the counterculture, laid the groundwork for the realms of *unofficial* and eventually *forbidden* activities. When Adam Michnik in a 1976 essay wrote, "The democratic opposition must be constantly and incessantly visible in public life, must create political facts by organizing mass actions, must formulate alternative programs," he was in effect laying out a design for the *unofficial* and the *forbidden* realms of activities.[8]

Guided by considerable self-restraint, the realm of the *unofficial* was above all a realm of language; though far from being capable of ultimate performativity, it was a realm of speech acts representing a large spectrum of uses: informing, deterring, warning, affecting, and persuading. Initiated in late 1975 with a classic "locutionary act"—a thing one does *in* saying something—in this case an open letter directed to the authorities, it developed further the historically known conventions of political speech acts through open letters.[9] The letter, known as the "Letter of 59" after the initial number of signatories, was then signed by several hundred intellectuals, artists, and scholars who questioned the wisdom of proposed constitutional changes. These changes, they argued—among them a constitutionally guaranteed brotherhood with the Soviet Union—would not only further limit civil rights but also dangerously deepen the existing chasm between the authorities and society. Immediately in the first paragraph of the letter the authors brought up the Helsinki agreement that Poland had signed several months before:

> *The Directives of the VII Congress of the Polish United Workers Party* contained an announcement of changes in the Constitution. After the conference in Helsinki at which the Polish government along with 34 governments of other states solemnly confirmed the "Universal Declaration of Human Rights," we consider that the implementation

of these basic freedoms should become a new stage in the history of the nation and the lives of individuals. Motivated by civic concern, we consider that the Constitution and the legislation based on it should, above all else, guarantee the following civic liberties.

The letter then discusses the urgent social need for freedom of conscience and religious practice, freedom of work, freedom of learning and teaching, and in its most elaborate paragraph, freedom of speech and information.[10]

Thus, the *unofficial* focused on building an alternative within the system by engaging in "doing things with words."[11] It exploited a gray area within the triangle of the preferred/permitted/forbidden within which it could, in effect, begin to function as a realm of gradual emancipation and dialogue. Its mode was best exemplified by Kuron's famous appeal about building and not burning committees.

The line between *the unofficial* and *the realm of the forbidden* is subtle and often difficult to pin down. In moving from the unofficial to the forbidden we are moving gradually from a realm dominated by speech to a realm dominated by action. Its aim: self-organization of a community taking positive, peaceful actions. The best example of a borderline initiative having the features of both is KOR—the Committee in Defense of the Workers—with its philosophy of self-limited action. It was Kuron, again, who warned against the syndrome of force and violence, as it never brings freedom, even if it changes the composition of the ruling group.

The move toward action and the constitution by citizens of a significantly growing *realm of the forbidden* were prompted by the June 1976 strikes in Ursus and Radom. In the similar protest at the Gdansk shipyards in 1970 several dozen workers had been killed while rushing for the morning shift. In June 1976 the police arrested 2,500 workers, and most of them were severely beaten. The crushing of this workers' protest bore fruit that was for the government bitter and most disconcerting: the establishment of KOR, a key step toward the upcoming social alliance between the intelligentsia and the workers.

And again speech actions, especially the two kinds discussed by Austin—illocutionary acts (informing, ordering, warning) and perlocutionary acts (acting *by* saying something: convincing, deterring, persuading)—constituted the core activities. The initiatives in this realm included the breaking of the state monopoly on information, through the dissemination in *samizdat* form of the statements of KOR, which were then broadcast from Munich by the popular Radio Free Europe; the launching of the increasingly sophisticated forms of *samizdat,* among them clandestinely published but widely circulated real books and periodicals; classes in history and politics taught in private apartments by the "Flying University" and supervised by academics from the unofficial Society of Academic Courses; the maintenance of contacts with foreign press and foreign correspondents in Poland; and the development of quick and dependable ways of transmitting news out of the country, especially to outlets that could broadcast it back into Poland.

This realm of the *forbidden* by the Communist state consisted then of any form of organized, institutionalized protest, which is why the workers' strikes in 1970 and 1976, which spilled out into the streets, had been met with force and severe retribution. KOR, in contrast, a grouping of highly visible public intellectuals and artists established to assist workers imprisoned for taking part in the protests, confronted the authorities with a curiously difficult case, for it tried to function openly and within existing law while at the same time keeping some aspects of its activities—though technically there was nothing illegal about them—highly confidential and necessarily clandestine. Everybody knew who belonged to KOR: their full names, addresses, and phone numbers—it is still hard to believe—were listed on all statements and newsletters. KOR's immediate goals were broadly publicized: initially to help repressed workers and their families, and eventually to force the regime to abandon the policy of repression altogether. What was not publicized were the names of thousands of people who donated money, the names of those who collected the money as well as those who delivered the money to Ursus and Radom, or the names of the families aided through KOR's financial, legal, and medical assistance program. KOR's activities and visibility set an instructive example, and even though its members were harassed, imprisoned, or fired from work, other civic organizations began to emerge, among them the Movement for the Defense of Human and Civil Rights (ROPCIO), free trade unions, the Farmers Self-Defense Committee, and the Students Solidarity Committee (SKS).

When the distinguished Warsaw sociologist Stefan Nowak analyzed Polish society of the 1970s, he saw it as a strange construction of those who thought about themselves either as members of strongly linked primary groups (i.e., family and friends) or, as Poles, as members of the Polish nation, whose identity is derived from a broad notion of the motherland. The "sociological vacuum" between the two sources of identity that Nowak discovered was in fact the absence of the *public sphere* that is characteristic of nonauthoritarian societies.[12] The vacuum, he argued, was caused by the lack of the kind of institutional guarantees that would make possible the rise of an actual *public sphere.*

Initiatives like the Young Theater, the Letter of 59, and KOR had begun to chip away at this vacuum, but the signing of the Gdansk agreement in August 1980 completely changed the definition of the situation, and the vacuum got filled up very quickly, rendering virtually obsolete the former modes of engagement. Solidarity emerged as both the ultimate incarnation and the guardian of a public sphere under whose protective umbrella a boom of professional associations, ecological clubs, new media, and initiatives in human rights and education took place. For example, the first public debate ever on the events of 1968 (including the anti-Semitic campaign launched by the Communist Party) was organized by the Solidarity chapter at Warsaw University, a startling and unforgettable event for all of us. And in the university courtyard I also remember seeing another startling first: an announcement about an upcoming meeting of feminists.

In order to take part in public matters, one had to make a decision to do so. The sheer numbers of those who joined the Solidarity union, even allowing for the inevitable infiltrators and opportunists, are very impressive, as they represented nearly ten million people, one quarter of the whole society, and an overwhelming majority of all those employed. Yet, even more remarkable was the sustained thrill and intensity of participation in public, which seemed to affect everybody and led to the emergence of a truly extraordinary sense of "we, the people."

SPEECH AND ACTION

Once the signing of the Gdansk agreement was seen on national TV, the unimaginable became real. The *unofficial* and the *forbidden* came out of their hiding places, along with the suppressed narratives—communicated now by an entirely new subject: the self-discovered, autonomously speaking "I." The visible public happiness that accompanied this shift from *private* to *public,* and from *I* to *we,* helped to create a widely felt belief in the invincibility of this new public collectivity that had originated in the shipyard.

It was the very first paragraph of the Gdansk agreement that established the institutional guarantee—in the form of the independent and self-governing trade union—for the emergence and existence of a free realm of engagement, a public sphere. When the mustachioed electrician who led the strike and then conducted the negotiations, Lech Walesa, spoke to the crowd gathered at the shipyard gate moments after signing the agreements, he said: "We will have our independent, self-governing trade unions; *Solidarity,* our own paper published here during the strike, will become our union paper; and we will be able to write without censorship whatever we want; we have the right to strike." This speech, filmed and a month later distributed throughout the country, became one of the most emblematic moments of performative democracy of the twentieth century.[13]

Walesa's speech was an act of creating a new space, outside of the homes, churches, and hidden sheds where news and poetry had hitherto been printed. This new space, located between that tight little *private* realm utilized by the civil society of the late 1970s and the *official* realm controlled by the state, was about to be carved out of the large dominions of the state and become lawfully inhabited. In this space it would be safe to discuss what Habermas calls "critical matters of general interest," and from this space citizens could keep a watchful eye on the authorities.[14]

The Gdansk agreement was a curious outcome for a workers' strike, unlike any previous outcome of collective bargaining. The demands were less about government doing things for people than about the removal of obstacles so that the people themselves could take care of things, and the government would not stop them from doing it. This newly opened space—aimed at addressing the issues, determining solutions, and implementing them—was a realm of positive action by emancipated private citizens on behalf of the public good.

The term *citizen* was rarely used by people in this context, as it had long since been appropriated by the regime and compromised by the tiresome frequency of its use in official speech. Yet it was precisely the self-discovery of one's *citizenness*, of being a part of the decisionmaking process, a "subject" in social life, and above all a distinct *speaking subject*, that was met with considerable emotion.

The performativity of Walesa's speech lies in the fact that—as Arendt would have said—it was action, disclosed by a word.[15] When he spoke, he represented the Interfactory Strike Committee, which, upon signing the agreement, acquired the status of the Interfactory Committee to Establish the Independent and Self-Governing Trade Union.[16] Closer examination of the relationship between word and action, and between action and knowledge, may help us to identify the conditions under which such action-facilitating disclosure could take place in—as the Poles called it—the new post-August Poland. First, it has to have the power to transform reality. The signed agreement had such power, as formal accords have to implement rules of performative word or utterance. Hannah Arendt would have added that the *word has to appear* in public, and it has to be a special word. Such a word cannot be a generic word; such speech cannot be "mere talk." In order to be a "word that does things," a word with performative qualities, it has to be permeated with truth and it must disclose a vital experience of the public. Such was the illocutionary preamble to the agreement, which began: "The activity of the trade unions of People's Poland has not lived up to the hopes and aspirations of the workers."[17]

Walesa's brief address was the complete opposite, in both form and content, of any scripted or unscripted performance by the government officials. Speaking from the top of a truck by way of familiar words and friendly gestures, he initiated a strikingly pure and dignified public conversation with the crowds on matters of critical interest. Common, truth-releasing words spoken in public have the power to diminish fear, strengthen connections between once-alienated individuals, and turn them into a community of speaking subjects who can themselves enact democracy. The obvious precondition for that to happen is freedom of speech. I introduce here the voices of several Poles to help us explore the word-action relationship. The first is the poet Stanislaw Baranczak.

A Poet

In the mid-1970s it was completely impossible to publish anything essential to society. Of course, it was possible to be published if the censor did not sniff in your poem or novel some allusions to reality. Literature has, of course, its own ways of deceiving the censor, to outsmart him, so to speak. But I felt sometimes that I am using metaphorical language not because I wish to use metaphors, but because it could pass the censorship much more easily. And I started to catch myself on this very early. Especially with a long poem, which was an image of an average day in the life of an average citizen. I was writing it, and I knew perfectly well that it is not going to be published in Poland, unless the situation changes, of course (but there was very little chance for that). I simply decided to finish it, and then to see what could be done with it. The first thing I've done, after finishing it—I typed it in ten or eleven copies and passed it to my friends. They passed it to their friends, some of those friends copied it, and so on, and so on. The circulation grew, and this was the first time I felt a genuine interest on the part of the readers.[18]

The original *samizdat*, single pages typed with carbon paper in batches of ten on the thinnest possible paper, were quickly superseded by hand-rolled mimeograph copying, then homemade printing machines, and eventually even faster and more efficient equipment smuggled from abroad. Thus the most visible element in the realm of the forbidden well before the Gdansk agreement was the surge in the number and quality of underground publications, which eventually achieved an almost semiopen status. Authors signed their texts with their own names, and ordinary people were less afraid of reading them, of passing the issues and volumes from one to another, of discussing them. Still, the whole process of printing, collating, and initially distributing, along with names, locations, and so on, was shrouded in secrecy. Even the recipe for homemade printing ink—unavailable from the state-run stores—was top secret.

When one looks at the landscape of civic activities in Poland in the late 1970s, one thing is obvious: for all their volume, scope, and vibrancy, activities within the realms of the permitted, the unofficial, and the forbidden all sprang from—and yet remained relegated to—the private sphere. So the Poles found themselves with an oversized, multifaceted, and multifunctional private sphere, which facilitated the emergence of what Robert Putnam calls "the networks of civic engagement."[19] And it did not take long for Western scholars to see in this highly articulated and mobilizable phenomenon—patiently constructed from below by horizontally linked primary groups—a revival of civil society.

This civil society of the late 1970s, which Poles generally referred to as their "unofficial culture," had already accumulated considerable social capital when it was tested during the first visit of the new Polish pope, John Paul II, in the summer of 1979. Enormous, record-breaking, but quiet and civil crowds were smoothly directed without incident by a small army of volunteer marshals. It was then—as many observed—that it became obvious that the authorities, for all their infrastructure, no longer had a monopoly on the organizing, launching, and controlling of large public events. Perhaps the most important outcome of the local invention of civil society—an outcome produced in the sphere of private initiatives on behalf of the common good—had been the accumulated human capital.

With the signing of the Gdansk agreement, this energy and human capital were reallocated into the public sphere, where they were multiplied almost overnight. As in the corporatist order of the medieval world, whose hierarchical ranks, privileges, fear, and social exclusions disappeared during carnival, the post-August situation had all the features of the Bakhtinian carnival.[20] The bottom ruled over the top, and the public square was presided over not by the king but by the jester, by the lowest of the low, a feisty, vernacular-speaking worker, an unemployed electrician. His frank and free gestures, his quick mind, his direct words, and his worries familiar to all, reduced the distance between him and everyone now assembled in the square.

In striking opposition to the medieval and renaissance carnival considered by Bakhtin, during which the church, its hierarchy, and its power were a target of the carnivalesque, the Polish Catholic Church, which was oppressed under the Communist regime, emerged in August 1980 as a part of this carnivalesque dissent. There was a spillover into the outside world of the imagery and behavior normally expected only inside the churches: those conspicuous displays of the icon of the Black Madonna; pictures of the pope; flowers and crosses; masses celebrated in the shipyards; people praying in public—and all of it part of this new upside-down world, all sharply challenging the existing order. For a careful observer, however, shipyards were also rich in typical carnavalesque contradictions and blasphemies: a religious cross positioned next to the bust of Lenin, portraits of the pope next to strike graffiti, a sign reading "Madonna on Strike!" that workers had put under the holy icon at shipyard gate number 3 as their response to the cautious tone of the church hierarchy, the outside sleeping shelters built from Styrofoam debris next to the shrinelike gate covered with fresh flowers and national flags, solemn images of workers receiving confession out in the open, and cabaret songs performed afterward over the loudspeakers. "A workers' revolution under the Sign of the Cross and the Pope's portrait—what a perfect example of history's merciless mockery of theory," observed Leszek Kolakowski.[21]

For such a carnival to take place, for performative democracy to occur, fear had to have diminished, or rather, a wall of fear had to have collapsed. Since the prior work of KOR, SKS, and the underground publishing operation NOWA (Polish acronym for Independent Publishing House), along with its numerous distribution points, had been prohibited, the continuation of this work depended on strong personal ties and could not have been accomplished without mutual trust, selfless assistance, and, simply, friendships. A society of civic communities is—according to Michael Walzer—the embodiment of Aristotelian friendship,[22] and in Poland these were sites where courage and commitment were daily confronted and challenged by fear and anxiety. For the society at large to transcend the wall of fear, Michnik argued, and to be effective in moving toward democratic forms, it needed the workers, the only social group that the regime was afraid of, and to whose pressures it had to give in.[23] Many Poles feel that John Paul II's famous words, "Do not fear," powerfully uttered during his first homily in Poland in 1979, contributed to a gradual shedding of fear throughout society at large. But in August 1980, much of it was, of course, still there.

A Shipbuilding Engineer

(addressing the government panel at the Gdansk negotiations, August 1980)

There is fear in society. There is fear. Fear of speaking up at a production meeting, at a union meeting, when submitting a more enterprising or audacious production proposal. And we have to get rid of it. You know it, and parts of Polish society also know it: the book that records the interventions of the censorship. There are entire volumes of these interventions. And we ought to discuss this, as this is a real picture of distortions and ignorance in which Polish society is kept. And this is a source of the biggest missteps. I'd like to suggest that all the things that took place until now ought to be published, made public, and that concrete steps be taken to prevent such things from happening in the future. This is exactly what you, Mr. Prime Minister, have said: censorship ought to be officially confirmed, and the rules of its operation—what is allowed and what is not—ought to be clear for the public.[24]

One of the most interesting questions is why the striking workers, whose protest had initially been motivated by specific economic and employment-related demands, ended up presenting at the negotiating table a position that put the larger public good over their individual interests as employees. Why did they present the government with a list of points that began with political demands concerning institutional pluralism, self-governance, freedom of expression, and human rights? After all, it was clear to everyone that those points, not the piecemeal ones about wages, were nonwinnable, impossible for the Communist regime to concede to, and therefore likely to jeopardize the entire negotiations.

The story of the shipyard strike reveals perhaps better than any other contemporary example the enduring validity of Hannah Arendt's insights concerning modern free laborers. The Polish workers understood their self-interest in winning the right to establish an independent and self-governing trade union, which—as Walesa reassured the crowds in front of the shipyard—would be the guarantee that public work outside of areas designated by the government would be possible. The imposed silencing of the memory of the workers killed in the 1970s was an example of the workers' direct experience concerning the absence of freedom of speech. Their emancipation from a repressive state took place when they insisted on being admitted to the political realm—though they were very careful not to use the term *political* in any public pronouncements coming from the shipyards.

Ironically—when one looks at the meager status of women in political life in Poland today—one should be reminded that the second phase of the strike with its key demand for freedom of expression would not have taken place if not for four women—a nurse, a tramway driver, a crane operator, and a newsstand vendor. At a time when the church hierarchy and even the leaders of KOR thought that the many workers' demands were unrealistic, these four women stood at the gates and convinced their colleagues that they ought to support other, smaller factories along the Baltic Coast who were still on strike and whose wrongs had not been addressed, and persuaded them to return to the shipyard to continue the strike.[25]

A Writer

(speaking during the Gdansk negotiations with the government, August 1980)
At the beginning of the current events there were efforts to steer the workers toward a discussion limited to the problem of wages. But the workers are full-fledged citizens who, with a full voice, are demanding full rights. Hence their demand for real, true trade unions independent from the state apparatus. Hence also their demand for an authentic regulation of the control over press and publications, so-called censorship, which in our case [the Polish case] is preventive censorship. We are fully aware of the complexity of Poland's alliances, and we know that the regulation of censorship ought to be regulated cautiously. But I want to emphasize that we—people associated in this Interfactory Strike Committee—fully understand the interest of Poland's security, etc. But we have to bring up the issue of publications, known as publications circulating outside the censorship. The point is that we have to find a way to implement a constitutionally guaranteed right for citizens to express their views publicly, and to publish books and periodicals. I would like to emphasize again that the workers associated with the Interfactory Strike Committee are full-fledged citizens, and they demand—with a full voice—their full citizens' rights. Thank You.[26]

The Poet

It was not just an abstract thought, that freedom of speech. The workers saw a connection between their economic misery and the lack of freedom of speech. They saw it because now some issues became better known. The reason for some economic disasters lay exactly in the lack of information about what's going on in the country.[27]

The Prime Minister

(speaking during the Gdansk negotiations with the workers, August 1980)
What I confirm is that the activity of censorship ought to serve the most indispensable matters of the state and social life.[28]

A Priest

(from a homily during a mass in the Gdynia shipyard)
Human rights, truth, and participation in spreading and supporting various forms of self-governance of the working people are guaranteed not only by natural, divine law, but also by a positive law, the international law signed in Helsinki, and the constitutional law of the Polish People's Republic.[29]

A Mechanic

(presenting the third demand of the striking workers during the Gdansk negotiations with the government, August 1980)
The government will bring before parliament within three months the draft of a law on the control of press, publications, and performances, based on the following principles: censorship ought to protect the interests of the state, i.e. state secrets of a political and economic nature, matters of the state's security and its vital international interests; it ought to protect religious convictions, as well as the rights of nonbelievers, and prevent the dissemination of morally offensive publications. The proposed bill will include the right to bring charges to the high administrative court against decisions of the office controlling the press, publications, and performances.[30]

The Prime Minister

Agreed. I accept this point.

The Poet

(recounting further)
During the Solidarity time everything changed literally from day to day. I could be a good example of it. After Solidarity was born I gave—in the first four to five months of Solidarity's existence—at least forty talks in various parts of the country, to various audiences: workers, intellectuals, students. I had a sense of reaching that audience, because one thing was the best proof of it: the lecture or a talk took one hour and the discussion went on for three hours. I gave a talk at the Cegielski Factory, a big train factory in Poznan, about censorship. Because the workers, and the people at large, were interested in publishing themselves. Every factory and office wanted to have their own newsletter, uncensored of course, being an organ of their Solidarity chapter.[31]

A Worker

We spoke openly about who is honest and who is not. About those who were supposedly honest, and were not.... You could read all about it in our bulletins.[32]

By the time Solidarity had enjoyed its nearly sixteen months of legal existence—well before the age of easy access to computers, fax, or Xerox machines, when the typewriter was still the main source of printed matter—there were about 200 different newsletters published by various enterprises, some issued in more than ten thousand copies. Most of the titles contained the word *solidarity,* followed by the name of town or factory (e.g., *Solidarity of Lower Silesia*), or names that reflected the need to address the shortcomings of the past, including the need for participation, such as *Free Word, Independence, Renewal, Rule of Law, Opinions, Concretely, Directly, Resonance,* and *Aspirations.* Sites of trusted information and debate on the work undertaken by the 10-million-strong Solidarity membership, the bulletins helped form public opinion and a culture of public deliberation. Importantly, they were published even in very small, provincial places (very much as in Alexis de Tocqueville's description of America, where there was scarcely a hamlet that did not have its own newspaper), far from industrial centers, where the local authorities were still very entrenched and did not accept the changes that seemed to be taking place at the top.

The bulletins were lists of initiatives and practical solutions and tactics applied by the unionists in various enterprises vis-à-vis hostile authorities, and they also fulfilled symbolic needs, often with the help of poetry. During the two weeks of the strikes in Gdansk, there was a raw strike poetry created on-site, expressing the convictions of the striking workers, printed in the bulletins and hand-copied by people.

Hannah Arendt would have found it particularly fitting[33] that poetry was there to encapsulate the years of humiliation, especially the hitherto forbidden poems of Czeslaw Milosz, whose Nobel Prize for Literature coincided with the birth of Solidarity. An excerpt from one of his poems ended up inscribed on the base of the monument erected in 1981—as guaranteed in the Gdansk agreement—in front of the shipyard to commemorate the workers killed there in December 1970:

> *You who have wronged a simple man*
> *Bursting into laughter at the crime . . .*
> *Do not feel safe. The poet remembers.*
> *You can slay one, but another is born.*
> *The words are written down, the deed, the date.*[34]

Poetry also fulfilled an important pragmatic function, as it assisted in a renewal of language, or rather its *parole* side, speech. The spoken and written language had been molded for decades by the official media to limit substantive expression and communicative function, successfully repressing the use of some words or divorcing words' signifiers from what they signified. Bulletins tried to use fresh, simple, and informative language, and everybody had an opportunity to test the freeing of oneself through it, while taking part in countless public discussions. The process of reversing public speech from the official, generic, and fuzzy to the informative, personal, and "familiar" resembled the processes of renewal that take place in the context of the carnival. The steel-mill workers from Czestochowa printed in their bulletin this excerpt from another Milosz poem:

> *We were permitted to shriek in the tongue of dwarfs and*
> *demons*
> *But pure and generous words were forbidden.*[35]

Milosz's poetry written in exile, a bitter testimony on the past, appeared next to the sermons of a Catholic philosopher, Jozef Tischner, written in a positive tone and very popular. "Dialogue," wrote Tischner, "means that people leave their hiding places, come closer to each other, begin exchanging words. The very beginning of a dialogue—leaving the hiding places—is already a big event."[36] Reprinted in thousands of newsletters throughout Poland, such texts provided enlightened guidance through the process of a collective discovery of self-expression.

A Printer

What did the preparations for printing these bulletins look like? We usually got together in my workshop at home. Typists from various enterprises and factories in our region brought the articles; I prepared a graphic layout for them beforehand with columns indicating where they are to type. So we cut the articles and pasted them up, and at 5 a.m. we got into a car and drove 100 kilometers east to a certain factory. And then when it suddenly turned out that we cannot use the printing facilities in this factory, we went to another one and so on. . . . Technically, every issue was completely improvised. Getting hold of paper was a miracle in itself. It is hard to explain because it is difficult to talk about those things publicly . . . how we got hold of paper, and so on. . . . But thanks to the help of the workers we were able to do the printing. . . . But a touch of danger entered our life, which had been placid until them. For instance, when the printing equipment was in our home, we were afraid. . . . What if the secret police would come, then what will happen? . . . Our first encounter with those sad people who will question us. . . . What is this machine for? What's it doing here? What are you doing here? We had never been involved in public life before. We were not even aware that it was "public life."[37]

RES PUBLICA

The Gdansk agreement signed in August 1980 was not a transaction—as in the case of the Young Theater movement—masterminded by the government and then put to good use by its other signatories. Rather, it appeared to be an accord initiated by the people who—in the context of real socialism and its alliances—understood the limits of their actions and took full responsibility for them. Their ostensible aim was not to overthrow the power but to deal with the problems of everyday life, to better the lives of all.

There were a total of eighty demands negotiated by the workers and signed by the government in late August at the large industrial sites of the major strikes in Gdansk, Szczecin, and Jastrzebie. Of these, fifty-four were concerned with issues such as truth, human dignity, freedom of speech, freedom of confession, the need to repair the economy, and democracy in general.[38] The dependent status of workers and intellectuals vis-à-vis the state, and the general conviction that the Communist authorities would do everything to humiliate them, prompted the demands for dignity. One can already see this in the August negotiations, when—in a situation of dramatic food shortages—the workers asked that only surplus food be exported, or that shops selling luxury goods for foreign currency be closed.

The accord was between people who refused to be treated as adolescents and rulers who were forced to see the unthinkable: a population that had just graduated into a citizenry. The publicity given this graduation, the spectacular character of its "space of appearance," along with the national broadcast of the signing ceremony as stipulated by the workers and featuring Walesa's conspicuous, supersized pen with the pope's image on it—all this instantly changed the definition of the situation.

Suddenly everyone was truly engaged in multiple roles outside the family: as employee, consumer, resident of a region, member of a professional association or environmental or cultural group, and citizen of the state. As difficult as it may be to imagine, most people abruptly ceased having private lives. They spent their time not only at work but at very lengthy though exhilarating meetings, lectures, and working sessions of all sorts to address the many challenges of their new public sphere: writing the bylaws of their new associations, discussing the priority topics to be raised in the upcoming issues of their countless factory or association bulletins and newsletters, developing new curricula in history and the humanities, dealing with surveillance or interference by the authorities or provocations by the militia, striving for transparency of decisionmaking in the workplace, or debating—for example—how to approach their traditionally Communist May 1 observances, given that May Day was ostensibly a celebration of the workers.[39] And then there was a profound need to "publicize" everything, to make sure that all of this was made public.

Unlike the case of the Young Theater, when theater became life, after August 1980 life in Poland became like a theater in which one felt as though one were at once actor and audience, taking part in new kinds of scenes, acting on many stages, playing different parts, listening to diverse voices, using new props. A collective and open participation in a sphere that used to be forbidden until now resulted in a special holidaylike atmosphere, in a carnivalesque world, as it was not only special but a franticly active, tireless, creative, nonviolent, unbelievable upside-down world. (It is not surprising that this was all very different from the way such freedoms have long tended to be taken for granted and left unused by most Americans, though possibly the Internet is beginning to change that.) The thrill of the newly gained right to speak, to communicate, to learn, found its expression in an intensive publishing and debating scene, providing an instant and constant social feedback, a key mechanism in any democracy. Factories, universities, and enterprises all had informal shops sponsored by the Solidarity Union where one could find out about lectures and meetings and buy uncensored books, historical documents, local bulletins, and poetry. The uniqueness of Solidarity—said Adam Michnik later on—lay in the fact that it made intellectuals out of electricians and drivers.[40]A peculiar feature of this body that, after all, called itself a trade union was that it was organized territorially and not according to trades, branches of industry, or professions. So truckers belonged to the same structures as teachers, nurses, and coal miners. This arrangement facilitated a broader sense of responsibility, solidarity, and reciprocity. Just as the striking shipyard workers demanded the freeing of political prisoners, at a time when many enterprises faced the resistance of local authorities in implementing the Gdansk agreement, the stronger industries went on strike on behalf of weaker ones. Some protested on behalf of those who—as Solidarity decided—should not go on strike because they served the most urgent social needs, like doctors or teachers.

Solidarity was a federation of people living and working in several geographic regions who often named their branches after the names of their respective lands, but its very foundation and the heart of the public sphere was the workplace—the mines, the steel mills, the factories. This is where people lived and worked; this is where they knew each other face-to-face. The circulating bulletins representing their respective work environments, visits of representatives from other regions, and the construction of many horizontal connections made Solidarity into an imagined, countrywide *gemeinschaft* of people who felt they knew each other intimately through their shared ideals and aspirations. Yet the publicness of this *gemeinschaft,* its preoccupation with larger public things, with the *res publica,* calls for an alternative designation.

The actual site of this large discursive sphere was almost identical with the one examined by Habermas, with one extra ingredient: its spontaneous enthusiasm. It was an extensive and uncensored press, with literary and political periodicals and occasional documents, either printed or mimeographed, and all widely distributed. The *res publica* was made possible in large part by a sudden and massive explosion in the previously limited and semiclandestine culture of self-publishing and low-tech in-house printing. This legitimate child of the mimeograph revolution of the late 1970s—this whole world of letters during the Solidarity period—quickly outgrew the reach, the size, and the impact of its forebear.

Had Tocqueville[41] had a chance to travel to Poland during the sixteen months of Solidarity's existence, he would have encountered an irresistible theater of democracy, driven by a recognition of human rights and fueled by a vibrant associational life, "the combined power of the individuals united into a society" with its passions and prejudices, not unlike those he had witnessed in America 150 years before. I am sure he would have agreed that the Poles had developed an enormous appetite for debate, and in a way had reinvented their own New England town meeting. And he would certainly see the enduring power of the phenomenon he discovered in America: the influence of the free press on the emergence of democratic culture, "for it accords a means of intercourse between those who hear and address each other, and without ever coming into immediate contact."[42]

In spite of a mushrooming infrastructure that issued and transmitted not only information but also statements of mission, bylaws, declarations, and projects—mostly related to self-government and self-management, and always taking responsibility for balancing the interests of the individual with the needs of the community—one could not easily detect a long-term program for Solidarity. This general programlessness supports my initial assumption that what was prompted by the strikes in the Gdansk shipyards was not a social movement but a public sphere introducing pluralism into all spheres of life. Rather than being an instrument for change, Solidarity was itself a change. The sense of responsible self-restraint, self-limitation, and the general support for a solution based on compromise remained an important principle of Solidarity despite the conviction—increasing with time—that the existing system did not lend itself to reform, that it was incapable of evolution.[43]

I do not want to argue that the public sphere that emerged in Poland closely followed the Habermas "script," or that it was founded on the basis of a rational-critical debate. The center of this morally sensitive public sphere was constituted by a debate on collective identity that strongly emphasized the commonality of values within the *res publica*. The model is perhaps better known from the writings of Vaclav Havel, but it was in Poland that it found its most massive application. In all the sociological surveys conducted at that time, Solidarity members declared above all the need for freedom and truth.

These declarations reflected the dynamic of the August strike in the Gdansk shipyard, where the workers stopped short of signing the economic concessions granted by the government and demanded the freeing of political prisoners, including dissidents "preventively" arrested in late August, a suspension of the repressions vis-à-vis independent publishing houses, and, above all, the establishment of trade unions independent of the Party and the state. It was Stefan Nowak who first noticed that one of the demands most crucial for the workers' sense of dignity was to have their own independent and self-governing trade union.[44]

Solidarity does not readily lend itself to coherent theoretical analysis, as it is a grand spectacle with Hollywood characters, opera-ready scenery, a multitude of exciting, dramatic threads, and a tragic though cathartic ending. Nevertheless, in many of its features Solidarity does resemble the Habermasian model of the public sphere: in its spontaneity, in its multiplicity of voices, and in the clear-cut emergence of an engaged social self, as Habermas puts it, secured by institutional arrangements and sustained by the print media. When Habermas, focusing in 1962 on a liberal model of the public sphere, questioned the possibility of its effective reconstruction, he had not envisioned, of course, the existence of a public sphere without the market. He did not see the possibility of a public sphere that could lose its links to the state and did not explore the possibility of a discursive sphere not driven by purely rational-critical arguments.

And yet, Solidarity, the *res publica* of 1980–1981, constituted just that kind of peculiar public sphere, with its unprecedented degree of high-spirited participation, responsible discourse devoted to public causes, and truly heroic efforts to fulfill its major role: relating the needs and aspirations of civil society to those of the state. This peculiarity was a function of the broader political and geopolitical conditions, under which the state in fact appeared to have less autonomy than the *res publica,* even though both were under constraints: the state under external ones and Solidarity under its own self-imposed limits.

The Gdansk agreement launched extraordinary societal transformation, but it did not transform the party-state into a rational, impersonal site of authority. Habermas's ideal of rationalizing the public authorities through the influence of informed discourse and reasoned agreement appeared to be—at least in the short run—unfeasible fairly soon after the signing of the Gdansk accords. Under mounting pressure from Moscow, and from its own party apparatus, the state became an increasingly hostile, unpredictable, incompetent, and uncooperative adversary. By the fall of 1981, the authorities did not want to negotiate, or even to talk, or even to listen.

Although the state disappeared as a partner in dialogue, *res publica* became a dialogue in itself, though one relegated to the fringes beyond effective politics, a dialogue in which sociopolitical concerns had to be replaced by moral questions. Solidarity was compelled to function as a highly mobilized polity that shadowed the state, creating its own authorities, experts, and domains of competence. And this is why the union was often referred to as an alternative society, or as "parallel structures." It was a train traveling down the tracks, as Kuron said, that officially just wasn't on the timetable. The 1986 Helsinki Committee Report concluded that during its legal existence, Solidarity did not work against the regime in most cases, but rather in spite of the regime, or simply aside from the regime.[45]

One way of thinking about that phenomenon, especially a posteriori, is in terms of Bakhtinian carnival, a time of all-consuming positive activity subjected to the laws of freedom; festive, not ordinary, time directed toward change and renewal and mediated by new types of communication and speech patterns.[46] In medieval towns the carnival lasted three months, and it offered what Bakhtin calls an extrapolitical aspect of the world, of man and human relations. Carnival is, after all, an *entr'acte* in reality, long enough for people to shed fear, to leave their hiding places, but usually not long enough to "straighten their backs" and to carry on them, as Tischner put it, "the heavy burden of another human being."[47]

The theoretical and practical improbability of anything but an *entr'acte* in the sociopolitical order of real socialism was grasped by Karol Modzelewski, one of the leading intellectuals in the movement, who during the last meeting of the National Commission of Solidarity in Gdansk and only hours before the imposition of martial law, said: "Society has organized itself democratically, but the system of power has remained totalitarian."[48] In the end, the Gdansk agreement turned out to be a case of unhappy performativity, with one side—though appearing to fulfill formally all the rules of the performative utterance (the accords)—being insincere at the moment of "uttering" it; that is, at the moment of signing it.

This unhappy performative, nevertheless, afforded the Poles an extended carnival, the Solidarity period, a lengthy *entr'acte,* allowing the *res publica* to emerge and considerable social and human capital to develop. The knowledge of the public matter, and the experience—not imagined but real—of acting in public did not disappear with the crushing of Solidarity on December 13, 1981, by the military dictatorship, the imposition of martial law, and the imprisonment of thousands of people. Bakhtin, a big believer in the power of plebeian culture, who thought about the carnival as a temporary liberation from tyrannical rule but also a threat to the existing order, would have welcomed the idea—not plausible at the time of the premodern monarchies and serfdom that he studied—of the carnival as a rehearsal for a change of systems. The carnival of *res publica,* a time of societal practice in public communication and agentic dialogue, developed a pool of local knowledge, which sustained societal hope. Eight years later the critical importance of that carnival was to be borne out.

4

Citizen Michnik

The cultural role of philosophy is not to deliver the truth but to build
the spirit of truth, and this means never to let the inquisitive energy
of the mind go to sleep, never to stop questioning what appears to be
obvious and definitive, always to defy the seemingly intact resources
of common sense, always to suspect that there might be "another
side" to what we take for granted.

—Leszek Kolakowski

Kolakowski's passage on the mission of philosophy in many respects
characterizes the work of his student, who, though not a professional philosopher, is a consummate thinker of action and an activist of thought:
Adam Michnik. It was the writings and rather peculiar projects—labeled
antipolitical—of Michnik, Vaclav Havel, Gyorgy Konrad, Jacek Kuron,
and Janos Kis that articulated an agenda for the democratic opposition in
Eastern Europe. It was their writings that became the center of attention for
the western Left as it searched beyond Marxism for new inspiration, for a
progressive, radical politics in a new key.[1] But it is Michnik's early essay "The
New Evolutionism" that opened up a new vista for dissident intellectuals
in the region, proposing a new, nonviolent strategy of essentially performative, speech-based, incremental transformations that—as envisioned by the
author—eventually led to fundamental changes in Eastern Europe.[2]

Though Michnik was hardly a pacifist, while imprisoned under martial law (altogether he spent over six years in Communist prisons) he argued
for a self-limiting revolution, renouncing revolutionary violence. Widely
perceived as the intellectual architect of the negotiations with the regime in
the spring of 1989 that launched the democratic transformation in Poland,
Michnik became an influential and passionate voice for a normal, "gray,"
ultimately liberal democracy in the post-Communist countries.

Ten years later, at the beginning of the twenty-first century, his writings are driven by what he sees as the troubling disappearance of the democratic debate, the fading of that initially promising grayness, and the reemergence of the simplistic dichotomies that, inundated with suspicion and devoid of generosity, explain the world in terms of black and white, absolute good and absolute evil. Wrestling with the ways in which the newly institutionalized democracy is allowing its promise and its spirit to be misled, he calls for courage, imagination, and mercy—important prerequisites for performative democracy. Another prerequisite, public space, even if less robust, is already there. In his most recent book, published in 2006, he confesses: "When I look at today's Poland, I feel a bit like a farmer after the hail has destroyed his crop and his livestock. But what does the farmer do when he sees this? The poet Adam Mickiewicz advised that the farmer begin seeding his fields all over again."[3]

Like his friends from the West, Ira Katznelson, Jonathan Schell, Daniel Cohn-Bendit, and Joschka Fischer, Michnik is a member of the 1968 generation. And though the students striking at Columbia University and those protesting on the streets of Paris in May 1968 only in the most general way shared the aspirations of students protesting in March 1968 in Warsaw, or resembled those of the participants in the Prague Spring, by the end of the century in each of these contexts the generation of 1968 had become more than just a legend. Havel was president of his country; Michnik was head of the most influential newspaper in the region; Joschka Fisher, leader of the Green Party, had become the foreign minister of a united Germany; and Ira Katznelson, who as dean had successfully rebuilt the Graduate Faculty of the New School, was now president of the Association of Political Science.

One of the leaders of the March 1968 student movement for free speech—the beginning, as he put it, of his generation's road to freedom—Michnik was expelled from Warsaw University and sentenced to three years in prison. For those like me who arrived at Warsaw University later, and therefore to our regret "missed" March 1968, Michnik was already becoming a distant figure in the early 1970s, as the university was cleansed of activists—many of whom were forced into exile, were sent to the army, or were about to graduate. The Michnik legend was there, but his face was not familiar anymore, and his whereabouts were a mystery to the average young student. I learned through a friend, a native of Warsaw, that when Michnik was released from his three-year sentence after a year and a half, he was banned from Warsaw University and sent for "resocialization" to the Rosa Luxemburg Lightbulb Factory, where he worked as a welder. Two years later he was allowed to commute on weekends to distant Poznan University, where he continued his study and graduated in history.

Adam Michnik, the dissident and the prisoner, was often referred to in the West as a historian. But there was something definitely missing in that description, the kind of thing that is easily overlooked if one is not

familiar with the local context. I am left with a similar feeling of dissatisfaction when I hear foreign scholars refer to the late Stanislaw Ossowski as
"a brilliant Polish sociologist." In Ossowski's opinion the professional duty
of an intellectual—and especially of a sociologist—was to think disobedi-
ently. Punished during the Stalinist period for his persistence in defending
fundamental human values, Ossowski is perceived in Poland as a person
whose very conduct was an answer to a situation in which many had felt
there was no answer. One of his students, Jan Strzelecki, wrote, "It seems
that this man achieved an extraordinary autonomy of thought and judgment
that is rare in our times and constitutes—in my opinion—not just his own
individual achievement but a common property of our society. Autonomy
here means an independent attitude toward the measure of human values,
toward the problem of good and evil, toward the measure of the true and
the false, of worthy and unworthy acts."[4]

A productive writer known for his integrity and for his exemplary and
autonomous conduct throughout the 1970s and the 1980s, Adam Michnik
is also an extraordinarily generous person and a tirelessly resourceful intellectual who has read everything, who remembers every word he has read and
every face he has seen, and whose contagious energy animates individual
people and group initiatives. Two volumes of his writings published in the
United States thirteen years apart, entitled by the editor *Letters from Prison*
(1985) and *Letters from Freedom* (1998),[5] provide a convenient time frame
in which to situate Michnik's work. But a whole host of subsequent reflections has not yet been available in one volume, one that might be called
Troubles with Freedom. It is here that Michnik has been trying—as patiently
as he can and with his characteristic use of historical analogies—to issue
dramatic warnings about the vanishing of democratic dialogue.

In writing about Michnik's work today it seems natural to distinguish
between his initial position as a dissident and political prisoner and his
later one as a citizen—and a very prominent one at that—in a democratic
state. At the same time, it is important to keep in mind that as a dissident
and prisoner he acted as though he was a citizen of any "normal democratic
country," and that now as a citizen of a democratic country, he is increasingly articulating a voice of democratic dissent.

Continuously central to his thought is a position that allows him to
make moral claims in politics while at the same time remaining receptive
to the necessity for compromise. But how successful is he in striking a
balance between moral principle and the indispensability of compromise?
The question is a contentious one, not just in his Polish context. Michnik
the citizen is also speaking and writing on problems faced by the world at
large. A recipient of major European awards, a mercurial political thinker
present in major international debates, he is a political figure who inspires
allegiance and provokes controversies both at home and abroad.

Finally, for me to write about Michnik is a daunting task. Along with
my friends at Warsaw University in the 1970s, I admired his brilliance,

his amazing knowledge, but also his independence, courage, and wit. I followed his writings during martial law from New York, and after 1989 I got to know him personally, as we often taught together at the New School for Social Research. For better or for worse, Adam Michnik has become a property of the society, both a national treasure and a target of hostile attacks, and though he is a friend, I shall try to look at him with some critical distance.

DISSIDENT

Michnik's project for a democratic and just society, expressed both through his probing writings and his own exemplary autonomous conduct in the 1970s, seemed both restrained and radical. His hope was to encourage a community of freer people, gradually capable of transcending the limitations set up by the system while quietly but systematically altering the immediate reality they lived in.

The project emerged in a context that for three decades had been dominated by a discourse exclusively conducted by the hegemonic party-state and based on the only "correct," scientifically argued laws of social development. By editing out most of Karl Marx's philosophy of activity and participation, and by postponing into some distant future beyond one's reach any vision of a society that might address the full spectrum of human needs, such a discourse locked people up in a realm of predetermined necessities and engendered the fatalistic self-image of a society that could not undertake anything on its own. The violently repressed citizens' protests of 1956, 1968, and 1970 in Hungary, Czechoslovakia, and Poland, all smashed even when the darkest Stalinist period was already over, seemed to corroborate this sense of hopelessness. "Totalitarian systems," concluded Michnik, "removed the possibility of average people exerting any real influence on social matters."[6]

He realized that to turn things around would require a concerted effort to create a new language that could name, represent—and help people think about—the reality they actually lived in. The task then was to come up with new words, categories, and images that could grasp and bring back to light active, autonomous minds that would stand for integrity and self-determination under the most trying circumstances. Ultimately, the challenge was to come up with a language in which the situation of captivity could be defined and alternative discourses could be articulated. Michnik looked for allies in constructing or reviving such language and found them among poets (Milosz, Herbert, Baranczak), people of the Young Theater movement, students, and eventually the younger generation of workers. "A society in captivity must produce an illegal literature"—wrote Michnik in 1973—"because it must know the truth about itself, see an unfalsified picture of itself, hear its own genuine voice. The existence of illegal literature is a prerequisite for the fight against the captivity of the spirit."[7] Published initially under pseudonyms, or in diasporic publications, from 1977 his own essays were distributed throughout the country by the underground press.

One of the first hitherto missing categories Michnik himself introduced was an abstract noun that conveyed a quality of a society capable of expressing its preferences and of determining its own creative actions: a society that is aware of the plurality of possible paths that could be taken, and one that is able to act upon the choices it makes. This noun, *podmiotowosc* in Polish and used by Michnik systematically since the late 1970s, has been given various renditions in its English translations (most frequently *self-determination* and *subjectivity*) that do not quite capture the power of what it signifies in the original. The very basis of that noun is another Polish noun, *podmiot*, which means *subject*, and *subjectivity* perfectly replicates the structure of *podmiot-owosc*. The emphasis is indeed on the subject, but not only on the character of its cognition but above all on its ingenuity, the creative aspects of its autonomous being. Thus the closest English-language signifier would be *agency*, indicating a capacity of individuals or collective subjects to be the authors of their own lives, capable of reflecting upon them, and capable of initiating purposeful, autonomous action to transform them. Furthermore, the Polish word—perhaps more than its English counterpart—is strongly associated with the sense of self-respect and above all *dignity*, even though there is a separate Polish word for dignity as well.

In order to build *podmiotowosc* we need a new language, new categories, new words, insisted Michnik.[8] Aware that words are not innocent, as they have a capacity to unleash both reconciliation and hatred, Michnik patiently dismisses the strategy for a change that resorts to the latter. Instead he explores the potential of the speech-acts that nurture the emergence of culture based on a dialogue, an exchange of different views and opinions. Contesting the opaque language of doctrinaire incantations and spells used by the regime, he discusses the liberating power of language and argues that language, a quintessential public good, is itself a form of freedom. On the pages that follow, I'd like to demonstrate that his own writings, which named things hitherto unnamed or unveiled things hidden, and which offered a rereading and a rethinking of stories and ideas long suppressed and unavailable to the average person, were performative, in that they made it possible for people *to be*, by creating the conditions for self-reflection, self-knowledge, and action.

The essential semantic ingredient of *podmiotowosc*, that of dignity, made Michnik's often-anonymous message understood and welcomed, and then it gradually spread beyond the circles of the secular intelligentsia to churchgoers and workers. Its performative power made the sense of *self*, and of subject, extend beyond the private. A large collective self saw itself physically during the new Pope's first visit to Poland in 1979, and heard together his memorable "Do not fear." New voices articulated themselves, and the construction of social communication on a large scale had begun.

Agency, as Michnik saw it, was above all an attribute of society, more specifically of a civil society, expressed "by building up *self-determination* [the translation errs here] in civil society, by creating associations from below and avoiding the intermediary role of the state institutions in public life"[9] The categories of *agency* and *civil society* helped to verbalize, and therefore to discover, and then to implement the new competence of individuals and communities to perform, to act vis-à-vis the structures of the party-state.

And when he and his friends in the region tried to reinvent politics[10] by encouraging the agency and civil society independently, scholars in the social sciences in the West began to conceptualize and theorize agency and structure, and returned to an exploration of language as a potent institution of social existence, strongly influencing social practice.[11]

"Freedom is identical with self-creation. I will sculpt my life on my own," Michnik wrote while in prison in 1982.[12] The performativity of Michnik's writings is that of both an instigator of the new civic knowledge and one of its key performers. When put behind bars to disappear, Michnik managed to make prisons his stage, his space of appearance. The enacting of this implausible, hidden-from-the-public, performative space was meant to carry on a discussion that could have happened under the conditions of freedom. Written in a conversational tone and smuggled from prison, his essays were promptly disseminated throughout the country by the underground press.

"There is no epithet in the Polish language that has not been spoken to Michnik's face nor a single plaudit that has not been cited in his honor," wrote the philosopher/priest Father Jozef Tischner many years later in an essay titled *Why God Created Michnik*.[13] The dissident historian from *Letters from Prison,* the volume that introduced him to the American public, Michnik has been perceived by his compatriots first of all as an exceptional man, and only then as a passionate writer, critic, and author of key reappraisals of Poland's past. Some Poles remembered his name from the relentless attacks by the press in 1968 calling him a "notorious ringleader of student unrest at Warsaw University," but few people knew what happened to him afterward. The broad public noticed his name again in statements on the activities of the Committee in Defense of the Workers (KOR, established in 1976 to assist imprisoned workers of Radom and Ursus), as a lecturer of the "Flying University," and as an author of articles in underground periodicals. Imprisoned in the meantime for shorter or longer periods, Michnik became a truly household name after the Otwock incident in May 1981. Though harassed and beaten many times by the police himself, he managed to calm a crowd enraged by a local instance of police brutality and thereby saved the lives of some policemen surrounded by the townspeople. When he arrived on the scene, his first words were exactly how the official press had labeled him at the time: "My name is Adam Michnik, and I am an antisocialist force," he said, in a striking instance of performativity, impossible for an outsider to understand. His very name, like a well-known and trusted brand, worked like a magic spell, a marvelous dream tool for conflict resolution.

The phenomenon of the "domestication" of Michnik's name and even veneration by his compatriots is reflected in a novel by a respected scholar and author, J. M. Rymkiewicz, titled *Polish Conversations: Summer of 1983.*[14] The plot is simple: on vacation in the Lake District, various people from the circles of the intelligentsia come together for conversation and chitchat. One character called Gienio refers to Adam Michnik using the diminutive form, "Adas," of the sort normally reserved for family members and close friends (the way a group of Robert Kennedy admirers might reminisce about "Bobby"). At one point Marek, a character who sometimes takes on the role of narrator, wonders why someone who does not even know Michnik personally would call him "Adas." Gienio would not have known him because he had spent most of his life in the merchant marine, was now a minor clerk in a local city hall, and during vacations earns extra money chopping wood. Marek comes to the conclusion that this is not so very odd after all. He himself refers to Michnik affectionately: "Adas wrote an article.... Adas was on the radio.... Adas got locked up.... They let him out.... Adas got locked up again.... Adas laid into Pinochet, and he'll give it to our Pinochet as well. Just wait'll they let him on the street again! ... Our sweet, strong, our very own Adas."[15] Marek knows Michnik personally, but he is certainly not so well acquainted with him as to have the right to call him "Adas." So both he and Gienio, in referring to Michnik this way—at least this is how Marek sees it—are expressing their affection for the hero of Otwock and their solidarity with the prisoner from the infamous Rakowiecka prison.

A little later Marek and Gienio are discussing the general situation under martial law. Michnik has been in jail for a year and a half, since December 1981, when martial law was imposed: "And turning homeward again Marek looks back at the axe stuck into the chopping block. 'You know, Gienio, I don't think this can go on much longer either. It has no right to exist at all'. 'Adas will fix them,' says Gienio happily, swinging the axe. 'I swear to God he will.' 'Only if we help him, Gienio. Only if we help.'" And discussing the relationship between Michnik and Jacek Kuron, another popular figure and longtime friend and collaborator of Michnik's, Gienio announces: "In KOR Kuron was always the brains, but Adas was its heart and soul. And when Kuron becomes Prime Minister—mark my words—he'll have Adas locked up. Because Adas simply will not stand for any injustice, even the tiniest."[16]

It is difficult to say how much of the above is fictional and how much is based on actual conversations. What is interesting in these remarks is not the accuracy of their political judgment but the fact that they reflect the close personal connection that many people felt for Michnik—one that transcended politics. He has been a hero who can do anything, as though there were a small bit of every Pole in him. He has been a man who can do no wrong in the most difficult circumstances and—what's probably more interesting—in the moments of greatest success as well. There has been this popular conviction about him that he is a strong, pure, incorruptible, indomitable, superhuman force for resistance.

The difficulty in explaining Michnik's position in pre-1989 Polish society lies in the fact that there was then no one with comparable status. To call him a historian places him in academic circles that indeed command respect and in some cases even reverberate in popular culture. But rarely do intellectuals become folk heroes as well. Yes, Michnik was also a writer, but a writer who has always tended to produce under more or less extraordinary circumstances. His very first book, *The Church, the Left, and Dialogue*,[17] was written during his visit abroad in 1976. A historical essay on Piłsudski, *Shadows of Forgotten Ancestors*,[18] was written under a pseudonym for a competition announced by the émigré Institute of Polish History in London (and won First Prize). Almost all his other pre-1989 works were written in various Polish prisons.[19]

His preferred genre, the essay, is packed with other voices and thoughts and has always thrived on questioning, comparing, contrasting, and identifying. His reasoning, dramatically constructed, makes the reader a participant in a sort of hearing. While he was in prison, it was mostly a hearing on the Polish past—conducted by the author in a very personal way. And the investigation was undertaken not in order to straighten out the historical record but to help in comprehending the present. In fact, every essay—even if "historical"—addressed some contemporary Polish dilemma, and Michnik readily admits that searching for analogies is what man's mind does.[20]

Nevertheless, the conception of history as having detectable rules and regularities is alien to Michnik. He would agree with one of his characters that history is *ex definitione* a discipline of unique facts, irretrievable hours, and unique characters. His historical essays offer a rereading of the Poles' modern political traditions and actions, which—since the partitions of the country in 1795—have been preoccupied with one major task: how to respond to captivity. In *Conversation in the Citadel*,[21] one of the essays that appealed to left-leaning thinkers in the West, Michnik reflects on the content of those traditions that originated at the turn of the nineteenth century with the National Democratic movement and with the independence-oriented Socialists. Those were two very different programs for building a sovereign state, and until now both remain potent sources generating aggressive nationalism, anti-Semitism, and political fanaticism on the one hand, and tolerance and pluralism on the other. This reexamination of past conflicts helped to crystallize for Michnik's readers in Poland the direction society should move in during the "state of war" imposed by the Polish military regime in December

1981: self-organization, a careful "politics of activism," and a national solidarity that respects differences.

Three generations before the National Democrats and the Socialists formulated their programs, in late November 1830, young Polish cadets in Warsaw disarmed the Russian garrison and seized the arsenal. The dramatic November Uprising against tsarist rule in Poland had begun. Exactly 150 years later, in November 1980, thanks to the freedoms won in August by the shipyard workers, Adam Michnik was able to give a public talk at the Jagiellonian University in Krakow, at the invitation of the students. We know the text of the talk, which was not written down, because it was recorded by the secret police and used as evidence against the speaker in a later trial. The lecture was called "November Uprising, Polish Questions," and here is how Michnik began: "'November is a dangerous time for Poland,' wrote a poet. And he was probably right. He was right, because after the 150 years that separate us from that November night, we are confronting the events of those days with our contemporary questions. We violate, thereby, the canon of historical science. We allow ourselves an impermissible actualization. We risk being accused of ahistoricism. But we cannot deny that after 150 years we are still confronting that epoch, those matters, and those supposedly departed people with our questions and complaints. Through them and through the perplexities they faced, we discover ourselves: our anxiety and our choices, our decisions, our backpedaling, our right to pride and our right to shame, our reasons for daydreaming." And near the end of the talk: "History either does not justify any attitude or it justifies every one. History, I believe, only lets us find in its pages ourselves."[22] And indeed it is in the creative tension with past ideas and developments, "in a dialogue with those who are now absent," that the new categories emerge that help us to grasp our own times. Still, Michnik incessantly distances himself from history seen as moving according to some necessary laws, as this "strips society of its agency ... and its capacity for self-determination."[23]

Michnik is fascinated by characters throughout history who have provided Poles with sterling examples of honorable action. He points out the significance of gestures that are important and indispensable in dark times yet are simultaneously constrained and tragic. In his essay *The Indomitable Londoner*,[24] he considers Rejtan, a deputy to the 1773 Sejm, who tore open his shirt and threw himself on the floor, blocking the exit and exhorting the other delegates to vote against the partition of Poland by three European empires. Such gestures in defiance of oppression are the only power the powerless have at their disposal in times of national misery. And this is why the vocation of the Polish intellectual, says Michnik, is essentially "Rejtanesque": "His lot endowed him with the privilege of speaking in a society whose mouth was gagged. For that reason Rejtan can still take part in Poles' late-night conversations, and his gesture still provides an ethical norm and a call for dignity."[25]

But Michnik will also argue that Rejtan's behavior cannot be reduced to a heroic gesture. This symbol of an uncompromising position has immense value for those who are condemned—by everyday reality—to compromises. In fact, Rejtan's gesture performs a very practical "cognitive" function. It identifies the realm of admissible compromise and helps distinguish compromise from treason. While discussing Rejtan, Michnik—himself always uncompromising, but stressing that "sacrifice one can only ask of oneself"[26]—acknowledges that people are born to compromise.

The problem of compromise was the central issue in almost every text written by Michnik the dissident. And the main question concerned the limits of compromise. His own discussion with the country's complicated past has been of service in the heated conversations about Poland's Communist present, or rather its various stages: that is, the post–October 1956, the post–March 1968, the post–June 1976, and the post–Solidarity 1980. In each of those periods the predicament of those who live under real socialism has consisted in having to contend with compromise. Michnik's lesson from the 1968 Prague Spring was "that change is possible, and that it has its limits."[27] "We have reason to be optimistic in the long run," he wrote, one year before Solidarity exploded in 1980, "but still we must count on acting alongside the governing monoparty."[28]

Michnik's big question is how to define the limits of permissible compromise. After all, he himself has been an advocate of the "solution by compromise" all along, calling it "self-limiting revolution," "a hybrid system" in which the state's totalitarian organizations coexist with society's democratic ones, or "solutions falling between conciliation and evolution." Free of the fanatical mentality of the professional revolutionary, he asks for patience and self-restraint in dealing with the authorities, who are weakened but still inflexible after August 1980: "We are all floating on the same raft and we may all sink with it."[29]

But does Michnik solve the question of compromise? Can this question, which both concerns the conduct of the individual and shapes the strategy for collective action, be solved on the level of discourse at all? Can the limits of compromise be somehow defined by referring to specific historical experience, that is, by pointing out that up to such and such a point we are dealing with acceptable compromise, while from that point on we are facing "manifest treason"? How high a price may one pay in order to be allowed to continue lecturing, publishing, or practicing one's profession?[30] Are there conditions under which a policy of conciliation with the Communist regime makes sense?[31] What is really possible today? Is "going for independence and parliamentary democracy" realistic in 1980?

Two months after the official registration of the Solidarity union as a legitimate organization under the law of the Polish People's Republic, Michnik, in his November 1980 talk at the Jagiellonian University in Krakow, addressed the issue of compromise in front of a huge audience. Reflecting on the mechanisms of servility, he said:

Compromise is a *virtue* for free nations, and a *requirement* for conquered nations—a requirement that is difficult to heed because it constantly poses the question of its own limits. So where are those boundaries of compromise? There can be no precise answer to this. Every answer is situational. But one thing seems to be certain: the boundary lies in the realm of language. Language is, in my opinion, an uncrossable border. Compromise at the level of language transforms the conciliation into a lie and leads to betrayal.[32]

A few years later, after the crackdown on Solidarity, whose institutionalized existence was an outcome of a compromise between the regime and the society, in one of his books written in prison during martial law, *Such Are the Times . . . A Word on Compromise* (1985),[33] Michnik addressed the problem again and made a temporary—but unusual for him—shift. For now the conciliatory voice was gone. When read for its ethical considerations, the book clearly embraces an ethos that refuses any possibility of conciliation or even negotiation with the devil. When read as a political treatise it seems to codify the rules of political behavior in accordance with the highest level of moral expectations. The balance between the need to keep one's own moral ground vis-à-vis a regime that overnight had multiplied by thousands the number of political prisoners and the need for compromise was upset. Yet it is not hard to predict the kind of criticism that such an "indomitable" position provoked: Michnik can afford to hold it, they said, as he has "those completely clean" hands, but this cannot function as the basis for a political program. This is moralizing, and moralizing as such cannot satisfy urgent political needs, the argument went.

Indeed, politics and morality, though not moralizing, are the most central issues in his writings. Still, generally considered a political animal par excellence, Michnik himself has said, "I am not a politician. I never wanted to be a politician. My political engagement is not the result of a chosen profession, but a result of both temperament and moral option. The world of political games has always repelled me—I feel lost and helpless in this world."[34] In fact, even during the Solidarity period Michnik never had any official function such as his older friends, Jacek Kuron or Bronislaw Geremek, had had as direct advisers to the Union. And his only effort in this direction before 1989, to become a delegate to the Regional Solidarity Congress in Warsaw, proved unsuccessful on a technicality. And after one term of office as a member of the Polish Parliament, he decided not to run again.

But despite some misgivings about taking part in direct political activity, Michnik cannot help but participate in public life. His is a world of adversaries and not enemies, and he wants to shape it by conducting a discussion on how to respond to the politics of restriction and confinement. He is one who adamantly seeks friends, not just allies—and he always finds friends: at the Rosa Luxemburg Factory, at the "young theaters" from Poznan and Lublin, students from Krakow, Catholic priests, Czechoslovaks from Charter 77, Hungarians from *Beszelo,* or leftist intellectuals from Italy. Instead of looking upon dissident Michnik as a political activist, or frequent prisoner of the Polish People's Republic (exemplary model of how to "sit" in prison), or intriguing historian or great writer, one should consider looking at him at that time as a social worker of the highest order: a character animating and bringing together different social and intellectual milieus, an actor who finds a stage and engages the public in the most trying circumstances (his own imaginative conduct vis-à-vis the police and in prison serves as a practical example), a speaker-writer whose speech acts make acts by others possible. Dissident Michnik, a facilitator of the small, incremental changes that make peaceful change for democracy possible, is a mastermind of performative democracy.

The key category in his writings of that time—and one that became an important item in Solidarity's vocabulary—is that of agency, with its implication that people who do not wish to live like objects can and should create an independent public life based on self-governing associations organized "from below." The broadening of this sphere of self-determination is itself the compromise solution. It is the kind of compromise that advances the ultimate goal of a democratic society by putting tolerance and pluralism into practice. It is also a kind of compromise that one can live with without compromising one's personal integrity. Daniel Cohn-Bendit named it aptly "self-limited Independence."[35]

While rethinking his Polish past, Michnik has written about issues that are concurrently experienced by people in different parts of the world: violence, life in the shadow of an empire, or the struggle to maintain one's dignity. He initiates his readers into a variety of ideas, but also—as a person of action—to practical solutions and realistic strategies of self-defense. He makes public certain venerable initiatives and actors hitherto missing from the well-censored historical record, most explicitly in his 1985 book, *From the History of Honor in Poland: A Prison Reader.*[36] The book is constructed as a counterpart to Czeslaw Milosz's *The Captive Mind.* Milosz took the case of four writers who were part of his own prewar literary circle and examined the methods and consequences—deception and self-deception—of their adaptation to the requirements of socialist realism. Milosz's book is a testimony to the methodical coercion of truth and individual spirit under totalitarianism.

Michnik, in contrast, most of whose works are written in a strikingly positive tone, offers a more uplifting picture as he examines the "Ossowski" strain among Polish intellectuals who during the 1950s resisted the pressures of Stalinist terror and evaded intellectual captivity. He presents the case of five authors: historian and agnostic Witold Kula; a Catholic intellectual and writer, Hanna Malewska; philosopher and humanist Henryk Elzenberg; the novelist Jan Jozef Szczepanski; and a poet, Zbigniew Herbert. Their writings, as quoted generously by Michnik, reveal the ways in which intellectuals confronted the end of one world and the emergence of a new one that justified itself through a faith in the laws of history. "Those people"—observed Michnik—"resisted not just the terror of the police, but also the terror of a certain historiosophy according to which the Spirit of History proclaimed mercilessly that historical necessity imbued the doings of those who had power."[37] These were his teachers, and Michnik saw in their works not just an effort to comprehend the new situation but a repertoire of techniques for self-defense that they made available—a precious heritage for all those who insist on retaining their own status as autonomous subjects capable of collectively launching self-determining projects—the seeds of a civil society.

Besides written works, there were various ventures—all speech-based, and today considered landmark initiatives—that Michnik initiated or coorganized, beginning with the letters of protest signed by major intellectuals in the early 1970s, the underground journals *Zapis* and *Krytyka,* the Flying University in the late 1970s, and semiclandestine seminars in the late 1980s. One of the latter was called the Democracy Seminars, a project at once modest and ambitious, proposed by Michnik in Warsaw, and extended to New York and Budapest to provide an opportunity for a sustained and uninhibited discussion of democratic theory and the prospects for democratization.

THE DEMOCRACY SEMINARS (A DIGRESSION)

It was the "suspicious" people who created the new quality. Out of small groups of friends, and a few communities of ideas, from private seminars, and primitive printing equipment, a social movement began.
    —*Michnik's lecture on the occasion of receiving an honorary degree*
    from the New School for Social Research[38]

When I look at that initiative now—and I was a member of the small New York seminar that met for a few years—openly, of course—in the Wolff Conference Room at the New School for Social Research—I do see it as one instance of those alternative activities outside the official structures of the state that added to the thickness of the pre-1989 democratic opposition in both Poland and Hungary. Excited about our exchanges, we did not think back then about this. Yet the Democracy Seminars, which in the pre-Internet and pre-fax era brought together independent-minded intellectuals in Warsaw and Budapest and linked them with their colleagues in New York, have earned a modest place in the history of the democratic opposition in the region. Michnik remembers:

> In apartments filled with cigarette smoke, in illegal self-education groups, we argued endlessly about everything: on the phenomenon of totalitarianism, on the condition of an intellectual caught up in politics, on what

it meant to be a Jew after the Holocaust, on the dynamics of the internal transformation of the communist system, on parliamentary democracy and the market economy, and on a process of transformation of the communist dictatorship that would itself be full of traps and new dangers.[39]

But these deliberations were rarely documented, as they were conducted verbally and necessarily "off the record." The main documentation of the democratic opposition, and of the whole alternative culture it nurtured, was provided by underground periodicals that came out of the same milieu as the Democracy Seminars—periodicals like *Krytyka* or *Res Publica* in Warsaw, and *Beszelo* in Budapest. It became the practice of these journals, as with the Democracy Seminars, to keep in touch with each other, introducing each other's ideas and presenting each other's authors. In that way the respective fields of discourse widened, along with a significantly widening and more diversified public.

The Democracy Seminars were different from other projects in the region in that they included an American partner, for whom, despite fundamentally similar values, the same books and concepts, considered under very different political and cultural conditions, had a very different resonance. For the Americans, the seminars offered an opportunity to discuss central aspects of their own normative tradition with people who had had profoundly different political experiences. The exception in all this was a very important bridge provided by the works of Hannah Arendt, writings deeply permeated with European history and philosophy, yet ultimately unimaginable without the author's intimate exposure to American culture and politics.

The earnest dialogue taking place in private apartments in Warsaw and Budapest and in New York—despite the exchange of brief summaries of the discussions—had a fleeting quality. There were no professional ambitions at stake, no selfish motives coming into play. It was clear that participation in the Seminars would not advance academic careers or make political heroes or public celebrities of any members; there would be no books produced, no public presentations, or articles in official or unofficial journals; nor was participation a substitute for political activity. It was simply to be a shared deliberation by engaged intellectuals on problems concerning political and civic engagement in their respective societies. The most exciting thing for us in New York was the very opening of these passageways, through which we all experienced each others' terms, semantic fields, moral and political concerns, and ultimately got insights into the confusing nature of modern European dictatorships. Though no one ever thought of preserving a complete record of the early seminars, there remain some bits of correspondence, as well as some reports from the discussions.

The story of the Democracy Seminars began on April 25, 1984. On that day, many of New York's intelligentsia gathered in the First Presbyterian Church on Fifth Avenue and 12th Street to celebrate the fiftieth anniversary of the founding of the University in Exile, the predecessor of the Graduate Faculty of Political and Social Science of the New School for Social Research. Among the extraordinary group of individuals awarded honorary doctorates was Adam Michnik, a name still rather unfamiliar to the American public.

Since Michnik was in prison, the honorary degree was accepted on his behalf by his friend, the poet and Nobel laureate Czeslaw Milosz, whose reading of Michnik's letter sent from prison to General Kiszczak "electrified" the audience, as the *New York Times* put it the next day on its front page. Several months later, when Michnik, as a result of a general amnesty, was again released from prison, a small group from the New School, including Jonathan Fanton, president of the university, and Jeffrey Goldfarb, a young professor of sociology, traveled to Warsaw to present him with the honorary doctorate personally. An informal ceremony was held in one of those densely book-lined private apartments. The presence of the major American TV networks recording the event may be what prevented a serious intervention by the security forces. Although the security forces, in fact, turned off the electricity, the TV crew equipped with portable floodlights was able to illuminate the entire apartment with impunity.

In a conversation following the ceremony, Michnik suggested to Jeffrey Goldfarb that a more substantive and durable form of interaction be developed—such as a permanent and more-or-less regular seminar that could be conducted in parallel sessions in, say, New York, Warsaw, and Budapest, to consider issues of democracy and to compare notes. Michnik's idea was simple: there are a number of useful books that we won't find around here, but which can be sent to us by the New York chapter. These books—he explained—if shared and discussed, could help us not only to explore the problems of democracy but also to consider the situation on both our own and each other's turf. And so we should exchange notes about these discussions. He suggested that Gyorgy Bence, a Hungarian philosopher and dissident already well acquainted with the New School and known to Poles, be asked to chair the Budapest chapter. And so began the Democracy Seminars.

The Warsaw group, finding Michnik, their chairman, taken off to prison yet again, began their work on a semiclandestine—or, in their own less melodramatic phrasing, private—basis under the leadership of a respected author and professor of sociology with a reputation for integrity and independence of thought, Jerzy Szacki. Gyorgy Bence indeed agreed to organize the seminars in Budapest. And in New York, at the Graduate Faculty, American scholars—frequently augmented by Hungarians and Poles on fellowships—worked under the chairmanship of Jeffrey Goldfarb. The New York seminar became a hub and clearinghouse of exchanges—as well as a "bookstore"—for the two European chapters.

The seminar in New York began with a critical reading of Hannah Arendt's works, and it was her books—requested by the colleagues in

Poland, as they had not been available there—that were the first to be sent to Warsaw and Budapest. They became a catalyst for what was an understandable preoccupation of the early Democracy Seminars, a discussion on the theory and practices of totalitarianism. Soon *The Origins of Totalitarianism,* with some help from the New York chapter, was translated into Polish and published underground.[40] The major challenges—apart from Michnik's frequent imprisonments—were problems with communication. That was a time—mostly in Poland and less so in Hungary—when mail was frequently searched, and movement in and out by people who could serve as couriers or liaisons was limited. The letters that have survived at the New School reflect the early efforts to find the most appropriate format and focus for the seminars.[41]

Like almost everything that Michnik envisioned, the initiative thrived and took on a life of its own. When Michnik went to prison in 1985, and when he went to parliament in 1989, the Warsaw seminar was taken over by others. After the final collapse of communism in the region in 1990, it turned into a loosely structured endeavor with more-or-less formalized chapters in fourteen countries of Central and Eastern Europe, along with the one in New York and annual joint conferences in the region.

CITIZEN

What was seen in the West as the miracle of the collapse of the dictatorships in Central and Eastern Europe was the outcome of deliberate civic actions, even though the strategy of the prodemocracy movements had been evolutionary, that of a "long march" in the course of which civil liberties were to be gradually recovered. One of its key catalytic events was a political masterpiece: the Round Table Talks between society and the Communist regime that facilitated a peaceful democratic transition in Poland. Michnik, with his long-argued strategy for replacing the principle of revolution with the principle of negotiations, became one of the key actors in the talks with the regime in April 1989. Soon thereafter he embarked on his biggest venture ever, putting together a new, above-ground daily, an outcome of the round table contract, *Gazeta Wyborcza* (Electoral Gazette), which had initially been launched to represent society in the preparations for the first, partially free elections to the Polish Parliament. The *Gazeta*'s task was to make known to the larger public the nonparty candidates, who would never have been covered by the official media. Elected to this Parliament two months later, this "antisocialist force," now Deputy Michnik, became a "citizen," and a passionate and influential voice for liberal democracy in the larger post-Communist bloc.

The *Gazeta,* the biggest daily in Central Europe, has become Michnik's main stage. Instrumental in crafting a language for grasping the new reality, and in its first fifteen years a forum for major debates on the democratic transformation, the newspaper was a key site for general education about democracy. It has also taken on the role of salient curator of the young democratic state, a controversial role for which it has been at times harshly criticized.

Early on, Editor in Chief Michnik made a decision to publish in the pages of the *Gazeta* authors who were rather unlikely choices for any regular daily newspaper, turning the newspaper into a school of thought and ideas. He introduced—perhaps to the largest public ever—his own mentors in the art of public deliberations: Leszek Kolakowski and Czeslaw Milosz; along with his multinational circle of intellectual friends: Jacek Kuron, Janos Kis, Vaclav Havel, Timothy Garton Ash, Jonathan Schell; and key contemporary thinkers such as Michel Foucault, Jurgen Habermas, Jacques Derrida, and, above all, Hannah Arendt. "If the 20th century world was a labyrinth ruled from behind the scenes by a horrible creature, then the works of Hannah Arendt," wrote Michnik, "were the golden thread of Ariadne, which helped us to depart for a deadly fight with the Minotaur, and then return to the human world."[42] Arendt remained for him a close intellectual guide since her work was first discussed in the Democracy Seminars, and then translated and published underground in the late 1980s.

One of his early, and now legendary, articles for the *Gazeta,* written one month after the contractual elections, argued for a change in the agreed mechanism of selecting candidates for the two key positions in the country, by allotting one to each partner in the round table negotiations. In the astonishing piece "Your President Our Prime Minister," Michnik suggested that power in the state ought to be divided between the Communist Party (the president) and Solidarity (the prime minister). Instead of having two generals that were both officials of the Communist Party, with Jaruzelski as president and Kiszczak proposed as prime minister, Michnik argued for keeping Jaruzelski as an assurance for the existing international and military alliances, and giving the task of forming a new government to the Solidarity candidate, who would have the support of society. He stressed that such an arrangement would have credibility both at home and abroad.[43] The performativity of this piece, or as Austin would have specified it, of this persuasive and happy *illocutionary act,* invited a response and took effect very quickly.[44] One month later Tadeusz Mazowiecki, intellectual, member of the Committee in Defense of the Workers, and editor of the *Solidarity Weekly* in 1980–1981, addressed the Polish Parliament as prime minister of the first post-Communist government in the Soviet Bloc.

But Michnik's idea of creating an alternative to the traditional party system, a nonideological, deliberative, broad civic force capable of shielding the process of reforms and inspired by the performance of Solidarity, did not turn into reality. He spoke about being disappointed with Walesa, who—after winning the presidential election in 1990—wasted this opportunity, more interested in introducing political conflict to quickly pluralize the political scene and to prompt the emergence of conventional political parties. This move, Michnik argued in his writings of the early 1990s, led to the balkanization of the political scene, as many of the fragmented post-Solidarity parties, unable to build a coalition, unleashed a divisive nationalist rhetoric, launched destructive decommunization discourse, and revealed fundamentalist and populist temptations.

Michnik the citizen remained faithful not just to most of his dissident ideas but also to the performances that they prompted and shaped. A decade into the transformation, the most contentious performance has turned out to be the round table, a highpoint in the history of dialogue, increasingly perceived as a compromising deal between the two elites, with too many concessions granted to the Communists. A patient defense of both the process and the consensus reached with the ruling party at the round table became a recurring motif of Michnik's recent writings.

His continuous commitment to dialogue and compromise has made him a firm opponent of decommunization, lustration, and various policies of retroactive justice toward former collaborators of the regime, its security forces, and its *nomenklatura*. Truth, yes—he kept insisting in various writings and public presentations—but revenge, no. Nothing should be forgotten, therefore "no" to amnesia, but "yes" to amnesty, insisted Michnik. "To move from dictatorship to democracy, we campaigned for compromise and national reconciliation with neither reprisals, nor winners and losers. Democracy, after all, is an endless search for compromise ... eternal imperfection."[45] In some arguments harking back to the nonviolent character of the 1989 revolutionary changes, one could hear a note of disappointment; after all, we were to be better than they were. Thus we have to be careful not to turn from prisoners into the prison guards.

In the mid-1990s Michnik's own ardent writings, and perhaps even more, some friendly gestures extended toward former political adversaries such as Jaruzelski or Kiszczak, began to divide his own admirers. Only a decade later, in a major assessment published on the fifteenth anniversary of the *Gazeta*'s establishment, he admitted, "I regret some of my exaggerated gestures and statements. Many of my friends held it against me. Many others misunderstood—and many condemned—me. I'll try to explain it, as I do feel guilty."[46] Later on, during a panel discussion in New York, he said that his mistake was not to recognize that for many people the process of reaching what he understood as "normal" takes much more time.[47]

One of the most emblematic writings of that period was a sizable article, branded by its critics "a manifesto," written jointly by Michnik and Wlodzimierz Cimoszewicz, once a member of the Communist Party, a cofounder of the major post-Communist party, former minister of justice, and a man who in five months would be appointed prime minister. The article, published on the fifteenth anniversary of the Gdansk agreement and soon after a postapartheid South Africa had launched its famous commission, was entitled *For Truth and Reconciliation*. Written in a very measured tone, the piece, which called for an end to the politics of toxic confrontation and a return to dialogue, caused considerable controversy even among Michnik's friends.[48]

How is it, asked Michnik and Cimoszewicz, that we Poles were able to conduct a very difficult dialogue leading toward the Polish-German reconciliation; that we've entered an uneasy Polish-Ukrainian dialogue; that we are talking with Lithuanians, that we launched a public discussion on Polish-Jewish matters opening up the possibility for a gradual overcoming of mutual prejudices, and yet we are unable to talk to each other?

Exploring the historical sources of sharp political polarization, the authors review distinctive chapters of the Communist past (the Stalinist period, October 1956 thaw, March 1968 student protests, the 1970 and 1976 workers' protests, the years of Solidarity and martial law) and the different ways in which society responded to the regime's shifting policies of repression and relaxation. Some, they wrote, chose engagement in the activities of the democratic opposition, some defended their own past and their power, and others were searching for increasingly difficult opportunities for reaching some reasonable, positive changes. They argued that it is the absence of a cathartic account of the past that makes dialogue and reconciliation impossible, and they concluded their cautiously balanced account with a proposal for establishing a group of people who have the public's trust and would prepare a "report for truth and reconciliation."

The intent was clear: the initiative would lead away from lustration and dependence on dubious files collected on the citizenry by the secret police while facilitating the opening of a badly needed dialogue. Though Michnik does not change his previous position to defend amnesia, his pragmatism resembles the over-a-century-old advice of Ernest Renan to those concerned with the successful coexistence of various groups within a modern nation-state: one has to forget about remembering past conflicts. But unlike Renan, who was referring to ancient wounds, the two authors neglected the fact that for many in Poland the conflicts, and resultant pain, were still fresh, that the efforts to acknowledge and repair wrongs appeared to be nominal, and that the legal procedures seemed cursory. Thus the question in Michnik's thought of a problematic balance between moral claims and the necessity of a compromise had resurfaced again. The article unleashes another downpour of polemics, all candidly printed on the pages of *Gazeta*. The critics suggested that the authors exaggerated the severity of political conflicts in the country, as Poland is not Yugoslavia and there were no signs of civil war in sight. But the main controversy centered on the way Michnik and Cimoszewicz, negotiating a version of history acceptable to both sides, assigned what many considered an all too charitably equal weight to each of two opposite kinds of engagement vis-à-vis the system: one rewarded by prison, the other by lucrative benefits and privileges. Perhaps such a version of history can lead to reconciliation—argued a popular journalist—but certainly not to the truth.[49]

Whereas the coauthored program for reconciliation ran up against a wall, the debate on the need for decommunization and the opening up of police files was gaining strength and became one of the most effective tools for political mobilization. The project of lustration reached its zenith in 2006, with the new right-wing government that won on a platform of "cleaning the house" of both corruption and the former regime's collaborators, on its pledge to make a policy of vigorous lustration its priority. Michnik, warning against trusting the records put together by the secret service and worried about unleashing the beast of revenge, made a dramatic move. After meticulous study of the records, he published in four installments an astonishing piece that reveals that the Polish national hero, the romantic poet-prophet, the epitome of patriotism and devotion to national causes, Adam Mickiewicz, was a documented informer of the tsarist police, the forces in service of Russia, the colonizer of Poland.[50]

In his cautionary tale he introduces what he calls a new hero of our times—the Grand Lustrator. That figure, explains Michnik, combines the fanatical zeal of an inquisitor with the cool cynicism of the interrogating police officer. And since his vocation—as Michnik acerbically puts it—is founded upon "detectivistic-al materialism" (his wordplay on "dialectical" works better in Polish), he looks for the sources of truth in the archives of the secret police. "Give me an individual, and I'll find a way to indict him or her," declares the Grand Lustrator.

Though the lustration of Mickiewicz was—as Michnik said—now only an intellectual exercise, reality caught up with the horror of it quickly. Several months later, a high-level governmental official, once loosely associated with the activities of the underground Solidarity, was—on the basis of available police records—charged as an informer. She was forced to step down from her ministerial post, but in a fairly prompt lawsuit widely covered by the media, a former secret service officer, called as a witness, testified that he had fabricated the record.

The lustration debate highlights the continuous presence of moral principle in politics, but now—as Michnik was already arguing with many of his friends in the early 1990s—the moral absolutism formed and cultivated in the antitotalitarian underground should not be automatically applied in a democracy, as it can easily turn into fanaticism. The Manichean vision of the world does not belong in a democracy, which, unlike dictatorship, is neither black nor white, but gray. Only in a world devoid of simple dichotomies and open to pluralism is compromise possible, and the compiling of proscriptive lists of witches, heretics, informers, is not. A measure of self-scrutiny and simple generosity toward others, even those who have erred, helps us better to understand the world. And later he will refer to Arendt's famous observation: "Forgiving serves to undo the deeds of the past whose 'sins' hang like Damocles' sword over every new generation."[51]

But when one looks at the landscape of Michnik's country, the grayness, the color of normality that he is so fond of, is increasingly losing to the crispness of black and white, the colors preferred by the Grand Lustrator. The lies and maliciousness that sustain a divisive perception of the world cannot be taken as a fully legitimate element of democratic debate, argues Michnik. One cannot get into compromise with a gutter: that is a road to nowhere.[52]

He condemns the call for moral revolution issued by the Polish right, which, by carrying out a "Grand Cleansing," promises to complete the still compromised task of building a better order.[53] To illuminate the problem Michnik turns again to the past and examines two positions articulated in response to the French Revolution, which, he argues, keep reappearing in new costumes, though in the same colors, throughout history. The first is that of the Jacobins, the *revolutionary ultras;* the second, that of the conservative "white Jacobins," or *reactionary ultras.* He patiently argues that both revolution and restoration have always been for their leading players too slow, not radical enough, unfinished, and eventually betrayed. Thus Robespierre and Saint-Just, on the one hand, and their counterparts, the "white Jacobins" like De Maistre, on the other, in their zeal to complete their victorious change, and suspicious of the secret "sects" of their political adversaries, both flooded the country with measures perfected by the Great Inquisition, thus launching reigns of terror that differed only in their ideological colors.

In conclusion Michnik wrote,

> We, the malcontents from the sect of those always disgruntled and terrified ... we do not want any moral revolutions, tightening of the reins, special commissions to track down enemies of virtue or of God's order, proscription lists of enemies, those who are suspected of animosity, or candidate enemies. We, the malcontents, dream about patching up a compromise and about common sense. We, the malcontents, do not want any new revolutions in a country which has not recovered yet from several previous ones.

One of the most intriguing questions—and one that still awaits serious consideration—is to what extent the promise of Michnik's thinking met the expectations of the fragmented and undermined western Left in its project of reinvigorating modern progressive thinking. Michnik was a perfect candidate here, with his early and enthusiastic exploration of Marxism ("as freshmen students we met in private apartments to discuss chapters of Oscar Lange's *Political Economy,* Paul Sweezy's *Theory of the Development of Capitalism,* and *Marx's Philosophical Manuscripts*"[54]); his rejection of the Party's paternalism ("I felt that Communist Poland was my Poland.... I believed that a Communist was someone whose mission was to denounce injustice. So I did."[55]); his attraction to early Polish socialist thought;[56] his affinities to the generation of 1968 in the West ("our common threads: an antiauthoritarian spirit, sense of emancipation, and the conviction that 'to be realist means to demand the impossible'"[57]); his cross-cultural language of rights, and the agenda of society's self-defense against the authoritarian system through pressure from below; his novel concept of self-limiting revolution, a strategy renouncing the use of revolutionary violence in the struggle for emancipation from a repressive power; and finally, as one who defined himself in terms of the Left ("the program of this Left is the program of antitotalitarian socialism"[58]).

Perhaps the most direct invitation to join forces in trying to reconfigure the project of the Left—more specifically, the American New Left at the end of the century—was articulated in 1996 by Ira Katznelson in his book *Liberalism's Crooked Circle: Letters to Adam Michnik.*[59] Katznelson, appreciating the movements in Eastern Europe that ended one-party rule there, presents a highly personal reconstruction of the twentieth-century discourse on liberalism and socialism. He revises some of their dimensions in a way that makes it possible for the two to complement each other, and to address the problems facing modern democracies: mounting inequality, problems of scarcity, issues of difference, and the situation of peoples' helplessness in much of the world.

Though Katznelson admits that his idea could be traced to the writings of older and newer classics, from John Stuart Mill and Karl Mannheim to John Dewey and Michael Walzer, it is clear that his project is very different. His proposal, an invitation to discussion, is based on a patient and open-minded rethinking of both traditions through the lens of recent developments in the former Communist bloc. His socialism is what he calls "self-limiting socialism," and his liberalism is similarly rethought. His is a project in which revised liberalism and socialism would enter into a dialogical venture, complementing each other's shortcomings. Such a mutually enriching partnership of two restructured precepts would not only provide a context for including a larger public than could liberalism alone, but its politics of caring would safeguard a space that could otherwise be taken over by unquestionably illiberal orientations.

Perhaps Katznelson's invitation to consider the possibility of creatively joining intellectual forces, offered in the sixth year of the democratic transformation project, was—from the point of view of those in the region— premature, and not just because the allergy to socialism was still at work. The post-Communist countries were struggling with the task of building democratic institutions, marketization was far from completed, and societal attention was focused on the burning issues of the crimes of the past, divided between those for or against the lustration law. A fundamental devotion to the building of procedural democracy, and a general sense that the velvet revolutions succeeded through a combination of irresistible civic spirit and negotiations with yesterday's adversary, made the ideological distinctions between Left and Right appear to be no longer constructive. The common desire was to depart from the past as quickly as possible and to join the structures of NATO and the European Union.

Michnik's skeptical response to Katznelson's project is a broad, mul-
tilayered account of the key dilemmas faced by the young democracies in
the region, an account that does not contain those issues that are central
for his American friend. His response is above all a strategic one, issued
by someone who, though he may not worry anymore that the changes are
reversible, is committed to seeing them through till fully accomplished.
Preoccupied with the primary agenda of reaching the benchmarks seen as
necessary for completing the systemic transformation, he sees a full freeing
of market forces and the liberated creativity of citizens working efficiently
in this new context as closely related. In this view, the social tensions resulting from the rapacious logic of the early market economy are the necessary
costs of transformation, and any serious critique of liberalizing policies is
ill-timed, as it further slows the reforms.

At the same time Michnik's vision of democracy, very much like his
earlier sensible program for the democratic opposition, is not a picture of
some blissful reality. It was in his 1996 response to Katznelson that he
praises *gray democracy,* which, though neither perfectly moral nor fair,
is—Michnik argued—the only system with a built-in mechanism for
self-correction. And it is clear that under this still-fragile democracy he
feels uncomfortable with thinking in terms of potentially divisive beliefs
and ideologies.[60]

But what happens when the normal, gray, pluralistic reality sheds its
grayness and under the full authority of the law overrides the principle of
a dialogue and implements one hegemonic voice? Five years later he will
confess that he watches the object of his dreams, a free Poland, with a certain anxiety. Though himself a loyal defender of the free market, he admits
that there is not enough space for debate on the kind of market Poland
is to have and how the market is to be corrected. The ideals of creativity
and entrepreneurship ought to be complemented by a sense of solidarity.
"Our democracy, here and now," said Michnik in a lecture at Warsaw University in 2001, "needs courage, imagination, and mercy."[61] Interestingly,
what he is calling for are the conditions that facilitate the emergence of
performative democracy, and not a self-correction mechanism automatically built in to any democratic order. But it was the younger generation
of progressive political thinkers in Poland, clearly fascinated by Michnik,
that came up with a shrewd critique of this 1968 student-leader. Afraid of
the national-Catholic right—they argued—Michnik had legitimized the
pragmatic post-Communists, making it difficult for the critical left to find
a space for itself.[62]

He returns to some of the questions raised by Katznelson in his essay
on Hannah Arendt, "Refusing to Bow."[63] He points out the illusions of
the Left invested in Stalin in the 1930s and those of the Right in the Nazi
Party. Arendt's mistrust of ideologies—argues Michnik—helped her to
avoid those traps and look at both as the rule of ideology and terror. And
he brings back a concept that is very close to him, even in the new context

of democratic Poland—Arendt's concept of the intellectual as pariah, who insists on maintaining his/her independence and dignity in a world of violence, cynicism, and deception.

The independence of Michnik the dissident has never been questioned. The independence and integrity of Michnik the citizen was confirmed when he refused to accept the lucrative shares in *Gazeta Wyborcza* that he had earned as one of its founders. But his writings and activities as a citizen throughout *Gazeta's* first fifteen years also reveal an imperative that overrides almost everything else: the imperative of a civilizing mission aimed at securing for the newly democratic Poland a place among select international structures such as NATO and the European Union.

Michnik's independence was demonstrated again when he exposed Poland's major corruption scandal, known as "Rywinsgate," involving an attempt to bribe *Gazeta Wyborcza* and a possible governmental cover-up.[64] It became clear that the overriding imperative, a concern for the well-being of the Polish state, became the argument for an order of higher necessity when Michnik made the decision whether to release this potentially damaging information just before Poland's final negotiations for entering the European Union.

The *raison d'état* did override other concerns, and *Gazeta* revealed the details of the Rywin affair four months later, in December 2002, after Michnik had completed his own journalistic investigation, and almost immediately after the return of the Polish delegation from successful negotiations in Copenhagen. Michnik confessed later: "Now, with Poland securely within NATO and EU, we can become a normal newspaper."[65]

The corruption scandal revealed by *Gazeta* turned into a major political watershed and led to the first televised parliamentary investigations in post-1989 democratic Poland. The hearings included many public and political figures, Adam Michnik among them. In the major piece published on the fifteenth anniversary of *Gazeta,* which he called "Poland at a Turning Point, *Gazeta* at a Turning Point," Michnik wrote bitterly:

> I am aware that never before did *Gazeta Wyborcza* pay such a high price for publishing something as it did for its coverage of the Rywin affair. This whole incident was a big surprise for us. We did not expect that somebody could come to us with a corruption proposal; we did not anticipate that we could be suspected of being capable of advancing our goals through bribes. It turns out that not only Lew Rywin and his principals presumed that we are capable of accepting a bribe, and that we are capable of despicable acts. It turns out that this opinion was shared by a significant part of the public in our country. Neither I nor anybody else at *Gazeta* foresaw this. For that error of imagination, and for that arrogantly positive self-image of *Gazeta* and its editor in chief, I paid a high price, and so did *Gazeta*. We got beaten up for that. I am sorry for any mistakes which may have confused public opinion, but I

am not sorry for our essential decision: that we documented an attempt at corruption, and that—by publishing the entire truth, we submitted the corruption to the judgment of the public.[66]

Michnik's independence, and his rejection of unqualified certainty, has always afforded him a position as mediator, someone who could bring together both the church and the Left-leaning intelligentsia, and who could negotiate with the adversary, the Communist regime. His independence, and his image as someone who is indomitable and untarnished, has also afforded him the position of somebody who could take sides to pacify the mob in Otwock, who could persuade the bureaucrats of the European Union that Europe is also east of Vienna, and who—to the dismay of his admirers in the West—could defend the 2004 invasion of Iraq on the grounds of his experience and that of his friends Vaclav Havel and Gyorgy Konrad. Theirs was the perspective of a prisoner in a Baghdad prison of the Saddam Hussein regime, "of the acute loneliness of people subject to totalitarian despotism and doomed to the world's indifference."[67] Yet, four years later, in a statement long awaited by many of his admirers, he admitted that the war in Iraq was a betrayal of the idea of humanitarian intervention.[68]

Rejecting the certainty of the determining laws of history along with the ideals of a perfect society argued through the Marxist tradition, Adam Michnik opens up for the powerless a whole new field of societal hope, residing in the power of argument, the power of imagination, anchored in friendship, and grounded in the realm of nonviolent action. His secular faith is in dialogue and in democracy, an imperfect *instrumentarium*, which nevertheless facilitates the exploration of alternatives and therefore the surfacing of gleams of hope.

One would think that the author of this old passage from *Maggots and Angels,* an essay in which Michnik defended those who did not have the nerve, or courage, for dissent, would make some of his recent criticism less vitriolic. After all, he does what he promised then when he said, "I am not an insane aesthete. I don't believe that all people can be well disposed toward one another all the time. But I do believe in the creative power of our actions. I do believe that we are capable of enhancing or diminishing the amount of hatred and intolerance in our public life."[69] Not a philosopher, this thinker of action hands to us the sparkling thread of Ariadne. The rest is up to us.

5

Furnishing Democracy

The Story of Two Round Tables

> The new always happens against the overwhelming odds of statistical laws and their probability, which for all practical, everyday purposes amounts to certainty; the new therefore always appears in the guise of a miracle.
>
> —*Hannah Arendt*[1]

The Round Table Talks that facilitated the democratic transformation of Poland's one-party state began in February and concluded in April 1989, at a time when the Communist system in the region had still seemed to be—even if not robust anymore—certainly irreversible. Yet clearly those talks were a lot less visually spectacular and telegenic than the joyous crowds hammering at the Berlin Wall half a year later. The talks that brought an end to apartheid in South Africa, though lengthy and dramatic, did not produce stunning images either: certainly nothing comparable to those one-person, one-vote bird's-eye shots of the winding lines of people waiting to vote for the first time in their lives. The real work of hammering out such agreements is simply not mass media–friendly.

Still, looked at from a distance of nearly three decades, the Polish Round Table Talks ought to be seen not just as the first instance of those velvet revolutions that, for the rest of the region, occurred only toward the end of that year. Rather, one should consider the fact that—very much like its South African counterpart a few years later—it became a new critical site, a *space of appearance,* in which both subjugators and subjugated were devising and testing a new formula for sweeping political change. It was a public, but local, site where a dialogue-produced word revealed its *performative* command, replacing the kind of violence threatened by the ubiquitous security forces. The very fact that the formula was worked out locally, with no external input, setting in motion the mechanism for negotiating the transformation of a dictatorship into a democracy, may be the

79

most precious political accomplishment of an otherwise dark century rife with wars, genocide, and an array of modern despotisms, the termination of which has too often been left to the mercy of multinational institutions and alliances.

The formula, which was driven by the idea of a dialogue at a round table, whether real or symbolic, and with no privileged seats, has the effect of safeguarding equality in communication when the word crosses barriers between the speech zones of the participating parties. Such participation, mediated by a reasoned and informed exchange, implies the possibility of learning, of self-transformation on the part of those participating, and therefore, the possibility of compromise.

The outcome of the round table—the dialogue-produced word—is a deprivileged consensual word, its lining woven from the thick polyphony of self-suspended words and voices that have conditioned and assimilated each other. There are words behind the consensual word; there has been a diversity of voices engaged in the dialogue behind it that licenses the consensual word as performative word. And it is the very social fabric of this lining that lends the word its performative powers. The round table mechanism is crucial here, as it facilitates the entry of words into dialogue within a defined spatiotemporal framework in which the construction of the consensual word—the accords that ultimately change reality—can take place.

The manifest publicness of Poland's Round Table Talks exposed the larger society to the broad foundations of democratic politics, serving as a tutorial in participation, deliberation, representation, and discussion. Like its older stepsibling, the New England town meeting, the round table instigates the art of dialogue and of compromise and further underscores the *performative* dimension of democracy-in-the-making.

The anxious monitoring of the talks by the public—including its frustration over their less-publicized parts—adds its own voices and gestures, expands the size of the theater of political negotiation, and enables a larger coparticipation in the round table talks. At the same time, the very mechanism and performance of the round table expands the stock of nonviolent settings and political idioms that facilitate democratic change in contexts that lack democratic institutions and processes.

Thus the round table provides tools for institutionalizing a dialogue between those who hold dictatorial power and those social movements that—though still illegal and often represented by people just back from prison or exile and labeled enemies of the state—are now acknowledged by the regime, however reluctantly, as the only ones able to bring credibility to the proposed dialogue and an eventual contract. The round table institutionalizes the dialogue by providing the *space of appearance* (a concrete temporal and spatial frame), by authorizing and legitimizing the actors, by necessitating the drafting of a script, by establishing the rules for the conduct of negotiations, and by foreseeing the need for a contingency infrastructure in which a lack of agreement or specific stalemates can be dealt with. In this situation the agreement expected to be produced at the round table represents more than what it states. The round table itself, however extraordinary it may have appeared, becomes an event staged according to agreed-upon conventions. And it is this very aspect of the whole arrangement that *makes* its performativity possible. As such, it acquires the status of an effective practice endowed with illocutionary force for changing the political system.[2]

What is most important is to understand that the launching of a dialogue is not the result of the "good will" of the ruling regime but a combination of factors, one of them being a recognition by the regime of a creative emancipatory invincibility demonstrated by society, the other party to the negotiations. It is important to observe that the invincibility reveals itself in a nonviolent way (even if—or especially if—the nonviolent approach is a recent one), and that it is not fueled by fear. The Spanish, Polish, and South African round tables were not generated by frightened, atomized societies deprived of any capacity to resist the dictatorial power. Instead they brought together a pragmatically motivated, and until recently, rather unlikely assembly of modern subjects, half of whom, representing the oppressed, were well aware of having been stripped of their basic rights and capabilities as citizens. The other half, representing the oppressors, acknowledged—even if reluctantly—that they were the keepers of a system whose very existence depended on excluding large parts of society from participation in the political decision-making process, and therefore from access to the resources and capacities needed to advance the well-being of both community and its individual members.

The unaccustomed new agency of the excluded is, in fact, grounded in the conduct over many years of wide-ranging activities directed against the regime that have resulted in the accumulation of considerable social capital and civic expertise. Beyond society's mastering of local ways of social self-organization in Spain under Franco's aging fascism in the 1970s, in Poland under Jaruzelski's compromised communism in the 1980s, or in South Africa under the desolate Botha–de Klerk apartheid of the 1990s, there was also a recognition on both sides of the pressures exerted by the international human rights community and by world public opinion, foreign governments, investment companies, and donor agencies.

But the cultures of civic knowledge and "practical consciousness" are not the only sources of local movements that aim at bringing solutions to injustices and human suffering. There are cultures mobilized by opposite premises, such as a people's sense of moral exceptionality, and a faith in divine forces backing their actions, historically known as the cultures of salvation. With their strong feeling of inevitability and mission, such cultures tend to engender violence whether revolutionary or counterrevolutionary, stressing the need for martyrdom and sacrifice for the sake of reaching an ideal whether located in the remote past or in an unspecified future.

Cultures of knowledge, whether locally generated or—as in the case of human rights—locally adopted and negotiated, engender solutions invested in the human capacity to communicate, to reason, and to compromise. These knowledge-based, solution-seeking sites locate their hope in communicative action that is focused on the here and now: current, nonviolent, discursive undertakings aimed at reachable change. A round table constitutes idiomatic expression of such an action. Its performativity, the very fact that it actually prompts democratic transition—that great change without the great utopia[3]—is perhaps the most encouraging feature of this political idiom.

The idiom emerged from what Michnik frequently refers to as a shift "from the logic of revolution to the logic of negotiation." It had been introduced in Spain in 1975 and tested in Chile in 1988, and it made possible the negotiated transitions in Poland and Hungary in 1989 and in South Africa in 1993. The idiom, facilitating the transformation of dictatorship into democracy, though in each case assuming local features, seems to transcend geography as well as the varied historical and political circumstances that brought about the varied forms of dictatorship.

Still, Laurence Whitehead is right when he insists that "context really matters" when it comes to political concepts, and, as I intend to show, the round table is a political idiom fully comprehensible only in its concrete social and historical context.[4] It is the broad fabric of socially diverse but interrelated voices as they react to a specific issue—this Bakhtinian heteroglossia—that gives meaning to any utterance, including one produced by a round table.[5] After all, the cases of Spain, Chile, Poland, and South Africa are hardly analogous. The one thing they had in common was, generally speaking, the ostentatiously nondemocratic character of their regimes, which were otherwise very different from each other. What may seem a paradox at first glance is that whereas in Poland it was the hegemonic Communist Party that was the ultimate confiscator of civil and human rights, in Spain and in South Africa it was the outlawed Communist Party that acted against their respective dictatorships of fascism and racial apartheid.

The two parallel stories of the Polish and South African round tables that I am considering here are put side by side not because of any similarities between the terror exercised by the apartheid regime on the one hand and the dictate by a one-party state on the other. I have looked at these two round tables because I am interested in the very mechanism of negotiated transitions. I would like to show that despite its context-dependent, locally produced, distinctive mode, the principle of the round table could be serviceable in a variety of circumstances. An examination of the existing instances indicates that the round table idiom has enhanced the world's hitherto modest repertoire of political tools and methods for ending oppression in a nonviolent way, and as such it deserves to be given more attention both by practitioners and theorists.

The main principles of the idiom, which received its impetus from an internationally reinvigorated human rights agenda, are rooted in the concept of choice-creating dialogue, which I see as the key site for emancipatory thinking. Negotiating in such a context, as Habermas observed while writing about new social movements, is not the old-fashioned kind of bargaining commonly engaged in by traditional trade unions and political parties. Mutual learning, conciliation, and compromise—though without mere conformity—are the engine that drives this kind of "negotiation-as-dialogue."

In both Poland and South Africa the actual negotiations were preceded by years of cautious contacts and informal, often failed, communication between the adversaries. And initially the real target was not the speed of change but its direction: always toward pluralism, a broadening of civic freedoms, and the enabling of "subjects" to stop feeling like objects, which in the case of South Africa meant nonracial democracy. The gradual regaining of real subjectivity, the process enabling members of society to become the agents of their own lives, was part and parcel of the negotiation process and radiated well beyond the space and the actors of the talks themselves.

In Poland there had been a long, "cold" civil war between the rulers and the people, launched with the imposition of martial law in December 1981, the delegalization of the Solidarity Trade Union, the establishment of internment camps for thousands of its leaders, and the immediate emergence of broad underground Solidarity structures through which society resisted the officially imposed martial law, called under Polish Communist legislation a "state of war." The real aim of institutionalized dialogue in Poland was to break the impasse of this "cold" civil war and to make peace on the basis of a new political accord between society and the regime. In 1989, eight years after the crackdown on Solidarity, the calculated price for this accord was compromise and concessions on both sides.

The direction and scope of change in Poland was negotiated during the continuous six-week Round Table Talks. The South African round table talks, interrupted by dramatic and unplanned intermissions, extended over twenty-three months. In the tense on-and-off multiparty negotiations, the original two-phase table, known as the CODESA (Convention for a Democratic South Africa), a forum that began in late December 1991,[6] collapsed in July 1992 and was then followed in March 1993 by a second, "refurbished" table called the Multiparty Negotiating Process.

Perhaps the most important question concerns the prerequisites, the preconditions, for entering the process of negotiating a transition. What does it take for a dictatorship to bend enough to open up for a round table or any other idiom that might facilitate a dialogue with an ignored society and its outlawed civic structures? What can persuade the oppressed—in fact, the very people, often yesterday's political prisoners, who are known for their indomitable tenacity—to sit at the same table with their oppressors?

It is important to observe that in such cases the ancien regime is usually in the process of weakening. Its core ideological motivations are long gone, or they are disoriented; it has trouble paying its bills and dealing with social unrest, and it loses its few foreign supporters. Fascism in Spain began to deteriorate in the 1960s. Communism in Poland lost face once and for all in 1981 when, unwilling to broaden the public sphere, it imposed martial law. In South Africa, the economic sanctions and international isolation began to take their toll on the apartheid government in the mid-1980s. In each case it took approximately one decade for the respective ancien regime to realize that it could no longer manage crises, and that the existing institutions of public life were unable to bring stability (let alone creativity!) to the economic, political, and cultural realms. Such governments still have considerable force at their disposal, which means they can stay in power but do little else.

It is also important to bring up the other, less frequently discussed element facilitating the round table: the precarious state of the antiregime movements. If there appears to be a possibility for negotiating change, it is probably because the other side as well—namely, the valiant society itself, with its movements, organizations, and leadership—is showing visible signs of fatigue. And it is precisely because of this kind of balance of weakness on both sides that the Polish Round Table was not only possible but in fact unavoidable. Adam Michnik put it this way: "Negotiations are possible when the resistance of the democratic opposition is strong enough that the dictatorship cannot destroy it completely, and when the dictatorship is strong enough that the opposition cannot overthrow it from one day to the next. The weakness of both sides becomes the national opportunity."[7] Joe Slovo, the legendary father of the South African Communist Party, announced boldly: "We are negotiating because towards the end of the 80s we concluded that as a result of escalating crisis, the apartheid power block was no longer able to continue ruling in the old way and was genuinely seeking some break with the past. At the same time, we were clearly not dealing with a defeated enemy and even a revolutionary seizure of power by the liberation movement could not be realistically posed."[8]

In the case of Poland, it was not just the toll of imprisonment, exile, and a growing sense that time was running out but also the realization that even the most spectacular activities of the democratic opposition were losing broad support. One Polish essayist observed bitterly that Solidarity had become a victim of its own strategy of functioning as an alternative society that no longer needed the regime. As such, it managed to keep going, but at the cost of becoming ineffective in dealing with that regime.[9]

In South Africa, a similar sense that time was running out was articulated by Nelson Mandela at the first plenary meeting of CODESA: "The risk of further pain and affliction arising from violence, homelessness, unemployment, or gutter education is immense. No country or people can afford the extension of this anguish, even a day."[10] A few months later, in June and September 1992, following the collapse of CODESA and a massacre in the township of Boipatong, near Johannesburg, the ANC suspended the talks, which were then formally resumed after a ten-month deadlock only after Mandela and de Klerk signed the joint Record of Understanding.[11]

As for the question of the oppressors and the oppressed sitting at the same table, Michnik writes: "The path of negotiations brings many disappointments, bitterness, and a sense of injustice and unfulfillment. But it does not bring victims. Disappointed are those who are, after all, alive."[12] Though the progress of South African negotiations was threatened by the use of force, and there were victims, a similar conviction was expressed there by Joe Slovo. In April 1993, just days after the assassination of Chris Hani, the charismatic leader of the South African Communist Party, a partner in the negotiations,[13] Slovo addressed a shocked and angry people, underscoring the need to continue the talks: "Any suggestion of calling off the negotiations would be playing into the hands of the murderers, whose purpose is to stop the process. We must defeat them."[14]

The usual prerequisites for launching a dialogue are the freeing of political prisoners (among them Michnik and Mandela); a stipulation that the negotiations will be preceded by, or will include, the legalization of outlawed organizations (the Communist Party in Spain, Solidarity in Poland, the African National Congress and other liberation movements in South Africa); and that they will establish freedom of speech and information. In South Africa an important condition was that both sides renounce violence, which in the case of liberation movements meant armed struggle and in the case of the apartheid regime meant the use of specialized state security forces. A separate and very sensitive stipulation concerned the past, that is, crimes perpetrated by the dictatorship and sometimes by liberation struggle movements: namely, a tacit understanding on both sides that a successful round table would exclude guillotines or Nuremberg Trials.

As the launching of a dialogue between enemies is a daunting task, an external third party, serving as promoter, guardian, or intermediary in the process, usually assists it. Interestingly, those are often surprising or even unlikely allies. In South Africa they were the Afrikaner nationalists, or more specifically the *verligte* wing of the governing National Party, enlightened Afrikaner intellectuals, mostly academics, but still loyal to the nationalist outlook. It was they who initiated and cultivated the early clandestine contacts with the ANC leaders in the late 1980s, and it was they who within their own party started the discussion on the necessity of reforms.[15]

Both in Spain and in Poland the third parties that exhibited considerable initiative in facilitating this experimental path were the ancient if not premodern institutions of the monarchy and the Catholic Church, respectively. Paradoxically, both those institutions advocating democratic change derived their own legitimacy not from the people but from divinity. Still, perhaps one should not wonder: after all, it was precisely these forces that in the past had paid the highest price in the course of modern revolutions.

The Polish and the South African negotiations were each additionally facilitated by an unusually favorable external context. In the case of Poland it was the only foreign context that mattered to the dependent societies of the Communist bloc: the Soviet Union and the changes taking place there. Gorbachev's policy of *perestroika* and *glasnost* echoed in Poland and severely shook the self-confidence of the hard-liners in the Communist Party. After all, the declaration of martial law in December 1981 had been explained and justified by the threat of Soviet intervention, and it had obviously strengthened the position of hard-liners. Now the reforms taking place in the Soviet Union disoriented the ruling camp in Poland, disarmed many in the party apparatus, minimized the possibility of blackmail of the more pragmatic wing of the party by the party hard-liners, and encouraged both the opposition and society.

The end of the cold war and the developments in Eastern Europe and the Soviet Union had an impact on the situation in South Africa as well. It not only further weakened support for the apartheid regime in some corners of the world (it could not exploit the fear of communism on the part of its few remaining foreign allies anymore), but it also terminated the support extended by the Soviet Union to the Communist Party of South Africa, an important actor in the antiapartheid movement.

Moreover, the Gorbachev reforms lessened the suspicions of the Pretoria regime that the antiapartheid movement was directed from Moscow.[16] More locally, the collapse of the socialist experiment in neighboring Mozambique and that country's devastation by a decade-long civil war served as warning signs for those in the liberation movements who insisted on achieving change through armed struggle. At the same time, the 1989 negotiation that brought about the independence of Namibia, administered until then by the South African regime, provided a positive example of conflict resolution. And one more factor favoring dialogue: the would-be negotiators both in Poland and in South Africa worked in a climate influenced by the presence of a new global actor, an increasingly influential human rights community, expressing itself through overlapping networks of nongovernmental, transnational organizations monitoring abuses and systematically reporting them to key international institutions and to the world at large.

Although at the time when the Round Table Talks convened in Warsaw, in the spring of 1989, the Soviet Union was still the hegemonic power within the region, objections to the negotiations were not voiced from Moscow. Rather, it was the southern and western neighbors of Poland—Czechoslovakia and the German Democratic Republic—that reacted to the Polish Round Table proceedings with vitriolic fury. Paradoxically, the political circle most sympathetic to the work of the Round Table was Moscow's political class, at that time introducing some measure of freedom through the policy of *glasnost,* which—according to historian Bronislaw Geremek, a seasoned dissident and one of the key figures at the Round Table—regarded the Polish Round Table as an experiment that might be worth repeating in Russia.[17]

Once the Polish negotiations were completed in the spring, the seeds of transition spread through the region and events moved quickly. Just two years later, in June 1991, the Association of Western Parliamentarians for Action Against Apartheid hosted in the capital of a newly democratic Czechoslovakia an international conference entitled "Eastern Europe and Southern Africa: Supporting Democracy and Development."[18] At that time the preparations for the first meeting of the South African round table, CODESA, were in full swing.

THEATRICS OF THE ROUND TABLE

Unlike any conventional theater play from *The Trojan Women* to *Mother Courage,* the theatricality of the round table is thoroughly modern. In Greek theater both the performers and the audience knew the outcome of the tragedy, as it was always based on a well-known myth or story. In the case of Brecht, at least both the actors and the director knew the lines of the entire play.

The round table is more like the theatrical performances created collectively by experimental groups in the 1960s and 1970s, among them the Living Theater, which built its performances around a baseline script. In such performances the key themes, and sometimes the outcomes of the actions, are agreed upon during rehearsals, but their actual execution depends on many additional factors, such as the events of the day, current public debates, or the chemistry among the actors and the audience and between the actors themselves. Thus in the round table, outside of the few prewritten threads, the rest has to be improvised, or "written on stage." That kind of performance requires enormous discipline, continuous research and training, a study of the new language, and a search for fresh ways of encouraging support from, and interaction with, the audience.

Although the Round Table process in Poland was not as telegenic as the festival taking place along the Berlin Wall, it was nevertheless—and despite its length (fifty-nine days)—an *intense political drama* with over 400 *performers* (a panoply of negotiating teams representing both sides), taking place sometimes simultaneously on *three round stages,* where *three separate ensembles* debated the problems of the economy and social policy, trade union pluralism, and political reforms. The site—or *the playhouse*—where the dramatic events took place was an impressive neoclassical building known as the Regent's Palace, which then housed the offices of the Council of Ministers and today is the official residence of the president of the Republic of Poland.

The main *prop* in this drama was, of course, the table, a huge one, open in the middle, and lying like a giant wheel without spokes, around whose circumference could sit fifty-seven people, and which was assembled from fourteen segments, prepared on special order by a furniture factory in Henrykow. About 26 feet in diameter, this elegant dark wood piece was assembled in the palace's Hall of Columns, and it "performed" only twice: in the inaugural plenary session of the Round Table Talks and in the closing ceremony.

In early 1989 in Warsaw it was the word and image of the "table" in its many various shapes and sizes that dominated both the political stage and the conversations of the public. It seemed as though the only world worthy of attention consisted of tables—a veritable archipelago of tables, or perhaps, more precisely, a neat hierarchy of stacking tables, with the grand plenary table at the top, and three somewhat smaller tables just below it for tackling three contentious issues: politics, the pluralism of trade unions and professional associations, and the economy.

These three tables dedicated to broad issues spawned eleven even smaller working tables—"subtables" as they were called in Polish, or one might be tempted to call them coffee or folding tables—which were established to focus on the specific questions of law and judiciary reform, mass media, local self-government, associations, education (including higher education, science, and technology), youth, housing policy, agriculture and social policy for the countryside, mining, health, and finally ecology. The full hierarchy of tables was served according to one count by 452 negotiators, experts, and advisers. And for those moments of crisis when the negotiations ran into an impasse, there was an extra side table available for less formal discussions between the two sides, at a small retreat, a government villa in a hamlet near Warsaw called Magdalenka.

In South Africa the stage for the negotiations was a "neutral" business space located in Kempton Park, known as the World Trade Center, on the outskirts of Johannesburg, on the way to the airport. The symbolic prop, the round table itself, was of lesser importance here, as the plenary meetings took place in a space designed for hosting large conventions, and to put together a large conference table at the World Trade Center did not take a lot of imagination since it had experienced professional planners. Judging from the pictures, the CODESA table in Kempton Park was assembled from smaller rectangular tables in the shape of a flattened, elongated circle, with empty space inside, affording a relatively good view for each participant. In comparison with its Polish counterpart it looked thoroughly modern if somewhat generic.

The two phases of CODESA talks (CODESA I and CODESA II) were conducted there, as well as the planning meetings and most of the five smaller tables, known as working groups, which conducted the bulk of work between the two plenary sessions. After the collapse of CODESA II, the refurbished round table, renamed the Multi Party Negotiating Process, worked in six technical committees and was coordinated by the Negotiating Council. The resumed talks took place in the same venue, the convention center in Kempton Park, and this is where the final agreements were signed on November 18, 1993.

DRAMATIC OVERTURE

The success of any negotiations depends on a careful, and often lengthy, preparatory process, a nurturing of "talks about talks" that brings the two sides together in informal settings and unofficial capacities. The Polish production of *The Round Table* was preceded by an *overture* that was facilitated by church officials, lasted at least four years, and signaled a growing realization on both sides that major change was indeed necessary and unavoidable.[19] In South Africa a similar process, usually referred to as "secret talks," also began about four years before the launching of the CODESA negotiations.

In Poland an amnesty for political prisoners was announced in July 1984, but the more solid signs of an imminent "overture" were two documents: a 1985 report published by the Solidarity leadership, "Poland 5 Years After August," and a 1986 secret report commissioned for the government by Interior Minister General Kiszczak. The conclusions of the Kiszczak report, prepared by his three trusted and capable high party officials—Stanislaw Ciosek, Jerzy Urban, and General Pozoga—indicated (not unlike reports by the Solidarity leadership) that the regime would have to share power and that it should begin to talk with the opposition as soon as possible. The recommendation to share power did not mean to scrap the system or to tolerate counterrevolution or revisionism. One should keep in mind that the word *opposition* here meant a group of people whose activities had been deemed wholly illegal. The same applies to the case of South Africa, where the ANC, the main opposing partner in negotiations with the regime, though acknowledged as a legal organization prior to the talks, was not a member of the parliamentary opposition.

One should note the role that diasporic leaders and the communities of political exiles had played in their respective overtures. The Kiszczak report was prepared in Warsaw not long after a Polish émigré publishing house in London came out with a book Michnik had written in prison in 1985, *Such Are the Times... Some Thoughts on Compromise*.[20] In his book, written with remarkable foresight, Michnik had sketched out what later became an accepted point of departure for setting up the Round Table agenda. It is difficult to know whether this was pure coincidence or whether the party leaders in their report were in fact heeding Michnik's suggestions:

> We are fully aware that within the totalitarian rules of the game, it is impossible to have the kind of elections that would prove that the ruling

Communists do not have the support of society. But the road to compromise should not be closed forever. The way out could be a solution that would enable society to make an authentic vote in the case of at least 30 percent of the seats in Parliament. But if society's candidates for that 30 percent of the seats were to be put on the same voting list next to people like Siwak or Urban [generally hated high party functionaries] it would only cause the authentic candidates to lose their credibility. The real road to compromise is in broadening the spheres of autonomy and not in buying votes and names for the price of a few seats in Parliament.[21]

Here Michnik also anticipated one of the main points of contention in the Round Table Talks, namely, the government's insistence on having all candidates for Parliament listed together, and Solidarity's demand for two separate electoral lists, one for the Communist Party and one proposed by Solidarity.

The long overture to the Round Table drama went into *allegro* in 1988. First, an interview with Geremek, whose name had long been banned by the official media, appeared by surprise in an official monthly. He spoke of the need for an "anticrisis pact" that would lead to the institutionalization of pluralism. Then two waves of clearly political strikes swept through Poland in May and August. Even though the strikes were not considered successful by the Solidarity leadership, they obviously prompted General Kiszczak, an *eminence grise* of the Party, not only to appear on national television with a vague offer of a meeting with the opposition, but also even to mutter the magic words, "round table." Finally Gorbachev visited Poland in July, and when in his address to the Parliament he said, "We are convinced that only through democratization can we move vigorously ahead, revealing the huge potential of the socialist system," and when he stressed as well the need for creating the rule of law, the promoters of the Round Table project on the party side felt they had received the backing they needed.

The first meeting with Walesa, working again as an electrician at the Gdansk shipyard, took place in a government villa in Warsaw on August 31, 1988, the eighth anniversary of the signing of the shipyard agreements, and it went on for three hours. One year later, on July 5, 1989, Nelson Mandela, still a prisoner, met with P. W. Botha, the man still presiding over the apartheid government of South Africa. The urgency of political settlement had been raised. A few months later, on December 13, at a time when the one-party state regimes in Eastern Europe were in the process of dismantling and many political prisoners in South Africa were being freed, Mandela—who insisted that he be released only after all the others had been—met Botha's successor, President F. W. de Klerk, to discuss the future of the country.

The early meetings were all small and private. Since 1985 Mandela had been meeting periodically, mostly one on one, with Kobie Coetsee, the minister of justice, police, and prisons. Only two other people attended the conversation between Walesa and Kiszczak, both secretaries: Secretary of the Central Committee Stanislaw Ciosek and Secretary of the Episcopate Bishop Jerzy Dabrowski. Walesa gives the following matter-of-fact account:

> General Kiszczak puts on the table some stiff conditions: the relegalization of Solidarity will be possible only after the Round Table talks are finalized with the signing of national accords; the current strikes have to end within the next 18 hours; we shall make our next decisions about the Round Table in two weeks, and in the meantime we shall prepare the initial lists of negotiators and advisors. Of course, I was not very happy about it, but there wasn't much I could do. A dozen striking factories are not the several hundred we had on strike in August 1980. And the General said straightforwardly that his party hard-liners were trying to torpedo any offer of talks with the opposition.[22]

In early September 1988, Walesa got a go-ahead for the talks from the National Commission of the still outlawed Solidarity. Thus the preproduction work on the Round Table was launched, with two main individual producers in charge: General Kiszczak, who had full authorization from the head of the Council of State, General Wojciech Jaruzelski, who was also first secretary of the Party, and Lech Walesa. The shipyard electrician Walesa, supported by his colleagues from the still underground organization, by all accounts made all final decisions during the talks with an unerring political instinct, even though—like Kiszczak—he did not take a direct part in the subsequent negotiations.

Walesa's first move was to invite about 90 people (a group later expanded to 138) to discuss the agenda for the negotiations and the composition of the Solidarity negotiating team. It was a kind of think tank, which, for lack of a legal entity with which to identify, called itself the Citizens Committee with Lech Walesa. A few days later, during a meeting with the government side at Magdalenka, Solidarity, though still not a legal organization, was recognized as the opposition side at the Round Table, and a mid-October date for the Round Table Talks was agreed upon. The grand circular centerpiece of the drama was ordered from the furniture factory and assembled in a government palace in Jablonna near Warsaw, where the talks were originally planned to take place.

It was at this moment that the overture became even more dramatic, as a result of major changes taking place *in the wings*. First, the cabinet of Prime Minister Messner collapsed, and he was replaced by Mieczyslaw F. Rakowski, an ambitious Communist also known as the editor of a relatively enlightened governmental weekly, *Polityka*. Rakowski had his own plans for dealing with the social crisis. The Round Table Talks were put on the back burner, and the prime minister announced that his government would now take the exclusive lead in introducing political and economic reforms that would be in the spirit of Gorbachev's *perestroika*. He promised almost everything but the legalization of Solidarity, as he was convinced that one trade union, the already existing official trade union OPZZ, was enough. Soon afterward, in a meeting at the Ursus Tractor Factory, an old Solidarity stronghold, Jaruzelski also put into question any likelihood of trade union pluralism. A few days later Rakowski made his first major political decision to close the Gdansk shipyards. Even though the decision was presented as having economic justification, it was perceived as a political provocation aimed at destroying the dialogue, a shocking blow at the cradle of the Solidarity movement and at Walesa's home turf and constituency.

Technical and organizational preparations for the Round Table Talks were nevertheless still going on—until the question of Adam Michnik and Jacek Kuron entered the agenda. The government side would not agree to their participation in the talks. These two most outspoken dissidents, longtime political prisoners, had been considered dangerous criminals and demonized in the official media for years as the most extreme enemies of the public order. Because of the unending campaigns conducted by the official media, for some Poles, especially in the countryside, Michnik and Kuron were perceived in about the same way Malcolm X was once perceived by "Middle Americans." But Walesa refused to agree to their exclusion from the talks. As a result, the big table waiting in Jablonna Palace was dismantled on November 24, and it looked as though the overture was not going to conclude with any raising of the curtain.

As in the past, the Catholic Church offered to mediate, and Archbishop Bronislaw Dabrowski asked to host one more meeting between Walesa and Kiszczak in the historic parish in Wilanow, a suburb of Warsaw. Walesa requested the presence of Gdansk bishop Goclowski and Tadeusz Mazowiecki, adviser to the shipyard workers in August 1980 and former editor in chief of the *Solidarity Weekly*. Kiszczak brought with him Stanislaw Ciosek, a member of the Party's politburo, who along with Father Orszulik, director of the press office of the episcopate, played the role of stewards of the pre–Round Table communication. The meeting, held for two days on November 18 and 19, brought reassurances that the shipyards, which would need restructuring in the future, would remain open, and the miners who were fired for taking part in a recent wave of strikes would be reinstated at their jobs. Yet, when it came to formulating a statement from the meeting, Kiszczak and Ciosek did not agree on mentioning the name *Solidarity*. They argued that the authorities intended to negotiate political pluralism first, and only later enter into the agenda the issue of union pluralism and the legalization of Solidarity. To keep the door to negotiations opened, the meeting ended with a vague statement about the need for further talks.

An amazing turning point occurred later that month, on November 30, during a TV debate between Alfred Miodowicz, head of OPZZ, the official Party-linked trade unions, and Lech Walesa. The idea for the debate had come from Miodowicz himself, a vain man in search of greater visibility and power, who had declared at a Central Committee meeting that he would "make marmalade of Walesa." But the expectation that Walesa, this uneducated electrician, for once entirely on his own before the TV cameras, would make a laughingstock of himself in front of millions of viewers went up in smoke. With his lucid, well-measured ideas that so effectively reflected the sentiments of the public, Walesa was extremely impressive and easily won against a man who was not only an "apparatchik" but also spoke like one, in an opaque language studded with newspeak. Walesa's famous sentence, "Europe moves by car, and we are trying to catch up with them by bike," disarmed the audience. He was clearly a leader, able to address people's anxieties; even the Party had to admit that. And suddenly the Round Table process was back on track.

On December 18 at a key meeting of the 138-member Citizens Committee with Lech Walesa, three commissions were created to address the economy, politics, and trade union pluralism, along with committees for the fifteen thematic subgroups destined for the various subtables of the Round Table. Still, skepticism about trying to negotiate with the Communist government was strong among a majority of the democratic opposition, and two familiar arguments were usually brought up: "The Communists never give up anything, especially on their own; and, on principle they do not keep promises." But Geremek would respond by saying, in effect: We do know that we are not talking with a credible partner. Internal tensions were further magnified by some of those who were not invited to the table and who circulated rumors about dirty dealings between the two elites.

As there is no clear agreement among the actors themselves when exactly the South African "overture" began, I highlight here one moment that I find symbolic: the 1985 visit of Kobie Coetsee, then South African minister of justice, to see Mandela in the hospital. It was followed by four years of what became known as secret talks between the ANC leadership in exile and *verligte* Afrikaners. The first meeting in Lusaka, Zambia, where most of the ANC leaders lived, was followed by twelve clandestine gatherings in England, gradually building a fragile trust between the key enlightened Afrikaner intellectuals (among them Sampie Terreblanche, Van Zyl Slabbert, Willie Esterhuyse, Whimpie de Klerk, and Michael Young) and ANC leaders (e.g., Thabo Mbeki, Jakob Zuma, and Oliver Tambo). All but one of the meetings were held in England at the Consgold estate in the village of Mells, near Bath. The intensely private encounters, discussions, and conferences influenced and shifted the mutual perception on both sides.

In the meantime, larger meetings between the two sides were arranged on the African continent, in Senegal, Zimbabwe, and Zambia.[23] Among the participating Afrikaners the key role was played by Breyten Breytenbach, a dedicated antiapartheid activist and novelist, and Van Zyl

Slabbert, a sociologist and leader of the parliamentary opposition who in 1986 resigned in protest from the Parliament. Van Zyl, who was now establishing the Institute for a Democratic Alternative in South Africa (IDASA), commented later on the 1986 antiapartheid cultural festival in Dakar, Senegal: "I think that Dakar contributed to a few defunct paradigms; it demystified the ANC, put an end to most of the stereotypes with which the South African regime had labeled it, and legitimized dialogue with the organization. It also did away with some prejudices held by the ANC about Afrikaners, especially those of the monolithic, obtuse, pap-and-worse, bully-of-the-Bushveld variety."[24]

The National Executive Committee of the ANC issued its first statement on the issue of negotiations in October 1987, and in October 1989 a much more measured statement indicated a need for "struggle by other means."[25] Although developments were taking place on several stages abroad, Nelson Mandela, still a prisoner, was visited in 1985 by Kobie Coetsee and developed an intriguing rapport with him. Coetsee reported:

> I had read a lot about him—all his speeches, and all these reports that came across my desk every day—and I was fascinated at what kind of man he must be to attract all this international attention and have all these honorary degrees and awards given to him. When I met him I immediately understood why. He came across as a man of Old World values. I had studied Latin, and Roman culture, and I remember thinking that this is a man to whom I could apply it, an old Roman citizen with dignitas, gravitas, honestas, simplicitas.[26]

The milestone move toward negotiations was de Klerk's televised speech opening the Parliament on February 2, 1990, in which he announced lifting the ban on the ANC, the South African Communist Party, and other opposition groups, and promised the unconditional release of Nelson Mandela, the halting of executions, the freeing of a number of political prisoners, allowing some exiles to return home, and partially ending emergency restrictions. The performativity of this speech was well grasped by Joe Slovo: "In a sense South Africa after February 2 will never be the same again: not because de Klerk has transformed it but because, objectively, it has been transformed."[27]

Once Mandela became a free man ten days later, after twenty-seven years of imprisonment, and when the trickle of exiled leaders began to return home, the road to negotiations was partially secured. But it was not until early May that year, when the future ANC negotiators met with the South African government (the National Party) at the president's Groote Schuur mansion at the foot of Table Mountain in Cape Town, and again in early August in Pretoria, for what became known as "talks about talks," that the overture was finally completed.

As a result of this still bilateral process, the two agreements, known as the Groote Schuur Minute and the Pretoria Minute, and directly facilitating the talks, were made public. The first one announced the opening of a path to negotiations right in its preamble: "The government and the African National Congress agree on a common commitment towards the resolution of the existing climate of violence and intimidation from whatever quarter as well as a commitment to stability and to a peaceful process of negotiations."[28] It established a working group to remove obstacles for ending the political conflict: the release of political prisoners, return of exiles, and introduction of the amendment of security legislation.

The second agreement, the Pretoria Minute, was a stunning and controversial move on the part of Mandela, declaring a unilateral suspension of the armed struggle: "In the interest of moving as speedily as possible towards a negotiated peaceful settlement, and in the context of agreements reached, the ANC announced that it was now suspending all armed action with immediate effect. As a result of this, no further armed actions and related activities by the ANC and its military wing Umkhonto we Sizwe will take place." The violence in various provinces was clearly a major concern in the Pretoria Minute, which stated, "The Government has undertaken to consider the lifting of the State of Emergency in Natal as early as possible in the light of positive consequences that should result from this accord."[29] Both the government and the ANC pledged to work on reducing the level of violence in the country. The path to dialogue was cleared, but the drama was far from over.

THE SCRIPT, MAIN ACTORS, ACTING STRATEGY, AND FIRST REHEARSALS

In Poland the two performance teams finally agreed on a baseline script for the Round Table Talks on January 27, 1989. Three main themes were to be played out at the three tables. The first, known as the political table, would negotiate changes in the political system of the state and innovation in the upcoming elections to Parliament. The second table would discuss ways to facilitate trade union pluralism, including the legalization of Solidarity. The third table was concerned with badly needed economic reforms. The general rules of the game included an agreement on the evolutionary character of the proposed changes, and on keeping at bay the looming conflicts over the past. Among more specific elements of the baseline script was the approximately 30 percent of seats in Parliament reserved for truly free elections. The opposition quickly realized that Solidarity would be legalized if they accepted elections that would be only partially democratic. That was the political price to be paid for bringing Solidarity back into the realm of the official.

And that is why the political table quickly became the center stage of the Round Table drama. Professor Bronislaw Geremek, a medieval historian and leader of Solidarity's team at the political table, decided that their best long-run strategy would be not to rush. At the opening meeting of his table he reminded his colleagues of the fundamental difference in priorities of the two sides: the government wanted to derive a degree of legitimization from its reform efforts, whereas Solidarity was trying to create the conditions for systemic change.[30] Instead of legitimizing specific changes, Solidarity wanted to put in motion *a process of democratization*.

Significantly, already in the course of the preliminary "pre-table" meetings, the Solidarity side had begun to notice with some surprise that the government/party side was making no reference at all to Communist ideology and that their argumentation was entirely pragmatic. In one of the informal chamber theater meetings in Magdalenka, Ciosek, addressing the issue of reestablishing the Rural Solidarity Union, pulled out a surprising argument when he said: "Did comrades from Solidarity, OPZZ, and the government read the Papal encyclical Laborem Exercens" and the document of the Primate's Council on the dignity of work? The matter of rural unions is clearly stated there."[31]

Among the key actors on the political team for Solidarity, the subject of a lengthy battle with the government, were both Jacek Kuron and Adam Michnik, along with independent intellectuals like Marcin Krol and Krzysztof Kozlowski, the widely admired worker/intellectuals Zbigniew Bujak and Bogdan Lis, as well as a specialist in local self-government, Professor Jerzy Regulski, the constitutional lawyer Janina Zakrzewska, and a Gdansk attorney, Jaroslaw Kaczynski (whose twin brother, Lech, sat at the union pluralism table).

The government side was led by Janusz Reykowski, a respected professor of psychology, and was staffed by the most talented Party leaders and its intellectually strongest players, with two younger members, Aleksander Kwasniewski, former activist of the Association of Socialist Students, now the minister of sport and tourism; and Leszek Miller, secretary of the Party's Central Committee; in addition to two prominent Party sociologists, Hieronim Kubiak and Jerzy J. Wiatr; and law professor Sylwester Zawadzki.

The table for negotiating pluralism of trade unions and professional associations was chaired by Tadeusz Mazowiecki on the Solidarity side and Aleksander Kwasniewski for the government. (The latter's position at two key tables was an indication that he was already a rising star in the Party.) Two well-known economists chaired the table on economy and social policy, Witold Trzeciakowski for Solidarity and Wladyslaw Baka for the government.

Politically representative, the Round Table turned out to be absurdly, and disappointingly, gender exclusive. Only five women were invited as negotiators at the three main tables: Janina Zakrzewska for Solidarity and

Zofia Czaja for the government at the political table, and three for Solidarity at the economy table: Helena Goralska, Grazyna Staniszewska, and Irena Wojcicka. Women thus represented just a shade more than 1 percent of the Round Table cast.

The arrangements for CODESA were more intricate, since once the overture was over—played almost exclusively by two players, the African National Congress and the Pretoria regime—seventeen other political groupings were invited to the table. Paradoxically, the South Africa of the 1960s, 1970s, and 1980s—an incomparably more repressive and predatory regime than those in Eastern Europe—nevertheless still exercised a limited, though racially based, democracy, with several parties, competitive elections, and an official parliamentary opposition. And though there were two leading actors in the South African talks, the ANC and the National Party, there were so many political organizations until recently outlawed and now participating in CODESA, as well as some regional and ethnonational organizations, and so many preexisting political parties, that the bilateral mode of talks, a feature of the Polish Round Table, was not an option in South Africa.

Thus the composition of the CODESA table was from the beginning more complex than the Polish one comprised of only two sides, "us" and "them." Around the CODESA table sat nineteen diverse political groupings, some with a broad membership base, with whom the delegates to the negotiations had to consult. This influenced the overall design of the round table, with an appropriately lengthy time frame, the two-stage process, framed by the two bookend plenary meetings.

The two plenary sessions of CODESA in Kempton Park, brought together mostly as a ceremonial body to ratify proposals sent by the working groups, were scheduled to take place five months apart and last two days each.[32] A Management Committee, composed of two members from each party, coordinated the work of the working groups carried on between the two plenary meetings. Just as in the case of the Polish subtables, the script for the CODESA talks was organized in five themes played out by five working groups, or in Polish terminology, five issue-focused tables. The task of the first group was to create a climate for free political activity. The second group was concerned with constitutional principles; the third with transitional arrangements; the fourth with work on the future of the "independent homeland" states; and the fifth with time frame and implementation. The groups were to prepare periodic reports for the Management Committee, which would assemble the agreements reached within the groups for presentation and ratification at the plenary table of CODESA II.

Not surprisingly, just as in Warsaw, the most contentious debate was conducted at the key political table, known as Working Group Two, negotiating an end to the apartheid laws, introduction of an interim constitution, and creation of a constitution-making body for a nonracial, democratic

South Africa. It was at this table that the cast was most impressive, as all sides appointed to it their most seasoned politicians. The ANC was represented by two negotiators in their thirties, the chief negotiator, Cyril Ramaphosa (raised in Soweto, a student activist, and most recently leader of the National Union of Mineworkers, the largest union on the continent), and Mohammed Valli Moosa (once a student activist at the University of Durban Westville and now a member of the National Executive Committee of the ANC). The third was a man of the older generation, an alumnus of the London School of Economics, politically skillful, fresh from exile, very experienced: Joe Slovo.

Two conservative members of the government, Gerrit Viljoen, the minister for constitutional affairs, and his deputy minister Tertius Delport, negotiated on behalf of the Pretoria regime. Ben Ngubane, a physician, was a senior negotiator representing the Inkatha Freedom Party, and Miley Richards of the Labour Party was the chairman of the group. Kobie Coetsee, the minister of justice and an early facilitator of meetings with Mandela, chaired Group One, concerned with creating an environment for free political activity and with South Africa's role in the international community. And Chris Hani, former guerrilla leader, now the secretary general of the Communist Party, was nominated to lead Group Three, discussing transitional arrangements, among them the ANC plan to suspend armed struggle.

As the working groups conducted their negotiations behind closed doors, much of the drama was hidden and had to be reconstructed from the fragmented statements of its actors. In this situation the attention of the public was directed onto the two main protagonists, Mandela and de Klerk. The striking no-show at the round table was Mangosuthu Buthelezi, a Zulu prince and the chief minister of the Zulu homeland, known as KwaZulu, and the head of the Inkatha Freedom Party (IFP). This man of many hats had expected to lead to CODESA more than one delegation, and when only IFP was invited to the table, he decided that he personally would not attend the negotiations.

Initially just 5 percent of the negotiators were women, also a very low number given the vibrant women's organizations in South Africa and the attention given to gender issues by the liberation movements there. Unlike what transpired in Poland, the absence of women at the negotiating table mobilized women across racial and political lines; they launched a nationwide organization to claim their civil rights and to fight against their conspicuous political marginalization. The newly established Women's National Coalition embarked on drafting the Women's Charter for Effective Equality, conducted strategic workshops, worked with the media (impressive ads appeared in the major newspapers protesting the exclusion of women from the momentous negotiations), pressured the respective political parties, challenged the talks by staging spectacular events in front of the Kempton Park buildings, and finally threatened to boycott the elections.

Helen Suzman, an outspoken member of the parliamentary opposition and a respected delegate to CODESA, spoke about the analogies between gender and race discrimination, and criticized sharply both her own party and the ANC. The concerted and resolute action by the Women's National Coalition, the Women's Lobby, and the ANC Women's League, supported by other women's organizations, added an extra layer of dramatic tension to the negotiation process.[33] The effectiveness of these speech-based activities is difficult to overestimate: not only did women members of all political parties force the delegations to reconsider the gender composition of their respective representations,[34] but above all the new South Africa established a Commission on Gender Equality. This constitutional body, a remarkable creation for a new democracy, secures a framework for the continuous mainstreaming of gender concerns into the institutions and policies of the country.

With the population of both countries nearly the same (ca. 40 million), the total number of actors, representing nineteen political organizations, was 228, almost exactly half that at the Polish table.[35]

THE SHOW: CURTAIN RAISER

On February 6, 1989, the first plenary session of the real Round Table, opened by General Kiszczak, was rebroadcast in the evening on Polish national television. The event was cochaired by two professors respected for their independence, Aleksander Gieysztor and Wladyslaw Findeisen. Kiszczak spoke first and made clear that consent for Solidarity's existence would depend on "the inviolability of the foundations of the socialist system" as well as "the nonconfrontational character of the upcoming elections."

Then the spotlight turned to Walesa, who began with his famous first sentence: "The side that I represent here accepts all proposals and suggestions presented by Mr. General." And later, apparently referring to the banner displayed on the façade of the Central Committee of the Communist Party, "There Is No Freedom Without Responsibility," Walesa added: "And there will be as much shared responsibility as shared participation."[36] After a break, seven speakers representing both sides followed. The three thematic tables and the eleven working groups at their subtables were to enter the stage within forty-eight hours. In the meantime, a new joke was circulating in Warsaw. "Why is the table eight meters in diameter? . . . Because the world record in spitting is seven meters!"

The inauguration of CODESA on December 20, 1991, took place with the full majesty of the law and according to a carefully prepared script. It was opened by the chief justice, Michael Corbett, and was chaired by two judges, an Afrikaner, Petrus Shabort, and the first nonwhite judge in the country, a human rights attorney named Ismail Mohamed. The program consisted of somber conventional speeches and was to end with a statement by de Klerk. Yet his speech was anything but generic, as he unexpectedly suggested that since ANC did not deliver its promise on disbanding its armed forces, the CODESA negotiations would not be fully binding.

The participants and almost 1,000 international observers were stunned. What had been thought to be a largely ceremonial script turned out—at least for the opposition—to have been tampered with. In fact, according to a quiet agreement between the government and the ANC from the beginning of the year, the army was to be dismantled at the time of transition to democratic government, and not before. An enraged Mandela requested time to respond: "If a man comes to a conference of this nature and plays the type of politics he has played, very few people would like to deal with such a man."[37] Despite the tense beginning, CODESA I managed to establish its working structures and agreed on a time for the second plenary, the CODESA II, during which the process was to be completed.

THE MAIN ACT AT THE POLITICAL TABLE

Whereas during the Polish overture it was trade union pluralism that was the greatest point of contention, the major controversy at the Round Table proper concerned the extent to which the democratic opposition, usually referred to here as the Solidarity side, would participate in the institutions of the state. The government offered to conduct earlier parliamentary elections, which—in accordance with the principle of "evolutionary change"—would be partially democratic, with about one-third of the seats (35 percent) allocated for fully free voting. However, not only would the remaining seats be reserved for regime-backed candidates, but the government introduced a new proposal not included in the baseline script: to create a new post of president, and to provide the presidency with very broad powers. This certainly appeared to leave all executive and all real legislative power in the hands of the ancien regime. The Solidarity side essentially responded, "No: we do not agree to play the role of an extra, with no influence on the most important institutions of power."

The stalemate was broken when Aleksander Kwasniewski, this wunderkind of the government side, came up with the idea of also creating a second chamber of Parliament—a Senate, to which elections would be completely free. In this situation Solidarity focused on turning the otherwise ornamental role of the proposed Senate into a substantive one, and it partially succeeded.

The drama at CODESA's political table, which was the stalemate at Working Group Two, took place just before the second, and presumably final, plenary session of CODESA II. With agreements completed by all other groups, the opening of the plenary session was postponed for seventy-five minutes, as the negotiators scrambled to make things work while assuring their waiting colleagues, observers from forty-two countries, and the anxious South Africans that they had the basis for reaching an agreement.

The disagreement was over what should constitute a majority on decisions about critical points of the new constitutional arrangement: more specifically, what percentage would constitute the consensus needed for a constitution-making body to reach an agreement. Should it be 75 percent, as proposed by the government/National Party and the Inkatha Freedom Party, or should it be two-thirds, or 66.7 percent, as suggested by the ANC? The matter was neither technical nor trivial, as getting a more sizable majority to agree on key constitutional issues could create a real impediment to the passing of a new constitution and delay the process of democratic transition. On the morning of the plenary session Cyril Ramaphosa said to the press: "We remain hopeful we can resolve this deadlock."

In the process of intensive talks the government side was willing to downsize the required majority to 70 percent but tied it to the creation of a second chamber, a Senate, that would also participate in the approval of the constitution. The Senate idea did not break the stalemate as it had in Poland, but prolonged it. One hour later, Rowan Cronje, Bophuthatswana minister of defense, said as he left the meeting, "We have absolutely agreed on nothing.... All I can add is that we have no progress report with an agreement to deliver to the second plenary session."[38] The lack of consensus in this vital political matter caused a major crisis and bitterness on both sides, reviving old prejudices and mistrust. Foreign Minister Pik Botha expressed this tersely when he said, "The ANC-cum-Communist-Marxist-school believes basically in winner-takes-all and grabs power and thereafter it's gone."[39] The crisis was partially arrested by the announcement made by Mandela to the plenary meeting that the Management Committee would immediately sit down to restructure the working groups and to establish a new mechanism for negotiations.

CHAMBER THEATER

When stalemates occurred in the Warsaw negotiations—and they began to occur as early as the beginning of March—a small group of key players, about ten from each side, would meet at the government villa in Magdalenka—but on these occasions with both of the producers and decision makers present, Kiszczak and Walesa. Without journalists, cameras, or tape recorders, and with a minimum of note-taking, these rather informal "summits" were attempts to unblock the impasse, break the stalemate, and move the negotiations on to the next stage. From here Kiszczak could phone Jaruzelski on short notice to get his go-ahead. The relative privacy and informality also helped to dissipate many of the prejudices that each side had had about the other.

At the same time, however, precisely because these sidebar meetings were conducted privately in rather inaccessible backstage rooms outside of Warsaw, they became the subject of speculation and rumor and gave fuel to the considerable buzz about secret agreements between the two elites in Magdalenka and about the signing of concessions.

In the course of the Round Table Talks, the sidebar in Magdalenka met five times, often for an entire day. Among the reasons for a stalemate were the determined efforts of the OPZZ, the only official, party-backed trade union, to assume the position of an independent player in the talks, and to block the relegalization of Solidarity. Another was a government refusal to give up its total control over radio and television, more specifically to give the Solidarity side access to other forms of media besides newspapers and periodicals. It was in Magdalenka that the offer of free elections to a newly established Senate made it possible for Solidarity to swallow the otherwise unpalatable new 35 percent/65 percent election law to the lower house, tied to a strong presidency.

The collapse of CODESA II—though mended at the end by Mandela's announcement on launching the work of refurbishing the table—constituted a warning sign. It became clear that for talks to resume and succeed, a temporary return to a bilateral mode might be desirable, with meetings conducted in a smaller, more intimate context more conducive to dialogue. Two chief negotiators—Cyril Ramaphosa, representing the ANC, and Roelf Meyer, representing the governmental National Party—were to work on rebuilding trust and reopening the paths of communication. Ramaphosa, recently elected secretary general of the ANC, and Roelf Meyer, more open-minded than his predecessors Viljoen and Delport and recently appointed minister of constitutional affairs, met alone in various hotel rooms in Johannesburg, re-creating common ground and planning the chamber theater dialogue.

Unexpected assistance came from Joe Slovo, one of the founders of *Umkhoto we Sizwe* (MK), the armed wing of the ANC, who in an article published in the August issue of the *African Communist* discussed the spectrum of permissible compromises that the ANC could agree to in negotiations with the government. One such compromise that would not be an obstacle for the future nonracial democracy was a deal that Slovo called the *sunset clause,* guaranteeing for the party still in power a fixed period of power sharing that would be only gradually phased out. The compromise he proposed, along with the patient work of the Ramaphosa-Meyer team and the September summit producing the Record of Understanding between Mandela and de Klerk, put the bilateral talks back on track.[40]

Two months later the ground was ready for meetings of the Magdalenka sort, with small groups of people representing the ANC and National Party. Three secluded meetings, *bosberaad,* took place in a governmental game lodge and were referred to by the press as the "bush caucus." In the pleasant surroundings of D'Nyala, in the middle of a mild South African summer, with breaks for swimming, fishing, and hiking, the joint positions were developed and the healing of the relationships between the two sides began. A few weeks later, at the beginning of 1993, it was clear that the multiparty talks would resume in Kempton Park soon. Gradually more and more of the players were invited to discuss the preparatory steps.

Such a chamber theater of negotiations, aiming against the odds to keep the dialogue going and though oriented toward a democratic project, is never inclusive, as it represents only a sliver of the round table. Its nonpublic mode produces controversies and resentments that could easily be revived and reintroduced into the political debates, questioning and undermining the negotiated settlement in years to come. In Poland, the talks in Magdalenka—especially for the right-wing populist parties, unhappy with what they see as inadequate treatment of those responsible for past crimes—are still a source of endless accusations of betrayal and conspiracy theories. Accusations from both sides about a conspiracy of elites have been no less common in South Africa, where the opaqueness of various segments of the negotiations makes it difficult to reconstruct their dynamics.[41] The term *trout fishing*, an activity considered elitist, entered the language of South African politics, very much as Magdalenka did in Poland, to indicate the murky character of deal-making between the elites.

THE REFURBISHED TABLE IN KEMPTON PARK

The Planning Conference for Negotiations, held in Kempton Park on March 4–5, 1993, was attended by twenty-six parties and organizations. They adopted a resolution to resume the negotiations and agreed that it would take place at the World Trade Center on April 1–2. The refurbished round table mechanism, the Multi-Party Negotiating Process (MPNP), consisted of a lesser number of direct participants than CODESA (208 instead of 238) but represented more political groupings (26 instead of 19). Only two major political parties refused to participate, the Azanian Peoples Organization (AZAPO) and the Afrikaner Resistance Movement (Afrikaner Weerstandsbeweging, AWB). The early protest over the meager representation of women—discussed earlier—changed the balance of gender in the negotiation teams.

The reconceived working groups, now called technical committees, were actually small groups (six persons each) of appointed experts, who—unlike their counterparts in CODESA—did not represent any political party or organization. In the frequently occurring stalemates, this new formula—explained one of the "technical experts" on the Bill of Rights, Hugh Corder—provided politicians on all sides with a convenient "face-saving" instrument, as they were now able to justify their decisions as based on the independent decisions received from the experts.[42] Their tasks were more sharply defined and focused on issues of violence, fundamental human rights, constitutional matters, discriminatory legislation, transitional governance, and media. The MPNP was supported by a new infrastructure designed to streamline the work of the technical committees.

The process was overseen by the Negotiating Council, a tighter (roughly half the size of the plenary table) but fully representative body composed of four delegates and two advisers per party. Meeting often several times a week, the council kept the nine months of the negotiations going, monitored the progress of the technical committees, and assembled the documents to be ratified by the plenary meeting of the MPNP.

Already at the first meeting of the Negotiating Council in the World Trade Center, in early March 1993, Meyer and Ramaphosa were playing the part of the breakers of deadlocks, acting as the emergency unit administering pragmatic reconciliation, as vividly described by one raconteur: "From day one the government and the ANC cruised towards the agreement, carrying most of the negotiating parties with them. As sticking points arose, one would see Meyer and Ramaphosa slip quietly from their seats to meet in a corner. A compromise proposal would follow. Or there would be an adjournment to allow for a longer consultation. The media dubbed it 'The Roelf and Cyril Show,' and it became the hub around which the entire negotiations turned."[43]

The Multi-Party Negotiating Process lasted four months and faced several challenges. Ten days after the first plenary meeting of the MPNP, on April 10, 1993, one of the most outstanding negotiators, the Secretary General of the South African Communist Party, a beloved hero of the black townships, and an embodiment of courage and dedication to a free South Africa—Chris Hani—was assassinated in front of his home in Johannesburg. A measured speech by Mandela delivered at Hani's funeral, held in a huge football stadium, helped to prevent major unrest in the country. In a separate televised appeal, Mandela, addressing both the black and the white communities, spoke of the assassination as aimed at destroying both Hani and the very advanced negotiation process: "As Chris has been saying, we should refuse to be provoked into any acts of violence, even if this is motivated by the desire to avenge his death."[44]

There was also a challenge presented by Buthelezi and COSAG, that is, Concerned South African Group, a peculiar alliance that brought together three territorial governments, the Inkatha Party, and two Afrikaner organizations, in a demand for federalist arrangements and therefore threatening the unity of a new South Africa. A shrewd Chief Buthelezi, though absent at the round table, was present in the media, giving expression to Zulu nationalism, evoking the right to self-determination of KwaZulu province, and alluding to the possibility of civil war and eventual secession.[45]

And there were parallel demands coming from the militant white AWB for establishing an Afrikaner homeland, an independent *volkstaat*. Once their demand was rejected by the MPNP, hundreds of members of the AWB, wearing camouflage and assorted short weapons, and joined by other extreme right-wing organizations, descended on the plaza in front of the World Trade Center. What began as a protest march, a show of discipline and determination, ended up as an unruly mob scene, leaving all parties to the negotiations outraged.

In early June 1993, the country learned that the Negotiating Council had agreed that the first fully democratic and all-inclusive national elections would take place in less than a year, on April 27, 1994. Though the protests continued, and rising violence spread anxiety and a fear of civil war, the negotiating parties made it possible for the disgruntled right-wing parties, including AWB, Inkatha Freedom Party, Pan African Congress, and AZAPO, to reenter the process.

BEST ROLES AND MY FAVORITE LINES

Some attention should surely be given to the unscripted content of the round table, those exchanges aimed at persuading and influencing both the partners in dialogue and the general public. These crafty, nonconventional speech acts, which Austin would call *perlocutionary acts,* are testimony to the intellectual and political savvy of the participating players.[46]

According to many observers, Adam Michnik was the most fascinating personality at the Warsaw Round Table.[47] Although widely known by name, until the Round Table Talks Michnik's face was not familiar to the TV audience or even to members of the government side. Nevertheless, when he spoke—because of the deft force of his arguments and the startling freshness of his language—all other conversations came to a halt: "There are three roads in front of Poland: we can take the one described by Konwicki in his novel *The Little Apocalypse*; we can take the Iranian road; or we can take the Spanish road, which means an agreement that can guide our country from totalitarian force towards the kind of democracy that need not grow by threatening anybody's interests."[48] A selection of other such remarks, all facilitated by the very convention of the round table, captures the underlying logic of the negotiations:

Professor Reykowski, chair of the government team: "We are only concerned that further steps in the direction of democracy not be steps in the direction of destabilization."[49]

Marcin Krol, editor in chief of *ResPublica*: "Only civil society guarantees stability. Any other situation guarantees revolution."[50]

Bronislaw Geremek, whose participation in the talks was resisted for a long time by the government side, has been acknowledged as a key mover toward a better understanding between the two sides, an understanding without which the agreement could not have been reached: "My problem is how to be coresponsible for my own state when I am completely dispossessed of it."[51]

Jan Baszkiewicz, historian of the French Revolution, and party member: "Poland.... But what Poland, gentlemen? A capitalist Poland? Please come out and say whether you are all for that kind of 'final solution'!"[52]

Tadeusz Mazowiecki: "I do not know whether Sweden is a capitalist state or Cambodia a socialist one. For me, and for many of us who sit here, far more important is the distinction between totalitarian and antitotalitarian rule."[53]

Adam Michnik: "We are to respect the law, yet you want to preserve the leading role of the party in the courts?!"[54]

Zbigniew Bujak, electrician from the Ursus Tractor Factory, Solidarity leader of the Warsaw region, and a legendary figure of the Solidarity underground during the martial law period, successfully escaping the police, and in hiding for over five years: "You are the experts on the police state, and we, on civil society."[55]

Krol: "If the government considers the question of elections to be part and parcel of our contract, then for us such a part and parcel means access to radio and television."[56] It was Krol who proposed that the Solidarity side be given the right to publish its own official daily newspaper through which to conduct its own electoral campaigning. It was he who suggested that the name of the paper be the *Electoral Gazette* (*Gazeta Wyborcza*).

Stanislaw Ciosek, an insider of the Central Committee of the Communist Party, in a conversation with Zbigniew Bujak, involved in setting up *Gazeta Wyborcza*: "Now, when you have your own daily, you'll make mincemeat of us in these elections. I do not have any illusions any more."

Joe Slovo, commenting on the criticism that the ANC was not grateful enough for President de Klerk's willingness to open a dialogue: "When a man has been consistently battering his wife, he shouldn't expect a bouquet of roses from her the morning after he promises to stop.... What have they really done? They've stopped battering us in the extreme way they did before, but beyond that, where are we?"[57]

Nelson Mandela in his address delivered interchangeably in English, Afrikaans, and Xhosa, to CODESA I: "Failure of CODESA is inconceivable; so too is consensus, without legal force. There is absolutely no room for error or obstinacy. The challenge which CODESA places before each one of us is to unshackle ourselves from the past and to build the new."

Allan Hendrickse, leader of the Labor Party, with mixed-race membership, in an emotional speech following the collapse of CODESA II, "It is not possible to understand the political debate today unless we examine the political consequence of the last 44 years of apartheid rule.... We are dealing with a National Party that has grossly abused their political power."[58]

Mandela at the dramatic conclusion of CODESA II addressing all participants of the failed negotiations: "From where can we claim the moral
right to assert that we need to move with less speed? Why do we put
off till tomorrow solutions that we can [achieve] today? The people
cannot postpone their hunger. Similarly, they do not want their freedom
postponed. Any one of us who acts to delay that freedom only serves
to perpetuate our bondage."

Mandela, turning to the government: "The time has come that you truly
cross the Rubicon. You must understand clearly that the days of white
minority domination are over. During that period of change and while
you remain in power, you cannot and will not be both a player and
referee. Whether you are genuine about the change will be judged not
by what you say but what you do. Let us move forward together as
speedily as possible to our common objective of a democratic South
Africa. Thank you.[59]

Cyril Ramaphosa amidst preparations for the refurbished table: "'Suf-
ficient consensus' means, if we and NP agree, everyone else can get
stuffed."[60]

Roelf Meyer on the chamber theater talks: "With trust, respect, and a common vision both teams could afford to spend time on serious, in-depth
dialogues instead of wasting energy on petty differences.... The reality
is that virtually all whites supported apartheid, including myself, and
it was very destructive. I mention this because it is important, I feel,
not to run away from this reality. For me it is fundamental to admit
that apartheid existed and that at one time I benefited from it, indeed,
that I was part of the structure upholding it. I want to stress, however,
that despite this it was possible for me, and for many others, to make
the shift from the old paradigm to the new, and so play an active part
in the establishment of a new democratic South Africa. My very last
remark, then, is that if the will and the faith exist in the possibility of
a sustainable peace, it is possible to resolve a conflict, even one that
lasted for more than three centuries."[61]

As noted earlier, the stars on stage during the South African negotiations were Ramaphosa and Meyer, who, at the refurbished table in Kempton
Park, had leading parts, revealing great improvisational talents, stamina,
and impeccable timing.

GRAND FINALE

On April 5, 1989, at 5 p.m. everybody sat down again for the second and
last time at the grand round table in Warsaw's Regent's Palace. After the
opening speeches by Kiszczak and Walesa, an unexpected break was announced. As it turned out later, the head of OPZZ, Alfred Miodowicz, who

had been assigned in Magdalenka to give the sixth speech, had threatened to leave the table if he were not given the floor as the third speaker. After an almost three-hour break, during which the whole country was close to a nervous breakdown—wondering what in the world was happening—the ceremony finally resumed. Miodowicz had prevailed on being third in line at the podium, and today nobody remembers his unremarkable words.

But the words of his predecessor on the floor, Lech Walesa, marked both the opening of a new era and the mastery of a new idiom of political/systemic change. "We are aware of the fact," he said, "that the Round Table Talks did not fulfill all our expectations, because it couldn't. But I want to emphasize that for the first time we have spoken to each other using the force of argument and not the argument of force. So we look to the future with hope."[62]

And so the agreements, all 271 pages of them, were signed. At some tables the protocols on differences were longer than those on the agreements themselves!

In the most contentious issues concerning the electoral law, the final agreement stated that the election to the 100-seat Senate would be free and that the Senate would have the right to issue corrections on legislation; and that the lower chamber of Parliament (450 people) would have 35 percent of its seats open to free elections, with 60 percent for the Communist Party and its coalition partners and 5 percent for the already existing official associations. As the Solidarity camp had demanded, the candidates from the two sides would be on separate lists. And finally, the president would be elected by the National Assembly—that is, by both chambers of the new Parliament. A Special Contact Commission for evaluating the implementation of the agreements was established.

Two days later these main decisions of the Round Table Talks were accepted by the still-incumbent Parliament of the Polish People's Republic. A former member of the Committee in Defense of the Workers, Jan Litynski, just elected a member of Parliament, welcomed the Communist Party's delegation with the words: "The representatives of the nation welcome to its headquarters the representatives of the powers that be."[63]

On November 18, 1993, in Johannesburg's Kempton Park, the sun was already rising when the exhausted Negotiating Council reached the final agreement ratifying an interim constitution, thus ending fifty years of apartheid rule and easing the way to democracy. The South African round table had negotiated a set of instruments and principles that were to determine and guide the country's transition to democracy, had set a date for the first fully democratic elections, and had agreed on a timetable for drafting a new constitution. This carefully designed two-stage process established a trajectory of changes that—as in Poland—did not interrupt the legal continuity of the state.

The plenary meeting of the MPNP ratified the transition package, known as the "six-pack" agreement, which included interim constitutional acts, among them the Transitional Executive Council Act, which set the rules for the structure and functioning of the existing government to be overseen by the newly appointed Transitional Executive Council. The Electoral Act determined the specific arrangements for organizing elections, both national and local. The Independent Electoral Commission Act established the institution that would be in charge of organizing and overseeing the elections. Finally, the Interim Constitution Act settled two contentious matters: how the transitional institution—that is, the interim government—should work, and how the work on the constitution should be conducted.

The agreements specified that South Africa's Parliament, the Constitutional Assembly, would have two chambers, composed of 490 members, 400 sitting in the House, and 90 (10 from each province) making up the Senate.

To satisfy the compromise concerning power sharing, and following Slovo's sunset clause proposal, the negotiating sides agreed that minority parties would participate in governance for the next five years, until the second democratic elections, which were to take place in 1999. Two deputy presidents would represent the minority parties in the cabinet. One would be appointed from the second winning party, the other from the party that gained more than 20 percent of votes.[64]

Upon signing the transitional act, de Klerk stated boldly that those "who are filled with anxiety about the uncertainties of the present and the future forget how desperate our situation was four years ago.... They forget how implacable the enmity was between our main political parties and groups; how seemingly hopeless the prospect was of finding any peaceful way out of the cul-de-sac of racial divisions."[65]

Mandela said, in a final stirring speech: "Together, we can build a society free of violence. We can build a society grounded on friendship and our common humanity, a society founded on tolerance. That is the only road open to us. It is a road to a glorious future in this beautiful country of ours. Let us join hands and march into the future."[66]

On November 18, almost exactly one month after jointly receiving the Nobel Peace Prize, Nelson Mandela and F. W. de Klerk signed the negotiated settlement at the World Trade Center. The Kempton Park structure was quickly compared to Philadelphia's Independence Hall.

The grand finales in Warsaw and in Johannesburg, played out in the full regalia of power and in full view of the public, completed the acts of the round tables while putting in motion the *performativity* of the agreements.

EPILOGUE

The main result of the Polish Round Table, the election contract, originally devised as a formula for ensuring the stability of a slow, evolutionary change, turned out to be a big time-saver. The June 4 elections were indeed a brutal test, as all of the seats in Parliament constituting the 35 percent designated for free elections were won by candidates from the Solidarity slate. As for the Senate, not a single seat was won by a candidate of the regime.

The extent of this electoral victory, which took place the same day as the shocking Tiananmen Square massacre in China, made many members of the democratic opposition nervous. The Communist Party had not expected such a smashing defeat, and it was not clear what the reaction of party hard-liners, the police, and the army would be. In response to the memorable article by Michnik, "Your President, Our Prime Minister," Tadeusz Mazowiecki, calling for political caution, published a piece entitled "Rush Slowly."[67] But within two months, the Communist Party's ornamental and hitherto passive coalition partners dared to leave it for the Solidarity side, and the terms of the Round Table contract began to lose their relevance.[68]

In September 1989, about five months after the signing of the accords, a new government was created, with Tadeusz Mazowiecki as the first noncommunist prime minister in the Soviet bloc. General Jaruzelski had been elected president in July by the new Parliament, but never in the course of his year-and-a-half presidency did he try to use any of the strong presidential powers negotiated by his party at the Round Table.

On December 17, 1989, a package of eleven laws fundamentally changing the economic system was sent to Parliament and voted in on January 1. On December 29 the Parliament changed the name of the country from the Polish People's Republic to the Republic of Poland. Though work on a new constitution was launched almost immediately, an interim constitution was not introduced until 1992 by the new Parliament, which also set up the Constitutional Commission. After lengthy public debate the final document was approved by Parliament in 1997.

Recalling Adam Michnik's reminder of the inevitable disappointments on both sides following negotiated settlements, I provide here a few closing words on some of those who were, "after all, alive."

General Jaruzelski was elected president of the Republic of Poland in July 1989 by a majority of one vote in the National Assembly. He served only sixteen months, succeeded by Lech Walesa, the electrician from Gdansk, Poland's first president to be chosen through fully free elections. Jaruzelski completed his memoirs, in which he insists that the imposition of martial law in 1981 was a necessary move to prevent an invasion by Soviet tanks. Adam Michnik, who conducted a lengthy interview with Jaruzelski, accompanied him—to the dismay of his friends—to Paris for the promotion of the memoirs.

Lech Walesa, after completing his presidential term in 1995, returned to Gdansk, where he established a foundation, the Lech Walesa Institute. His book, *A Way of Hope,* has been published in many languages.

Professor Bronislaw Geremek became a Member of Parliament and as head of the Constitutional Commission oversaw the drafting of the new constitution. As Poland's foreign minister (1997–2000) he chaired the European Commission on Security and Cooperation. After Poland joined the European Union in 2004, Poles elected him to the EU Parliament. In the summer of 2008 he died in a car accident while driving to Brussels.

Adam Michnik, who was elected to the lower chamber of the Parliament in the first June 1989 elections, remained one of the most influential political writers in the country. With a staff that included old friends from the underground, he established *Gazeta Wyborcza* and became editor in chief of this very successful—also in economic terms—daily. The recipient of many international prizes, in 2001 Michnik was awarded the prestigious Erasmus Prize, given annually to a person who has made an exceptionally important contribution to European culture, society, or social science. An unwavering defendant of nonviolent political solutions in general, and of the Round Table negotiations in particular, he is a frequent object of sharp criticism on the part of those who thought that the Round Table was a conspiracy of the two elites.

Zbigniew Bujak, the worker from the Ursus Tractor Factory, graduated with a master's degree from the Department of Political Studies at Warsaw University and was appointed chair of the High Chamber of Tariffs and Border Control. He is working toward his doctorate in political science.

Stanislaw Ciosek completed in 1999 an almost decade-long tenure as Poland's ambassador to Russia.

General Kiszczak lost in the 1989 parliamentary elections. Appointed by Jaruzelski as prime minister, he was unable to form a government, and after three weeks Tadeusz Mazowiecki replaced him as the first post-Communist prime minister. He retired from politics, published his memoirs, and is frequently called upon to answer questions before the Polish courts.

Aleksander Kwasniewski succeeded Lech Walesa as president after winning the 1995 elections. A popular political figure, he was reelected in 2000 for his second and final term as president.

The epilogue of South Africa's round table was somewhat similar. Three weeks after the signing of the agreements on December 6, 1993, the newly appointed Transitional Executive Council, made up of eleven representatives of all major parties and equipped with considerable powers, began to monitor the work of the government that remained in place until the elections. Four months later, on April 26–29, South Africa held its first democratic elections, an extremely moving occasion, with millions of people standing in long lines to vote for the first time in their lives. The world watched the collapse of another wall, that of apartheid—a quiet dismantling, this time.

There were nineteen political parties participating in the elections, and 22 million people cast their votes. The African National Congress won overwhelmingly (though not reaching a two-thirds majority) with 62.65 percent of the vote, followed by the National Party with 20.39 percent, Inkatha Freedom Party with 10.54 percent, Freedom Front with 2.2 percent, Democratic Party with 1.7 percent, Pan-Africanist Congress with 1.2 percent, and the African Christian Democratic Party with 0.5 percent.

The outcomes of the elections determined the composition of the new South Africa's Parliament, more specifically its House of Assembly, with the ANC getting 252 seats, the National Party 82 seats, the Inkatha Freedom Party 43 seats, the Freedom Front 9 seats, the Democratic Party 7 seats, the Pan-Africanist Congress 5 seats, and the African Christian Democratic Party 2 seats. The ANC won in seven out of nine provinces, losing Western Cape to the National Party and KwaZulu /Natal to IFP.

Two weeks later Nelson Mandela, South Africa's first democratically elected president, was officially installed in office. Mandela, known as the "shepherd of South African democracy," quickly became an unquestionable global actor with an influential and universally respected voice. According to schedule, two years after the elections the Constitutional Assembly adopted the text of a new constitution. A few months later, on December 10, 1996, which is International Human Rights Day, President Mandela signed the Constitution of the Republic of South Africa into law—a document admired worldwide for its progressive recognition of diversity and its fostering of dignity and integration. South Africa's rule of law, articulated in fourteen chapters of the constitution (with a Bill of Rights being chapter 2), initiated the supremacy of the constitution in providing guidance-solving for the most contentious problems, under the watch of the strong powers of the Constitutional Tribunal. This whole process, which had been given the highest attention in the course of the South African negotiations, was completed one whole year before its counterpart in Poland.

And on October 29, 1998, President Mandela received the main Report of the Truth and Reconciliation Commission (TRC), 3,500 pages describing findings of gross human rights abuses committed during the past thirty-five years of apartheid. Born out of the spirit of a political compromise, the TRC helped to build a bridge between both sides of a sharply divided society, and between the past and the future. After intensively canvassing the entire country—public hearings that included both the victims and the perpetrators, with large parts televised and broadcast by radio—the TRC facilitated the process by acknowledging the atrocities and granting amnesty to those who confessed to crimes.

Mandela's successor as president in 1999 was Thabo Mbeki, a member of the younger generation of the ANC leadership in exile, and educated at Sussex University in England. A member of the initial talks about talks in Zambia and in Senegal, he was a key negotiator in Kempton Park. Picked by Mandela in 1994 to become deputy president, he was elected president of the ANC in 1997. A powerful political broker in Africa, he became a subject of criticism at home, especially over his skepticism (and ensuing policies) concerning the sources and treatment of AIDS. He modified his position, and after the overwhelming victory of ANC in March 2004, he was reelected for a second term as president of the country.

Frederik Willem de Klerk, "the overseer of the transition" and co-recipient of the Nobel Peace Prize, remained president of the interim government. Following the elections, as the representative of the second biggest parliamentary grouping, the National Party, de Klerk became the second deputy president (Mbeki being the first). Although in 2000 he established the F. W. de Klerk Foundation, whose motto is "continuing the miracle into South Africa's second decade," and published his autobiography, *The Last Trek—A New Beginning,* he has virtually disappeared from public life. His only presence today is on Noble Square at Cape Town's waterfront, where his full-figure sculpture is positioned in a row along with three other Nobel Peace Prize winners from South Africa: Nelson Mandela, Desmond Tutu, and Albert Luthuli.

Kobie Coetsee, an early facilitator of the talks, became president of the Senate, a position he held until the new constitution was ratified in 1996.

Mangosuthu Buthulezi, upon meeting Mandela and de Klerk, and nervous about the prospect of being marginalized in postelection South Africa, decided—in the very last minute—that the Inkatha Freedom Party would participate in the elections. That decision reduced political violence in the country almost immediately. Appointed minister of home affairs in the postelection government of National Unity, he also became chair of the KwaZulu/Natal House of Traditional Leaders Executive Committee. The 1998 TRC report held him, as leader of the IFP, accountable for the violence committed by members of the IFP against their political rivals and for collaborating with the state security forces.

Joe Slovo, whose conciliatory voice at the round table was a surprise for many inside and outside the country, ran on the ANC ticket in South Africa's first multiracial elections in April 1994 and gained a seat in the Parliament. Appointed minister for housing in the postelection government of National Unity, Slovo held the position until his death from leukemia in January 1995. At his funeral, President Nelson Mandela praised Joe Slovo for his achievements in the struggle for democracy in South Africa.

Cyril Ramaphosa, secretary general of the ANC, and the star of the round table show, was elected chairman of the Constituent Assembly (a body of 490 members representing seven parties in both houses of the Parliament) and was made responsible for the two-year project of drafting South Africa's constitution. In 1997 he resigned from politics and moved to the private sector, where he became director of South African Breweries. A successful businessman, he is a member of the ANC's Executive Committee.

Roelf Meyer, the other leading player of the negotiation, appointed for the first postelection government as minister of provincial affairs and constitutional development, became in 1996 the secretary general of the National Party. Frustrated by the party's resistance to undertaking major self-reform, he stepped down and cofounded the United Democratic Movement (UDM) in 1997. Elected to the Parliament on the UDM list, he served until his resignation from politics in 2000. Subsequently he lectured at Harvard University in 2001, held the Tip O'Neal Chair in Peace Studies at the University of Ulster in Northern Ireland, and became deputy executive chair of TILCA Infrastructure Corporation in Cape Town and chair of the Civil Society Initiative of South Africa.

NO CURTAIN CALLS

Although in both countries the agreements negotiated through their respective round tables are now harshly criticized by many for their variously perceived shortcomings, it may be useful to remember the wise observation made by Adam Michnik that "disappointed are those who are, after all, alive" and to recall Mandela's vision: "We live with the hope that as she battles to remake herself, South Africa will be like a microcosm of the new world that is striving to be born."[69]

6

Provincializing Global Feminism

The polis was distinguished from the household in that it knew only "equals," whereas the household was the center of the strictest inequality. To be free meant not to be subject to the command of another and not to be in command oneself.

—Hannah Arendt[1]

BITTER FREEDOM

Once the Round Table Talks were concluded and the new political contract negotiated between society and its last nonelected regime was signed in May 1989, Solidarity, which at that point still meant the majority of society, had only one month to prepare its first election campaign. With very limited access to the state-run mass media, and with its only daily newspaper in the process of being organized, Solidarity looked to the streets again as its preferred setting for a battle. But this time it was a battle of posters. Huge posters and banners with the familiar Solidarity logo covered all empty spaces on walls, fences, trams, and the windows of stores and restaurants.

At that point it was not only a matter of *time*: who would be first to put a poster on a still available space, Solidarity or the authorities? It was also a matter of *glue*: whose would hold the best so the competition couldn't tear it all down? And it was a matter of *wit*: whose handwritten puns and comments on each other's posters were the best? The poster wars were about how imaginatively the available wall space could be used to convince the biggest public.

The most emblematic poster for Solidarity's campaign was a full-size black-and-white picture of Gary Cooper from *High Noon,* walking alone to his final confrontation with the outlaws. On the poster the pistol in his hand had been airbrushed out and replaced with a paper ballot, and above the sheriff's star on his chest he wore a red-and-white badge with the familiar Solidarity logo. The caption below read "High Noon—the 4th of June, 1989." Whether he was Solidarity bracing to clean up the place or a citizen heading for the voting booths at this climactic moment, it was probably the most talked-about image of the campaign.[2]

The poster became an instant hit, and everybody reveled in how well it captured what people felt at that time: dramatic tension, affirmation of justice, a sense of agency, and the assurance of a successful performance. The message was right on target, and only from the perspective of time does it reveal one discrete trait of the democratic transformation project: its maleness. In opposition to the gendered image of the nation, which has been always female, the gendered image of the newly institutionalized democratic state in Poland, the source of societal hope at the end of the twentieth century, emerged unquestionably male. And at that time nobody, not even Polish women, seemed either alarmed or even aware of being excluded. What a pathetic case of false consciousness, some would have said.

A partial explanation for such a state of affairs, a subject of disbelief for my feminist friends in the West, could be found in an April 1989 survey. A team of Warsaw sociologists asked a representative sampling of Poles to choose from a list the one category that best defined their identity. Gender came in last place, preceded by, in order, human being, Pole, parent, and occupation. The survey, however, was conducted at the time of the Round Table negotiations, when a sense of solidarity of *all* citizens in challenging the regime was particularly strong, and, in this challenge, all parts, all social variables including gender, were of lesser importance than the whole.

When I first returned to my native and already virtually "postcommunist" Poland in the summer of 1989 after eight years in New York, one of the things that struck me most vividly was that in the new and exuberant public life of the country there was an almost total absence of those capable women who had played such an active and essential role in the clandestine operations of the prodemocratic movements of the 1970s and 1980s. I knew many of them well and had been active along with them, but I realized that like them, I had never defined the critical problems of the society in which I lived in terms of gender. The primary objective of every social protest and movement then was to fight for the political rights of *all* members of society. All other issues seemed to be of secondary importance and could be dealt with after the battle for democracy had one day been won. But now, watching the freewheeling debates in the new Parliament and the quickly emerging institutions of public and political life all staffed by men, I found myself wondering where all the women were. Democratically, but quietly, women were being squeezed out of the new polis and sent back to the household.

During the first four years following the collapse of the Berlin Wall, while visiting various countries of the region, I could sense tensions building around "the problem of women." On the one hand, the issue of gender, never really discussed in those countries before, was quickly emerging as a response to the deteriorating legal and economic status of women. On the other hand, in those first years of transformation, there was enormous sociocultural and political pressure coming from both men and women to disregard the issue and even to ridicule those involved in discussions of it.

I also observed a pair of striking paradoxes concerning the situation of women throughout the region. First of all, for many in public life the most politically rewarding behavior in the first years of postcommunism seemed to be that which focused on eradicating all remnants of the previous system, which included, ironically, its never-fulfilled commitments to human rights in general and to women's rights in particular. The second paradox was that the spheres of relative freedom available under Communist rule—those provided by the church in Poland, by the so-called second economy in Hungary, and by the family in Czechoslovakia—had now—for women—become spheres of constraint.[3]

The whole situation was additionally complicated by a priori negative attitudes toward feminism in this part of Europe. Both the old and the new constitutions guaranteed fundamental rights and freedoms for all, yet equality for women did not extend much beyond their participation in employment—a result of the postwar industrialization, ideology, and the need to supplement family income. Additionally, it was only in the late 1980s that it became obvious that there was no language that could be used to initiate a debate on women's rights. The very word *gender* does not exist in any Slavic language, and initially the only option for those interested in the analysis of gender as a social construct was to use the term *sex,* and to qualify it at each and every use.

The word *feminism,* which exists in those languages, is so pejoratively loaded that it was considered political suicide for a woman active in public life to identify herself with feminism and feminist issues. Until the mid-1990s it was still the exception rather than the rule that the small number of women involved in politics paid any attention to the mounting problems facing women, or acted on behalf of their lost rights. On the contrary, there was an assumption at work among women policy makers that women's problems are inseparable from the problems facing society as a whole. It would be premature to say that the silence concerning women's problems was orchestrated or imposed, but it did not take long for women to speak up.

"Until recently," confessed Olga Krzyzanowska, a physician who in fall 1992 was deputy speaker of the Polish Parliament, "I never divided issues into male and female issues. Now I am noticing that actual women's rights in Poland are being threatened. So women's issues have faced me right here on our own front doorstep, and not just slipped in through the international back door."⁴ Krzyzanowska's admission reflected a larger process, which slowly, in the face of much resistance, took place throughout Central and Eastern Europe: the process of discovering and acknowledging that there is a problem of women in the first place.

Already in the mid-1990s in Warsaw, Budapest, Prague, and Bratislava—places where the political scene was being looked upon more and more frequently with disappointment and disgust—one could detect the emergence of a new *public-spirited ethos* exemplified more often than not by certain individual women and women's groups. Such an ethos combined the experience, commitment, and unselfishness of former dissidents with a readiness to address imaginatively the unfamiliar challenges of new political and economic circumstances. And it was speech in a variety of its forms, as I will try to show later, that brought women back to the political realm. Gradually, and not without resistance, they began to be accepted, and sometimes even respected, both by the broader public and by the political elites, either because of, or in spite of, their commitment to women's issues.

This experience of women organizing themselves in the countries of post-Communist Europe, in spite of the feminism-hostile context, substantiates further the reasons given by Ann Philips as to why feminism ought to be interested in a conception of civil society.⁵ Indeed, contemporary feminist thought does need to examine closely the concept itself, as well as the ways in which women in different local contexts have organized themselves to mediate with the state the key issues of rights and gender equality. And yes, the feminist conception of civil society has to be broad and generous in providing space for diverse responses to the challenges occurring locally. There is no one blueprint for civil society, and in many parts of the world there may be neither a need to copy Western civic know-how or forcibly adjust theory that neither recognizes nor informs local realities. Also, in the so-called new democracies, once imaginative sites of civic movements and initiatives, the current much more rationalized and professionalized civil society organizations, identically designed and governed, are a source of disenchantment on the part of those who built the hard-to-imitate structures of civil society under the constraints of nondemocratic regimes.

Perhaps the usefulness of the broad civil society concept is best seen in instances of local feminisms, which, whether in democratic or nondemocratic states, found themselves marginalized by the gendering of politics anchored in local culture. The broad concept of civil society, not identical with what is commonly known as the NGO sector, neither prescribes one best way of action nor enforces any one agenda. Rather, it provides an inclusive space for diverse, indigenously inspired initiatives to conduct public dialogue with a concrete state, which in the case of women's organizations means negotiating matters of gender justice in specific social and cultural contexts.

This is why knowing that civil society in Poland was conceived in the 1970s and 1980s in a search for consensus rather than confrontation with the regime may be of assistance to those of us who want to understand the strategies behind women's initiatives there, and it may protect us from the pitfalls of appearing patronizing. One of the responses to systemic transformation in the region was the mobilization of women's civil society, driven by a newly initiated discourse on the deteriorating status of women and grounded in locally cultivated civic experience. The agenda and praxis of this feminism were less concerned with issues of identity and more with equal participation in social and political life. As such they were close to what on an analytical level is proposed by Nancy Fraser when she suggests treating recognition as a question of social status.[6]

The more recent response to globalization has opened yet another opportunity for the mobilization and further articulation of local feminism in this part of Europe.

ECONOMIC TRANSFORMATION MEETS GLOBALIZATION

Is globalization a threat or an opportunity for local feminism?

In Poland, the processes of globalization intersect with three relatively localized political and cultural processes: the post-1989 systemic transformation, the process of integration into the European Union, and a celebration of certain elements of the national past long censored and now retrieved. When one looks at these processes through the lens of gender, one ends up with if not necessarily an unclear, then certainly a perplexing picture, the dynamics of which are driven by various paradoxes, by contradictions not easily reconcilable, and by the coexistence of different pasts and bizarre figures. The relationship between globalization and feminism in Poland makes me think of the murals of Marc Chagall: thoroughly modern but idiosyncratic, and, as such, not founded on the premises of modernity.

The process of accession to the European Union revealed some new aspects of the systemic transformation in the region, which in the first decade of the twenty-first century is by no means completed. One of the main foundations of the liberal-democratic order was an economic reform that led—through the structural privatization of enterprises and entire industries—to a market economy. Thus both processes, the so-called transition to democracy as well as globalization in post-Communist Europe, are processes unfolding in the context of extensive privatization and the dismantling of centrally planned economies. What has followed in the mid-1990s was the mismanaged and famously corrupt privatization of state utilities and enterprises,[7] commonly known as the "privatization" or the "propertization" of the Communist nomenklatura, accompanied by the collapse of whole industries, economic dislocations, unemployment, and the rapid impoverishment of entire regions. The jury is still out on whether these are all just the necessary costs of a transformation that will eventually bring economic rewards and a degree of equity to the affected population.

At this point it is difficult not to observe that there is a very close connection between the devastation of the national economies and the emergence in the region over the first decade of transformation of a certain massive profit-making option: trafficking in women.[8] There is also a close link between the illegal trafficking in women and their powerlessness in the face of new and confusing, but still gendered, realignments in the marketplace. The UN Office on Drug and Crime has been warning—since the beginning of the century—that the trafficking in women is now the fastest-growing business of organized crime, and its rate of growth is fastest in Central and Eastern Europe and the former Soviet Union. According to estimates, the industry is now worth several billion dollars a year. Russian trafficking victims working in the sex industry in Germany reportedly earn on average $7,500 a month, of which the exploiter takes at least $7,000.[9]

This trafficking is obviously a global phenomenon. It moves across borders, continents, and oceans. And Central Europe, at the interface between the wealthiest and the poorest countries of Europe and Asia, is the point of passage. As economic differences between the countries of the former Communist bloc become sharper, the trafficking runs not only from east to west (Ukraine to Germany) but also from east to east (Bulgaria to Poland), because even within "The East" there is always some place west—or north—having relative economic success, proximity to the European Union, greater density of international transit on major highways, or greater strength of the local currency vis-à-vis the dollar and the euro. Hence victims trafficked to (and through) Poland come mostly from rural and impoverished regions in which trading is the only occupation, and for a young, unemployed woman with little education, the only merchandise available for trading is her body.

They come from Russia, Belarus, Ukraine, Moldova, Romania, and Bulgaria, and—what is rarely mentioned—increasingly they turn themselves desperately into wares to improve their own and their families' impossible living conditions. The most common end goal of the growing trade in women is forced prostitution, which is often characterized as an organized crime, to be addressed in legal terms and to be prevented by a further tightening of the borders between the European Union and the rest of Europe. Such a response comes from people who would seem to prefer to be blind. The countries of the EU are not interested in seeing that the traffickers are not the sole culprits, that it was not they who coerced women into bonded labor abroad in the first place, even if it is indeed the work of criminal gangs and unscrupulous male traffickers who profit from all this enormously. Yet it is obvious for key international organizations that "the search for work abroad has been fueled by economic disparity, high unemployment, and the disruption of traditional livelihoods."[10]

The response of women activists in the region was to launch La Strada, a dynamic network of women's organizations in Central and Eastern Europe established in 1995 to fight the trafficking in women. La Strada increasingly sees the trafficking in women and children not just as a result of powerful criminal networks operating in this part of the world, or in terms of violations of human rights, but above all as a violation of social and economic rights.[11] Saskia Sassen, a scholar with a critical activist edge, struggling to define the trafficking in women, said, "This is not crime, this is something else." And this "something else" will remain with us until some vast campaign is undertaken to improve the condition of women—and men—in the poorer countries.[12]

The major enlargement of the European Union in May 2004, which included eight post-Communist countries evaluated as the most advanced in democratic and economic reforms, created a new divide, this time among the countries of the former Communist Bloc, between the lucky ones who made it to the club and the poor, unlucky ones who did not.

THE POLITICS OF EUROPEANIZATION

The goal of European Enlargement is to equalize the differences between the eastern and western parts of the continent.
—*Sueddeutsche Zeitung, April 2001*

The eastward enlargement of the European Union, the most significant growth it has experienced so far in terms of both scope and diversity—from fifteen to twenty-five member states—has obviously had enormous implications for the applicant countries. Of the ten countries invited to take part in the lengthy process of preparations and negotiations for EU entry, completed on May 1, 2004, all but Cyprus and Malta were former members of the Communist Bloc.[13]

Poland completed its negotiations with the European Union on December 13, 2002 (for Poles an interesting, though pure, coincidence—that being the anniversary of the 1981 imposition of martial law that temporarily crushed Solidarity). Although the talks had been stormy, as the Polish negotiators frequently rose from the table, ready to break off the talks, it was finally agreed that Poland had met the EU criteria for membership, which were organized into three clusters of requirements and thirty chapters of negotiations focusing on various areas of EU law and policy. The first cluster called for stable democratic institutions, founded on the rule of law, human rights, and respect for and protection of minorities. The second group required the existence of a functioning market economy capable of coping with the competitive pressures and market forces within the Union.

The third cluster included the ability to take on the responsibilities of membership, which include adherence to the aims of political, economic, and monetary union.[14] The return of the Polish negotiating team from Copenhagen, with Prime Minister Miller at the helm, was greeted with considerable euphoria, especially by the liberal media. On April 16, 2003, the ten applicant countries signed the Treaty of Accession in Athens.

It is widely believed—at least among the original EU members—that the carrot of membership contributes to a strengthening of the causes of democracy and tolerance within the applicant countries. Women's groups in Poland—the country known for its regressive policies concerning reproductive rights—had been following the process of negotiation closely, in the expectation that the process itself, and the very act of joining the European Union, would force the Polish state to adjust its laws to the standards and norms of the EU, including Europe's provision for comprehensive gender equality, or what they call *gender mainstreaming*. In short, women have been actively anticipating that this European approach will become a commanding guarantor of gender justice in the region, and that the principle of gender mainstreaming will gradually produce a major change in mentality, especially within the Polish political class.

Gender mainstreaming[15]—actively promoted in the 1990s by various intergovernmental organizations in Europe, especially the Council of Europe—is a strategy aimed at integrating the gender perspective into every fiber of society. More specifically, it means incorporating a gender-equality perspective into all policies at all policy-making levels, primarily by those who deal with the given policies (i.e., in education, health care, transportation, etc.). Gender mainstreaming—as defined by the Council of Europe—is the "reorganization, improvement, development, and evaluation of policy processes, so that the gender-equality perspective is incorporated in all policies at all levels and at all stages, by the actors normally involved in policy-making."[16]

One would think that the painstaking process of negotiation would have provided the EU with an excellent opportunity for the coherent introduction of the principle and culture of gender mainstreaming to each country through its extensive teams of experts negotiating separately in thirty different policy areas. One would have thought that this was a major opportunity, since the applicant countries were adjusting and reorganizing their structures, learning to take on new responsibilities, and at that very sensitive moment having to exhibit their political goodwill. But a closer examination of the thirty chapters of negotiations on the conditions under which applicant countries can join the EU reveals a priority given to economic issues over social or political concerns.

And under the pressure exerted by the EU to synchronize the legal, social, and economic spheres, gender was not the primary or even a secondary lens through which these were examined. In fact, women's issues appeared in only one of the thirty areas of negotiation, specifically in the thirteenth, concerning the problems of social policy and employment. And there were no negotiations concerning the question of gender equality as such. This prioritizing makes one think about the double standards already applied now vis-à-vis candidate countries. After all, the EU has been for many years openly promoting gender mainstreaming among its original members, setting aside human and financial resources to ensure the implementation of policies that support further equality for women. The applicant countries, however (or rather, their women's rights groups)—it was tacitly decided—ought to be satisfied that the employment status of women has been considered.[17]

Ironically, for the EU to highlight this partial standard is not just misleading but also can undermine the efforts of the local women's movements in the new member countries. A high level of women's employment (70–80 percent) and education was experienced by two generations of women and is generally taken for granted in the region. Although the current inequalities between men and women in the labor market are widely recognized by Polish society, it is also clear to women that equality in the labor market, still very high in Poland, does not automatically advance their equality in other spheres of life.[18]

The main preoccupation of the EU negotiations—the policy of equal opportunity for men and women in the realm of employment (on the premise that women can handle simultaneously both household responsibilities and full-time employment), argued Polish scholars and activists, does not actually address the real problems faced by women in Poland. Such problems are issues of importance to current members of the European Union, where even a few years ago the participation of women in the labor market was much lower than in Central Europe. In Poland women had been managing double duty for years, and now many of them would prefer to have some flexibility in making their choices, especially at a time when the state is pulling back from its provision of support systems for working mothers.[19]

The absence of such flexibility on the part of Brussels, and the insistence on selected, mostly economic standards that were devised in one context and cloned for another, may help in forcing women in Central Europe to retreat into the roles envisioned for them by the Church, as mothers and homemakers. As one of the most perceptive feminist writers in Warsaw has bitterly observed, the EU may simply be willing to accept gender discrimination in Poland as a matter of local color: "The French have their cheeses, the Brits their Queen, and the Poles have their discrimination against women."[20] She said this in 1999, and it now seems that what sounded then like a sardonic observation about a misapplied idea of the cultural rights of the community has turned—or is turning as we speak—into an accurate prediction.

One may argue that the principle of gender mainstreaming has been unevenly realized among the member countries of the EU itself. Whereas it seems to be fairly well entrenched in Germany and in the Nordic countries, its realization in France, for example, seems to be taking place mostly at the local level. But the lamentable absence of any general discussion with the applicant states on the strategy concerning gender issues—a comprehensive strategy that for the member states is already a guiding strategy—has already had detrimental effects. Perhaps such a discussion could have helped to create a larger consensus around the need to introduce gender-equality policies, or at least discourage manifestations of openly antiwomen attitudes that originate in official circles and constitute a further assault on the women's rights community.

As one might expect, the reasons why Polish feminists looked with hope toward Poland's entry into the European Union were the very reasons cited by the local conservative groups in warning against accession. The growing split between the progressive and reactionary publics, the latter spreading fear about accession and further aggravated by the patronizing stance of some Western politicians vis-à-vis the "New Europe," put the government negotiating the accession treaty into a state of anxiety, especially in view of the June 2003 national referendum in which Poles were to cast their votes for or against the accession to EU. And paradoxically, Polish feminists were nervous that even if accession were accomplished, they might discover that the EU had been stinting all along on the question of women's rights when it came to the "New Europe."

The feminists' disappointment with the EU approach toward the candidate countries, which applied scrutiny to everything except women's rights broadly understood, was based on a decade of either unworkable or straightforwardly hostile relationships between the women's civil society and the state. Following the 1997 elections, the Polish government replaced its office dealing with gender equality with one called the Governmental Plenipotentiary for Family Affairs, whose representative, sent in June 2000, to the UN conference "Women 2000," spoke out against women's rights without hiding her disdain. But the hard work of women's organizations paid off in 2001, when women candidates won 22 percent of the seats in the parliamentary elections and a new Office of the Governmental Plenipotentiary for the Equal Status of Women and Men was established. Its appointed head, Izabela Jaruga-Nowacka, a longtime leader of a women's organization affiliated with a left-wing party, announced that her office, which would also defend men's rights (including those related to reproductive health), had taken upon itself, as one of its goals, a campaign to liberalize the antiabortion law. She pointed out that this very strict law had resulted in the massive emergence of underground abortion clinics and dramatically affected the lives of thousands of women, particularly those who are less affluent. Making her first major presentation of the program in January 2002, she set the stage for acts of constructive performativity, making it clear that she intends to work toward liberalization of the law criminalizing abortion through dialogue and the building of societal and political consensus around the issue, rather than through a declaration of ideological war against the conservative, populist faction in Parliament.

Yet Jaruga-Nowacka's refreshingly independent position and visible presence in public debates soon began to be perceived not only as a threat to those at the right end of the political spectrum but also as an *obstruction* to the work of the new government, which—despite its Communist pedigree—liked to present itself as an enlightened, European-style social democracy. Nevertheless, a governmental spokesman, during the plenipotentiary's January presentation, immediately stated that the Council of Ministers had no plans to revisit the antiabortion law in 2002.[21]

Soon afterward, in an interview given to a Warsaw daily, a Polish bishop who had been generally considered one of the most reasonable and moderate[22] came out with a surprising statement, calling the new Governmental Plenipotentiary for the Equal Status of Women and Men "a feminist hard-liner who will not change even under hydrochloric acid." This tipped the scale, and the bishop's vitriolic remarks were immediately greeted with a barrage of criticism in the media, including the voices of well-known professional women who had never associated themselves with the feminist movement.

In early February 2002, more than 100 well-known women—intellectuals, scholars, and artists, including a Nobel Prize laureate—signed a letter of protest written by a widely respected senior professor and literary critic, Maria Janion, and addressed to the European Parliament and to Anna Diamantopulou, the EU's Commissioner for Labor and Social Policy (the very area—chapter 13—which considers women in the enlargement negotiations). The letter, widely circulated throughout the country and abroad, expressed distress over the direction of the debate on the situation of women in Poland and suggested that behind the scenes in Poland's negotiations with the EU some very specific trading in women's rights had taken place.[23] And looking at the entire political stage from overseas, one could not help thinking that the government's caution about not antagonizing the Church hierarchy was closely related to its anxiety concerning the issue of European enlargement. Popular support for joining the EU had been steadily dropping in Poland (from 80 percent in 1996 to 55 percent in 2001),[24] and it became clear that the post-Communist government had been courting the church to gain an advocate vis-à-vis its large rural constituency, which was most resistant to the idea of enlargement.

At some point it seemed as though this disturbing antifeminist alliance might only have been a temporary strategic constellation: this alliance of globalizing Eurocrats, cloning their mostly economic laws and regulations for others but unwilling to see the candidate countries as they really were and to set in motion the general idea of gender mainstreaming; individual governments that were itching to join the European club and that to get there were willing, despite earlier promises, to close their eyes and sacrifice women's rights; and the "universal" Catholic Church, which—at this historic juncture—was happy to play its illiberal card openly, hoping to hinder at least for a while the unavoidable.

Even though the process of European enlargement has not provided the expected program of prerequisites, instruments, and climate that would empower women's rights groups in the region (certainly nothing comparable to CEDAW), membership in the EU inevitably has to open up access to the broader family of standards implied by the notion of gender mainstreaming, and to provide mechanisms through which their implementation could be monitored and accounted for. But the mechanics of enlargement, as seen through the lens of gender, reveal major flaws and deficiencies in the European institutions themselves. When in July 2002 the European Parliament accepted a resolution recommending that abortion be legal in the candidate countries, the Polish Episcopate retorted: "We do not need any instruction from Brussels in order to learn when one can kill a baby. We know that one cannot do it ever, and that's it. It is a scandal that the European Parliament is trying to intervene in countries which are not even members of the EU."[25] And yet as soon as the government delegation, with Prime Minister Miller, returned from the final accession negotiations in Copenhagen in December 2002, Church representatives expressed their satisfaction and support for the successful conclusion of the process.

Later the government—pressed by the Episcopate of the Catholic Church—was trying to hammer down a separate protocol (like the one forced by Ireland in Maastrich) to be added to the Polish treaty, stating the inviolability of Polish antiabortion law. And Prime Minister Miller—even though he knew from the opinion polls that the overwhelming majority of Poles support a liberalization of the antiabortion law—announced that in today's Poland the conditions were not right for a modification of the abortion law.

THE POLITICS OF LOCALITY AND ITS GENDER IMPLICATIONS

In the mid-1990s one could still observe a considerable discrepancy between the dynamic growth and vitality of women's civil society in the new democracies of Central Europe, and their virtual exclusion, for all practical purposes, from access to policy-making circles and their consequently limited impact at the national level. In the early transitional period the NGOs in general, and women's organizations in particular, tend to be given the "Hyde Park Corner" treatment, as an outlet for nonthreatening, nongovernmental initiatives. Thus women's organizations—though performing a crucial role as incubators of women with leadership skills—have generally been seen by their own members as fenced playgrounds within which women can do what they want but from which they cannot graduate.[26]

But a few years later a first and very impressive cohort of women finally "graduated" in Poland and began to enter into the politically relevant public sphere. There were several points of entry: at major universities women have managed to establish varied and impressive Gender Studies programs, popularly known as "gendery" (for lack of a Polish word, giving the English a Polish plural ending); they have developed shrewd media strategies; there is a remarkable phenomenon of conceptual women's art, causing major controversies and debates.[27] Women have appeared in politics, in business, in the arts, in academia, they have organized themselves in women's or feminist organizations, and they cannot be ignored anymore. The feminist debate has gone mainstream. In June 1999 *Gazeta Wyborcza,* the major Polish daily, published an extensive and provocative essay analyzing the nature of patriarchal rule after communism.[28] In the course of the next two months, thirteen sizable articles followed—polemics and counterpolemics, not just letters—a phenomenon so striking that it was eventually noticed by the American media.[29] Since then feminist writing has been flourishing in the press, everything from regular columns to very readable essays obviously addressed to a broad, intelligent audience.

There has also appeared a rising tide of sophisticated books produced by this first cohort of local feminists, often witty and always a "good read," widely discussed and reviewed, and often nominated for major awards. The books have generated new knowledge, and as they discuss the subordination of women, using categories and cultural references that are immediately recognizable by Poles, they have generated a new, informed, and critical public. The titles, which sound better in the original Polish than in these translations, convey a combination of freshness and savvy: *A World Without Women: Gender in Polish Public Life*; *Cinderella, Frankenstein, and Others*; *Sparrow with a Broken Wing [...] or, A Shot of Vodka; Constructions of Femininity in Polish Post-War Visual Culture*; *Ladies, Knights, and Feminists*; *Body, Desire, Attire*; *Lipstick on the Flag*; and *Silence of the Lambs: The Thing about Abortion.*[30]

Women's NGOs—300 of them—as strong as they are diverse, have become recognizable actors on the Polish political stage, even if their influence on the politics of the state is still relatively limited.[31] And finally, even though this does not necessarily translate itself into increased gender sensitivity, women have made enormous strides in entering the world of politics and the economy. Both the 2001 and 2005 parliamentary elections significantly raised the number of women in both chambers of Parliament (from 13 percent to 20 percent). Women run the largest news organizations, they constitute about 30 percent of the country's managers, and already in 1998 they owned 20 percent of small companies (those with eight to twenty workers).[32]

All these advances in the presence of women and women's issues are accompanied by an increasingly sympathetic climate for an albeit moderate feminist agenda. There is a steady decrease in the number of those who support the traditional role of woman as homemaker, including those who still in the early 1990s believed that women ought to sacrifice their professional careers for the sake of their husbands.[33] And according to a 2002 opinion poll, 92 percent of Poles wanted the government to put on its agenda the issue of equal status for women and men.[34]

These gains, which serve in the West as markers of women's relative success, are accomplished in a sharply gender-contentious context, in which the state with its successive governments and parliaments, no matter whether right-, center-, or left-oriented, has bred a political class and perfected a party system that is still virtually closed to women. Other elements of this context are harder to translate, as they cannot be readily understood in terms of categories designed to grasp Western patterns of subjection and oppression. Such a mechanical application causes real problems for the practical work of women in the region. One of its results is the EU's mishandling of the gender question in the process of European enlargement. Another is the tendency to look at the trafficking in women exclusively in terms of women's human rights.

Gendering Idiom

The feminist agenda and discourse—radical as it might have appeared to many in demanding a firm institutionalization of gender equality in all spheres of life—became gradually informed by exposing the cultural sources implicated in the gendering of political life in today's Poland. Bypassing the debates of the region's feminists on the colonization of thought by the West, the Polish feminists focused on the reconstruction of the local cultural idiom that elucidates the tricky position of Polish women and helps to frame the challenges of local feminism.

The exploration of the gendering idiom was from the very beginning a highly strategic enterprise and not just a "celebration of difference." Reconstructed from familiar cultural particulars that revealed the pattern of dependencies and subjugation hidden in a culture that ostensibly venerated women, the unveiling of the idiom helped to validate the local feminist agenda while making the discourse more inclusive and accessible to a larger public. Obviously "larger" does not necessarily mean sympathetic. But it became clear that more women now relate to the debate, and in more meaningful ways. Even a few years ago, the more abstract categories of rights seemed for many not only abstract and alien but also bearing too much resemblance—at least rhetorically—to resented forms of past ideological indoctrination regarding women. This attitude has been changing now. The sizable, diverse, and dynamic women's civil society that has emerged across the country, the surprisingly thriving programs of gender studies, and the literature with its cogent exploration of the gendering idiom at work here together constitute the distinctive local face of contemporary Polish feminism.

That prevailing idiom has a relatively recent nineteenth-century pedigree, as it is generated by a cluster of sociohistorical circumstances that the Poles have had to face, and by the strategies they have developed for coping with them. The circumstances for most of that time were the loss of statehood, followed by political and cultural subordination to, and economic exploitation by, the three continental colonizing powers. As the nineteenth century was the age of the formation of the modern nation-state, the loss of political sovereignty put Poles outside of the processes of political and economic modernization then taking place in Europe. Even though insurrections and uprisings against the colonizers did not bring results comparable to those in Greece, Italy, or Germany, as they did not lead to the reestablishment of a united and independent Polish state, the romantic paradigm disseminated by the prophetic literature of the period—with the cult of the woman as a key to nature and the cosmos—endured as a part of Polish culture for almost 200 years.[35]

The Poles' experience of conspiracy, imprisonment, a clandestine schooling system, political exile, confiscation of property, the smuggling in of forbidden books printed in Polish abroad, the organizing of various self-help societies—all this was memorialized through a literature written mostly in exile, through drawings, Chopin's polonaises, and countless family stories. Those elements constituted for Poles in the twentieth century the master narrative of national chivalry and a repertoire of heroic-civic roles, available mostly to the impoverished nobility-turned-intelligentsia.[36] Hence the struggle for national and political emancipation has become a way of life for several generations of Poles, the very core of their cultural ethos, and an important point of departure for any feminist analysis.

One of the recent "gender boom" books argues that the emancipatory feminist discourse in Poland, even if confronted by a variety of other possible discourses—liberal, socialist, ecclesiastical, national—has one feature in common with all of them, which is the nobility-derived gender contract between knights and ladies. "In the liberal discourse the knight is a gentleman attending and admiring his 'lady'; in the socialist discourse he is a courteous party activist distributing to his female coworkers red carnations on March 8, the International Women's Day; and in the national-religious version of the discourse, it is a woman attaching ribbons to the chest of a man, in a gesture of encouragement as she sends him off to fight for the motherland."[37]

Gender Adoration or Gender Discrimination?

However, the Chagalesque visual representation of the idiom that frames the Polish feminist discourse has more than just two figures. In addition to the *knight* and the *lady* (in their various ideological embodiments), there are also the figure of a *peasant*, the figure of the Virgin Mary (i.e., *Maryja*), and the figure of *Matka Polka*, or "Mother Pole"—a womanly symbol of patriotism not to be confused with the Motherland, the Virgin Mary, or Polish mothers as such.

The courtly ethos, with its gender implications, has its chivalrous analogue in a peasant culture, where the object of adoration is also a lady, the lady of the Catholic Church's icon: Our Lady of Czestochowa, Our Lady of Ostra Brama, or *Maryja*. The Marian cult, most pronounced in peasant-rural societies, represents a religiosity that fulfills itself through collective pilgrimages and processions, adorations of iconic representations, and rosary chants. The place where public adoration takes place is a holy manor, a church. As in any folk culture, the reasons for adoration are usually very specific. *Maryja* is the mother and caretaker of those who have suffered wrongs. She offers consolation and protection. She is sometimes represented with a sword in her hand, a female knight. The Black Madonna of Czestochowa, with a slash on her cheek and a baby in her arms, is said to have saved Poland twice from foreign invaders and is thus intimately linked to the national culture of suffering and struggle.[38]

Thus the contract between the knights and the ladies is further reinforced by the peasant-rooted Marian character of Polish religiosity and by the intelligentsia-rooted collective ethos of struggle and sacrifice, with women—or more specifically, "Mother Poles"—as its moral guarantors.

A more thorough "unpacking" of this indigenous, overbearing, and heavily gendered cultural idiom, which embraces the entire society from knights to peasants, might help one understand the difficulties faced by Polish feminism. A concerted effort is being made by Polish feminists to reveal the opaqueness of gender discrimination, which—whether quite unconsciously or sometimes even half-consciously—masquerades as gender adoration. And gender adoration in Poland is seldom recognized as patronizing or condescending.

The First Gender Revolution

The nineteenth-century version of the idiom went through various modifications during the century just past, beginning especially with World War II. This war, launched by the Nazis into Poland first, confronted them with the longest-running resistance movement of all. It was on Polish territory that the biggest atrocities on a civilian population were committed, but it was also there that the largest anti-Nazi underground emerged and functioned for five years.

During World War II, Poland's widespread, youth-based resistance movement instigated what may well have been the most far-reaching cultural and gender revolution in Europe. The rules of conspiracy broke and eventually eliminated the prewar standards of propriety, including the roles traditionally assigned to women. Young men and women disappeared together in the thick of the night with concrete covert assignments. Women were no longer just the moral guarantors of their sons' and husbands' courage to sacrifice: they fought and thus participated in direct self-sacrifice next to the men.

The experience of war, occupation, and in particular the resistance challenged, altered, and liberalized traditional perceptions of the gender dichotomy in Poland, bringing about a whole generation of independent and audacious women and opening up for them beyond family, motherhood, and church a space in the midst of public matters, that is, at the center of *res publica.*

Growing up in Poland in the 1950s and 1960s, my own identity was shaped by a culture that offered an expanded repertoire of choices, thanks not to any immediate Communist policies but to the deep gender rearrangements that were a by-product of the war and the anti-Nazi resistance movement. I remember being impressed with various women, friends of my father from the underground, visiting our home, and conversations we had at the dinner table. I remember trying to bargain with my father, a former officer in the Polish underground in the 1940s, for some position in a clandestine resistance unit when the next invasion came. And in fact the air was full of war and the fear of war. Thanks to the state propaganda, there was no doubt that we were already surrounded, and the question was not *whether* "they"[39] would invade but *when.* I needed to be assured by my father that when war came I would not be a nurse, the traditional role for a woman in wartime, but somebody dealing with arms and logistics, maybe even a *laczniczka,* a courier running between units of the larger underground army operating in the deep forests near my hometown in central Poland.

The equality in a time of anti-Nazi struggle did not invalidate the contract between the ladies and knights entirely, but the pronouncements of the postwar Communist regime introducing gender equality were taken for granted and did not sound as progressive as had been expected.

The Gendered Dialectics of Freedom and Equality

The Communist system throughout the region, although based on the same political, economic, and ideological postulates, did not generate identical outcomes. Despite pressure from Moscow, each state within the bloc developed certain peculiarities of its own. In the Polish case three well-known specifics stand out. The first was that most of its farmland did not undergo forced collectivization, and that most individual peasants thus remained owners and managers of their own farms, guaranteeing them a measure of economic independence from the state, with a fairly equal division of labor between members of the family. The second was that the Catholic Church, too, had retained much of its autonomy, as the only national institution to survive the nineteenth and twentieth centuries intact. The third specific, not entirely unique to Poland but certainly far more pronounced there, had to do with the frequent changes in political climate. When periods of extensive ideological frost were followed by thaws, there were variably extended periods of relaxed censorship, curbed secret police activity, freeing of political prisoners, openings to the West, a green light given to associational life, a more outspoken press, foreign movies, and translations of Fromm, Tocqueville, or Beckett. Thaws were a time for people to get a taste—however limited—of freedom and the possibilities for greater self-realization. The question is whether everybody participated in these moments equally.

In analyzing the gender composition of Communist-era parliaments, Malgorzata Fuszara, Poland's major academic and civic feminist, discovered a negative correlation between the times of political thaw and women's representation in Parliament. In the two most memorable periods of political relaxation, after October 1956 and after the Round Table negotiations in 1989, the percentage of women parliamentarians dropped sharply, from 17 percent to 4 percent in 1956, and in 1989 from 20 percent to 13 percent (and eventually, in 1991, in Poland's first fully democratic elections since the war, to 10 percent!).[40]

When Fuszara says that the participation of women in Parliament decreases abruptly when the Parliament itself gains an unaccustomed degree of power, or when it in fact acquires true legislative power, her observation rings a familiar "bitter freedom" bell for the region.[41] But what is interesting in Fuszara's analysis, examining as it does both the Communist and the post-Communist periods, is that it debunks a lingering belief—still prevalent especially outside the region—that the disappearance of the Communist system is solely responsible for stripping women of their status and the opportunity to participate in political life.

Freedom, or the relative freedom during Communist thaws, rarely created the conditions for equal participation by women in the institutions of political life. In Poland, paradoxically, it was in periods with drastically curtailed freedom—in particular the Nazi occupation in the 1940s, and the period of martial law in the 1980s, known in Poland as the "state of war"—that women came closest to earning equal status with men.

There is a growing body of literature analyzing the key role played by women in mending the banned trade union Solidarity after the devastation it suffered as a result of the military coup in December 1981, and in reconstructing its civic activities and structures underground.[42] As all this was highly illegal activity in defiance of harsh military law, it required the most rigorous conspiracy, and in part because the identities of female leaders (like those of the men) were kept secret, they rarely got any credit for their efforts afterward.[43]

Nevertheless, the experience was an extraordinary demonstration and test of their political wisdom, leadership, fiscal responsibility, and management skills, as well as their creativity in the realm of communications and logistics—not to mention ordinary courage. In effect underground, Solidarity brought to light and developed an impressive human capital in women that had not been recognized before.

This participation in the struggles for freedom was never really translated into participation in power when freedom finally came. In South Africa, women ANC fighters talk about a similar experience following the end of apartheid. This is also strikingly analogous to the history of African American men repeatedly demonstrating their patriotism and sacrifice in war after war, yet returning home to second-class citizenship and racism.

In early 1989, when the Communist government was ready to negotiate at the Round Table a compromise with the still delegalized Solidarity movement, only one woman was actually seated at the Round Table (on the Solidarity side), and in the several separate subtables only five women took part (four of them on the Solidarity side). No woman was included in the informal negotiations in Magdalenka, where decisions were massaged and finalized.

Though it may not be a uniquely Polish experience, it has gradually become clear to many Polish women that they were really good for the tough times of struggle, but now they are told to relax and go home. The men could take it from there and continue their battles in the Parliament under the shield of procedural democracy, now the almighty lawmakers in a democratic state. The government soliciting church support for accession to the European Union and trading its earlier promise given to women to liberalize the abortion law provides another case of male-dominated democracy, gendered ownership of the rule of law.[44]

Ironically (or perhaps not), it was precisely a women's issue that became one of the key battlegrounds in the last Communist and all succeeding post-1989 Parliaments. That battle, part of a more extensive cultural war, was over a woman's right to self-determination, and specifically over her reproductive rights. The key soldiers of this legislative battle—just to expand upon the metaphor, mind you—arrived in Parliament armed with the paraphernalia of the Polish idiom: as if "dressed" as knights and ladies, as peasants hiding behind the icon of the Madonna, with male politicians cross-dressed as those patriotic "Mother Poles," and finally bishops—not as shepherds but as the sheep dogs of a Poland lured by the New Europe.

And all the rigmarole of this pageant turned out to be very expedient. In the favorable context of the fresh and authentic gratitude that society felt toward the Church for its long service on behalf of the survival of the Polish nation, harsh antiabortion measures were voted into law in 1993. Abortion was virtually delegalized, sex education was removed from the schools, and state subsidies for contraceptives were cancelled. Now the Polish abortion law is becoming a "cultural specificity," an exception protected in accordance with the principle of a multicultural Europe.

In an annual feminist demonstration on a Sunday in March that marks International Women's Day and is commonly known as a *Manifa* (a term of endearment for "manifestation"), proceeding theatrically along the major streets of Warsaw, one could see among the posters and banners the declaration, "I've had enough," signed, "Mother Pole."[45]

A Digression on a Manifa

In March 2006 I had an unexpected opportunity to join an especially witty parade in Warsaw that began in front of the Parliament and turned into an event that many joined who several years before would not have cared to do so. This time, dissatisfaction with the prevailing political discourse, dominated by the dogmatic and divisive voice of the ruling camp, turned the Manifa into a setting for the expression of a broadening discontent about growing discrimination not only against women but also against various open-minded groups in the society who feel increasingly marginalized and whose voices are officially considered perilous to the health of the country. A colorful group of a few thousand women and men gathered in front of the Parliament and then advanced through the main street of Warsaw in a carnivalesque parade of popular dissent, under banners that sharply attacked government policies, spelling out "We are equal, we are different, and we are in solidarity." And what was perhaps most interesting of all, the Manifas had spread throughout the country. But that is a different story.

* * *

Paradoxically, it was the country's democratic transformation that for some political forces opened up an opportunity to rebuild the wall between the polis and the household that had been perforated during the time of the self-limiting revolution. It was Poland's accession to the European Union—in particular the favor expected of the Catholic Church to support the accession and to convince the people to vote "yes" in the upcoming referendum—that postponed any revisiting of the antiabortion law. And it was the process of European enlargement that made it difficult for local feminism—with its impressive analysis of Poland's indigenously gendered culture—to "undress" the pageant and thus to disarm it.

One could, of course, toy with the idea of a radical unilateral rejection by Polish feminism of the entire idiom, but that would include its other modern and often whimsical elements, which, like the experience of World War II, the Solidarity resistance, and the street theater of the late 1980s, remain for many women in Poland a source of autonomy, agency, creativity, and strength.

It is particularly important under present circumstances to consider that the response to such a unilateral rejection may come from relatively recent ideologies based on ultraconservative values—mostly religious and national—from populism, or fundamentalism. Thriving in times of rapid social change, such ideologies provide emotional, cognitive, and political answers for those whose own modernizing efforts have been challenged and systematically frustrated. Poland's own systemic transformation, its opening to markets, ideas, and people, as well as its joining the European Union, provoked a manageable measure of moral-majority and populist-fundamentalist response.[46] The real danger may lie, rather, in impoverished, isolated, and autocratic places like Belarus or the countries of Central Asia.

The response of Polish women to their exclusion from the institutions of democratic governance and policy making was manifold, and their actions resided in speech: the resolute media performance, books and journals that reached an ever-increasing audience, carnivalesque street performances, seminars, letter campaigns, legal clinics, hotlines. Though not contractual or declaratory, not immediate, purely illocutionary acts, these action-oriented utterances have been implicit performatives, utilizing in a new political context the strategies of the civic movements of the 1970s and 1980s that women had cocreated, to reenter the public space, to retrieve the weakened status of cocitizens with access to power. Just as before, in the time of self-limiting revolution conducted by civil society, their current speech actions were mostly of the *perlocutionary* kind. It was acting by saying something; acting to convince and to persuade that produced follow-up consequences.[47] One set of performative actions was generated by articles, TV interviews and panel discussions, "gendery" seminars, and above all by books disclosing the cultural blueprints that had facilitated the removal of women from the newly created polis. The other was generated by massive letter campaigns, theatrical manifas taking place on the streets of the cities, legal actions undertaken by women's groups and concluded by rulings on behalf of women (including the victims of trafficking), and finally voting for women in the Parliament.

At the same time, a major change took place on the level of language, both its vocabulary and grammar, where new gender-specific words—mostly nouns, gradually invented, translated, or adopted—entered linguistic usage. The most striking but also the most visible in the bylines of the press articles were the new words designating the professional or occupational status of women. In a conspicuous difference from their pre-1989 position, women acted to be recognized for who they are as women. Instead of a *sociolog* (sociologist), which used to indicate—as in English—both male and female, a grammatical female ending was added, and a woman sociologist, especially the independently minded and feminism-friendly one, now called herself *sociolo-zka* (psycholozka, or antropolozka), an initially awkward-sounding but now popular and progressive form of expressing both gender and occupational identity.

The growing and better-connected civil society organizations provided local feminism with the community and space where actors could be raised, issues identified, "subversive" strategies addressing the gender-exclusive, male democracy worked out, and actions launched. The media, not particularly friendly but initially curious about a few women authors, were then compelled to open a space of appearance for savvy local feminist discourse. Only in such an accepted setting where conventional language is invoked (in this case the language of rights) could performative utterances take place. The public revelation of the once-unnoticed exclusion of women from institutional democracy, done in a powerful combination of conventional and fresh words, was a key to felicitous acts of performative feminism. Such local feminism-in-the-making, far from reaching its goals, managed to transform the climate surrounding women's issues in post-1989 Poland.[48]

CENSORING FEMINISM IN CENTRAL EUROPE: PARADOXES OF THE WESTERN FEMINIST CRITIQUE OF LIBERALISM

There is now a considerable literature by American authors focusing on the systematic tensions between Western and Eastern women (N. Funk 1994); the jamming of communication while trying to translate western feminism into postcommunist realities (B. Holmgren 1995); the difficulties in discussing gender issues in the region (A. Snitow 1993); the prospects for feminism after Communism (J. Goldfarb 1997); or the straightforward rejection of feminism in Eastern Europe (P. Watson 1997). Similar literature has also been produced by women from the region who address questions frequently asked by Western women: "Why Am I Not a Feminist?" (M. Marody 1993), "Why Feminism Is Not Successful in the Czech Republic" (J. Siklova 1996), "How to Smuggle Feminism Across the Post–Iron Curtain" (J. Smejkalova 1996), "Gender and Citizenship: Contentions and Controversies in East/West Debates" (J. Siklova 1998), and "The Social Construction of Women in Hungary" (M. Nemenyi 2001).[49]

Paradoxically, the relative success of Polish feminism in its efforts to find a voice that allowed for such a compelling Polish debate is also one of the reasons why Polish feminism is the most open to the West. Yet there are some latent issues that are continuously causing tension and misunderstanding in East-West debates and that are rooted in the different evaluation of liberalism offered by feminists from the East. To list some of the contentious issues may open up possibilities for future discussion. And liberalism is important here not because—as the exact opposite of communism—it has to have some bearing in the region on new directions in thinking, but because liberalism is also, of course, a convenient vehicle for globalization, or "universal" civilization, with its emphasis on universal standards, free markets, individual freedom, individual rights, and the rule of law. This underscores one of the seeming paradoxes, mentioned earlier, that characterizes feminism in Poland: the attention given simultaneously to the specificity of the Polish idiom formed by the politics of locality, and to the language of universal human rights and consensus-based civil society. Here are some issues that further explain why Polish feminism reacts so differently to liberalism.

Issue one: liberalism never really made it to Poland, but nationalism did. The cultural idiom, which has framed gender relations in Poland, is not only the outcome of a particular historical and cultural experience but is heavily oriented toward collective rights and community needs, above all the needs of the national community. Trying to free themselves from such constraints, which are experienced in Poland as the constraints of nationalism and a recently vibrant populism, it is difficult for local feminists to enter into a Western feminist discourse that talks predominantly in terms of collective rights. It would also bring them dangerously close to those populist sentiments.

Two: although the biggest foe of globalization may be religious nationalism, one of the main foes of liberalism—and the biggest factor impeding the reception of liberalism in Poland—has been, and remains, the Catholic Church.[50] Whereas in the most difficult times the Church provided Poles with a space in which they could experience personal freedom and dignity, since the collapse of communism it has become the major antiliberal force redefining the role of women in terms of motherhood and family responsibilities. Thus in Poland the liberal principle of keeping the Church away from the public is considered both attractive and progressive; and so is the liberalism-rooted critique of the Church, which rejects all forms of dogmatism and any limitations on discussion and criticism. This is at a time when Marxism-derived theories are simply not an option in this part of the world, particularly as they are now often embraced—under various guises—by the populist right.

Three: the absence of a liberal tradition, along with the specific political circumstances prevailing in Poland for fifty years (1939–1989), has made the private-public divide postulated by the liberal tradition a useless tool as far as feminist theory in Poland (and most of its discourse) is concerned. Poland's politics of locality required a peculiar merger of the private and the public. The boundaries had already become blurred in the nineteenth century. Education, art, and self-help organizations—all activities that in a normal society constitute the public sphere but that in Poland were illegal throughout the nineteenth century and both World Wars—had already moved into the domestic, private sphere long before communism was installed there. It was the extended family with its close circle of friends that hosted and cultivated a public sphere within the private. The public became private, whereas the so-called publicness of the sphere sponsored by the state was staged, as Habermas might put it, "for manipulative purposes."[51]

From the 1970s on, for a growing number of Poles the private sphere developed into a civic realm inhabited by private agents acting on behalf of the public good. Were the seminars of the *flying university* that were regularly organized in private apartments and announced through the underground press public or private? Were the studies and research on Polish society, conducted by private groups of university professors called *Experience and the Future* and published by the underground publishing house NOWA, public or private? What about the private performances of the Eighth Day Theater, or poetry readings at home, in churches? Yes, it was all unofficial, very often illegal, but it did not easily fit the Western notion of a private sphere. The private spaces became public as they blurred the lines between exclusively personal or domestic matters and public matters and agendas.

What looks like a paradoxical privatization of the public (closely related to "depublicization" of the official), or a going underground by the public, does not make it a lesser public. The names of the editorial board of the biggest underground periodical, called *Censored,* were openly printed along with their home addresses and phone numbers. The general rule was that "things may not be normal here but we have to act as though they are normal." To expand in this way the realm of the private in order to accommodate the public was, in effect, to dissolve the boundaries between the two spheres, or at least to install multiple openings between already porous walls.[52]

Four: acknowledging this peculiarly Polish experience of a private but public sphere helps us to understand the emergence here of civil society, which is the domain of an expanded private sphere. As western social science theorists have suggested, Poland was the place where civil society was reinvented. The lack of a liberal tradition and liberal discourse in Poland did not become an obstacle to devising a set of practices in the 1970s that later came to be labeled by westerners "civil society." Obviously civil society in the late 1970s was an emancipation project, empowered by the notion of human rights as adopted in the Helsinki Accords signed by the Polish government in 1975. Yet this paradigm of civil society did not prescribe as best any one way of acting but recognized the value of locally cultivated civic imagination and homegrown initiatives. It was, and is, a specifically Polish experience of applied liberalism, closer to the democratic potential of Habermas's theory of deliberative action than to conventional rights-based liberal theory.[53] This also sets it apart from the populist environment dominated by a monological black-and-white vision of the world, an environment in which fear reigns supreme.

In a society where democracy is a reasonably well-functioning mechanism, civil society functions as a partner of the state. Women's organizations in Poland, although amazingly numerous, as they are still building their home base, are still not strong enough to be recognized as a full partner of the state, but—with or without the help of the European Union—they are getting there. The problems begin when gender—by becoming an issue-driven grant vehicle—often creates conditions in which a comprehensive, locally derived agenda for women's groups clashes with the programmatic guidelines of some Western donors. This asymmetrical relationship causing multilateral dependencies is very much a feature of globalization.

THE CHALLENGE OF TRANSLATION

While pointing out both the understandable liberal leanings of Polish feminism and its seemingly antiliberal imperative in exploring local idiom,

I tend to agree with Ann Philips when she observes that "the universal discourses of rights are often formed in context, and they often fail to engage adequately with difference."[54] At the same time I would like to emphasize that the work Polish women do on disarming the cultural idiom is strategic, as it directly addresses the sources of violations of rights and gender equality. Hence, it is important to caution against the natural temptation to translate regional or national differences into terms that are our own. To understand the nature of their distinctiveness, yes; to extend what Ann Snitow calls "hermeneutical generosity," yes.[55]

Feminism is a political and cultural project of global dimensions, but with its own local expressions and accomplishments that do not always lend themselves easily to exact translation. And perhaps feminism's biggest strength is its polyphony of voices and strategies. Even within the *local* there is a variety of feminisms. Just as there is the organization Women Under Muslim Law, a sizable network of women's groups in India, there are in Poland women intellectuals and theologians associated with the movement called the New Feminism, concerned with recognizing men and women as equals in both theology and everyday life.

Though the notion of local multiple feminisms does not necessarily deglobalize feminism as such, it does *decenter* it, or *provincialize* the center,[56] which is where Western/Northern feminism tends to locate both itself and most of its discourse. These local feminisms operate within the same set of concerns but address them through indigenously developed strategies. Such strategies may be, as in the Polish case, a mixed bag of blueprints developed under Communist rule by the democratic opposition in the 1970s and 1980s (if you cannot talk to your government, talk to foreign media or international institutions, e.g., the UN Human Rights Committee) and by local gender studies programs (if you cannot reach a wider public using the detached language of rights, gradually create a thicker feminist culture by launching a critical debate on the gendering outcomes of the core cultural tradition). Saskia Sassen talks about the importance of multiple microinterventions, which have, in fact, a global character even if they are not thoroughly cosmopolitan.[57] I think we should take her advice.

The Polish feminists discovered how badly they needed a language and some key concepts to make their efforts both understandable at home and connected to other feminisms. *Gender* is one of them; *civil society* and *women's rights* may be others. And perhaps such feminisms—provincialized, decentered, but linked to each other, and seeking indigenously based solutions to global problems—could serve as an attractive, inclusive, and less arrogant model for globalization itself.

EnGendering Democracy

Women Artists and Deliberative Art in a Transitional Society

> Works of art are thought things but it does not prevent them from being things.
>
> —*Hannah Arendt*[1]

One decade after the Poles successfully negotiated their transition to a democratic order, art by women, especially conceptual art, has become a major field—as well as an instrument—of contestation in the astonishing struggle to save and sustain a barely reestablished public sphere. And it is above all the women artists, through their dialogical and often unsettling artwork, and through the discursive web it has stimulated, who have contributed to an "enGendering"—in both senses of the word—of public discourse, this important principle of democratic politics.

* * *

Two decades earlier, in 1978, a young artist known as Natalia LL—now considered Poland's pioneer feminist artist—organized in Wroclaw the first significant exhibit of Polish women artists, entitled simply "Women's Art." Two years later another artist, Izabella Gustowska, presented in her Poznan gallery a second group show under the same unpretentious title. She organized three more women's exhibits there between 1987 and 1994: "Presence" I, II, III. Today one can talk about a solid tradition of group shows by women, with a roster of more than a dozen major exhibits throughout Poland, augmented by numerous presentations abroad—one of them, entitled "Architectures of Gender: Contemporary Women's Art in Poland," mounted in the spring of 2003 in New York.

However, despite the fact that some of the exhibits were presented by Poland's main national museums and galleries, this new wave of women's art has not been accompanied by serious critical analysis and, until recently, has been virtually ignored by the mainstream media. No doubt a part of the reason has been the well-known, sharply gender-contentious cultural context, which has cultivated an allergy to anything that could be suspected of having an association with feminism.[2] This context was freshly reinvigorated by the kind of patriarchal discourse that is often a characteristic of societies driven by rapid change: in the case of Poland, by radical systemic transformation after 1989. One of its early fruits was the passing of the very strict antiabortion bill, prepared by the last Communist parliament in 1989 and voted into law by a democratically elected one in 1993.

It took a decade of persistent work by women's NGOs, feminist scholars, and activists for the issues of gender to be presented in nonderogatory terms in the mainstream press; for senior scholars or public figures to dare to identify themselves as feminists on national TV; for feminist writers to be invited to publish their weekly columns in high-circulation newspapers and magazines; for feminist books to be considered for major awards; and for gender programs to be launched at major universities.

Almost parallel in time, in the late 1990s, a fairly dramatic entry of women artists and their art into the public life of the country took place. This could be only partially explained by the surge of information about the successes abroad of works by Polish women artists or by the gradual mainstreaming of a public debate on women's issues at home.

The entry of women's art into Polish public life coincided with the eruption of major corruption scandals involving public figures, an accompanying loss of societal trust in new democratic institutions, and a fear on the part of society that an uprooting and dissolving of national identity would result from joining the European Union. In this situation the public debate generated by artists and their artworks revealed the underlying tensions between democracy and culture and posed the challenge of establishing a new public space for addressing these tensions.

I would like to discuss the artists' strategies for generating this discourse, and to examine the ramifications of their participation and their substantive contribution to an encouragement of democratic culture in Poland. The main source for my discussion will be the exciting art presented at a 2003 group show in New York, a multigenerational,[3] multimedia, multithematic show by sixteen women artists representing postconceptual art, broadly defined. To complete the picture I will also "visit" selected art events and related debates in Poland. I will argue that the very language of installations that the artists use facilitates their entry into a direct debate with the public, the media, political and cultural organizations, and, finally, with the past. I intend to show that Polish women artists today have launched a major effort to rework a syndrome of Polish culture that has been dominant for two centuries, by moving away from a preoccupation with issues of national identity and sovereignty to an attention given to active, postnational citizenship, the key agency in a democratic polity.

THE LANGUAGE

The art that will be discussed here provides a conceptual space for physical representations in the form of installations and performances. The spatially organized works are usually less portable and decorative than colorful canvasses and are designed—as is any conceptual artwork—to discourage the public from judging it according to aesthetic criteria. The artists play with space, they take it over and insert into it images, light, sound, objects—whether familiar or created for the occasion—or even sometimes themselves, in order to pose questions, present ambiguities, and illuminate disturbing truths. Like the artists themselves, I am not concerned with the autonomous, traditionally "artistic" value of the works themselves. It is, rather, the issues raised and ideas and reflections generated by the works that are of importance here.

Conceptual art challenges the core traditions of artistic representation anywhere, but particularly in Poland, where the use of romantic-symbolic language endured to the end of the twentieth century, while the various efforts to see art as an autonomous realm of purely aesthetic values, a formal game with colors or shapes, have always found themselves on the defensive. The dominant historical narrative of the tortured, partitioned nation with its sacrificial national uprisings led to the model of a heroic, insurgency-style mentality, with the Motherland at its center, which dominated both Polish political experience and cultural imagery until 1989. A part of this narrative concerned the unusual role of the arts and artists (and especially the poets) who, in the absence of the institutions of a sovereign state, exercised their only available legitimate power over the nation: that of spiritual rulers who provided a badly needed sense of group identity and solidarity.

Conceptual and postconceptual art[4] not only questions this artistic canon for its devotion to national community but also reacts against the easy marketability of patriotism as commodified in this kind of art. Installations, even when displayed in traditional art institutions, such as museums or galleries, are distinguished by their transitory, impermanent, and theaterlike character, which makes them destined for the general public rather than private collectors. And it is not just the individual artworks, but increasingly the exhibitions as such, conceived and executed by creative curators, that constitute—and function as—elaborate cultural performatives. They do not just say something; rather, *by* saying something these "things of thought" launch an intervention into existing reality. This was the case with "Architectures of Gender: Contemporary Women's Art in Poland," which was authored by a Polish curator specially for the new site of New York's SculptureCenter, and which was to live there for just six weeks, thus marked from the very beginning by acute transitoriness. The exhibition catalogue and assorted documentation are usually the only residue of such exhibits. But when they are actually on display, more than with any other form of contemporary art, they constitute directly discursive spaces in which the discussion of public issues takes place. Thus the American visitors at the show entered into a conversation essential for their own society, another evidence of the arts' general reach, though I would argue that these works were both mobilized by developments taking place in the context of the new Polish democracy and aimed at a local public.

In Poland, where the post-1989 civil society—with some noticeable exceptions, among them the vibrant women's groups—has been channeled into a neat network of formalized, highly specialized nongovernmental organizations, the public sphere has become increasingly thin and nearly atrophied. In this context the art cultivated by a sizable number of women artists has generated precisely the kind of thicker, alternative discursive space in which sensitive contentious issues, silenced in the dominant public sphere, are posed and can be debated.[5]

CIVIL SOCIETY CHANGES GENDER

Beginning in 1999, particularly after the spectacular success of "Men's Bathhouse," presented by Katarzyna Kozyra at the 48th Venice Biennale, the media, no longer able to ignore art by women, came up with the catchphrase "Polish Art Changes Gender," followed by many other headlines, often sarcastic, that ended with a question mark.[6] The changing gender of Polish art has been framed as a ridiculous women's rebellion, a conspiracy by irresponsible, immature, publicity-seeking, senselessly provocative female artists. The emergence of a discussion on women's art was thus neither the glorious growth of a young democratic culture in which gender prejudices were finally discarded nor a final victory of emancipatory feminist discourse in Poland.

The works by women featured at the New York exhibit, as well as the many other installations presented by women artists throughout Poland, have nevertheless ignited the most contentious and significant debates concerning the limits of free speech, artistic expression, censorship, public sponsorship of art, and responsible citizenship. A frequently disconcerting realization emerged in the media that women in the art world—women artists, women curators, and women gallery directors—were launching a resolute intervention into an increasingly shrinking public sphere, entering into play with a coercive cultural system in order to pluralize discourse. And once this intervention became not only controversial but also exceedingly public, it could not be ignored anymore.

It is difficult to escape a sense of irony when one looks back at the inventiveness and glorious booming of civil society in the nondemocratic Poland of the 1970s and 1980s and now observes its current degradation. Though the pre-1989 "public sphere" generated by civil society was not exactly public, it was vigorous and thriving, and most certainly it was civil society that unfurled the democratic changes. Fifteen years after the momentous negotiated settlement with the Communist regime, a public sphere, now truly public and free, has found itself in circumstances similar to those of the now professionally streamlined civil society, which—allotted an appropriate slot within the framework of a formal democracy, as the so-called third sector—has lost much of its vigor and critical voice. The last big event staged by the pre-1989 civil society was the Round Table Talks with the regime, in which a process of gradual democratization was negotiated and put into motion. Once free elections took place and political parties emerged, the role of the reinvigorated citizen ended at the voting booth, as all decisionmaking was left in the hands of representative institutions.

Paradoxically, but perhaps understandably, the new democracy, busy as it was with setting up procedures, mechanisms, and institutions, disarmed and marginalized its own midwife: civil society. It soon became clear that institutions and procedures alone do not make a democracy. There is no democracy without people who stand for, and argue, its values, principles, and ethos. There is no democracy without people who are ready to internalize the principles of pluralism and equality under the law. There is no democracy without enlightened, critical, tolerant citizens.

The newly official public sphere, with its gradually diluted discursive dimension, became mostly a playground for the profit-motivated and often politically implicated media, and is now challenged less by the heavily politicized institutions of the state, especially a Parliament increasingly driven by populist forces demanding circumscriptions in various spheres of cultural and social life.

To explain this peculiar downsizing of the independent public sphere and its voice, one could seek answers in two closely related factors. The first was the very way in which the transformation processes were conceptualized. In this process the establishment of a procedural democracy with parties and elections was given—perhaps understandably—priority over a substantive democracy, in which civil society and a robust public sphere, concerned with issues of liberty, equality, pluralism, and tolerance, would be assigned a vital role.

A second answer can be found in the political landscape as it has emerged in Poland since 1989. The crowning moment of Polish civil society, the so-called first Solidarity (1980–1981) that put the first serious crack in the system, was itself an alliance of various forces united only by their broadly anti-Communist attitudes. Its three main original constituencies were the workers at large enterprises, bringing a populist hue to the language of material claims and entitlements; the secular intelligentsia, including many lay Catholics, speaking the language of human rights, cultural liberties, and strong democratic commitments; and many in the broader Catholic milieu who were unambiguous about their national colors, speaking the language of national values and claims. In the political scene of the late 1990s and early 2000s, that second current, representing a civil-society-based agenda of human rights, democratic practice, and civic responsibility, seems to have been gradually marginalized, especially in the Parliament. It was overpowered by the two pillars of the various ruling coalitions, namely, the so-called post-Communist left, "reformed" in its dissociation from any Communist principles and in its support of a free market and accession to the European Union; and the radical right, which had emerged, in turn, through a kind of symbiosis between the first and third constituencies of Solidarity—that is, the proletarian/populist and the Catholic/nationalist groupings.

The resulting civic vacuum is only partially filled by the existing NGOs, with their separate niches of expertise, often performing auxiliary functions for the various governmental agencies. Even though they greatly enhance the institutional landscape of democracy, the public debate that they generate is fragmented and limited to their specific concerns, often driven by external funding agencies. A visible exception to this vacuum is the still fairly young but vibrant Polish feminist movement, along with the more general phenomenon of women's art that gets exhibited throughout the country.

There is a striking structural-functional resemblance between the artistic activities proposed today by women and those activities developed two decades ago in the struggle of a dissident culture with the officialdom of the Communist regime. Both pre-1999 art and pre-1989 civil society were cofounded and advanced by women, but indeed the women rarely received full credit for their contributions.[7] However, I believe that today women artists have managed to expand the fragmented civil society and have forced others to notice that, indeed, civil society changes gender, too.

If the comparison with its original model, the civil society developed in predemocratic Poland, is correct, then the alternative discursive sphere opened by women artists in the late 1990s is also analogous to those civic and cultural initiatives of the 1970s (e.g., student theater), which did not belong to a sphere that from the point of view of the regime was "preferred and rewarded" but operated on the borderline of initiatives that were either "permitted, but limited," "unofficial," or "forbidden." Their art constitutes a new realm of dissent, emancipation, and dialogue.[8]

At the turn of the twenty-first century, conceptual art by women creates a space linked by a series of sites and related discussions in which art objects and art processes assume ideational status, and—as I've already mentioned—are not considered for their aesthetic but above all for their cognitive and—as I would like to argue—deliberative functions. Public circulation of their art has made possible a revival of the discursive aspect of civil society and a broadening of its public sphere. It is the women artists who, by entering into an open debate with central elements of the Polish cultural tradition, pose the main questions concerning the nature of democratic citizenship and the closely related matters of toleration and pluralism. It is their art that affirms the principle that plurality and dissent enrich both individual citizens and the democratic polities in which those citizens live.

Some argue that the conceptual art presented in SculptureCenter's exhibition, part of a larger phenomenon that has emerged in Poland over the last several years, looks like a Polish version of U.S. culture wars.[9] I would like to suggest, rather, that in the Polish context it resembles the culture of dissent of the late 1970s and 1980s, with its citizens' initiatives directed against an authoritarian state, and managing to create a culture that was independent from the system.[10]

However, there is a very important difference between the culture of dissent and the heavily gendered civil society expressing itself through the arts twenty years later. When one looks at the scene of civic activities in Poland in the late 1970s, one thing is apparent: for all their volume, scope, and vibrancy, activities within the realms of the permitted but limited, the unofficial, and the forbidden all sprang from—and yet remained relegated to—a peculiarly enlarged private sphere.[11] The initiatives of the post-1989 women artists have been taking place—though with increasing difficulty—in the public sphere proper, in which—under the conditions of a formally consolidated democracy—art has become a realm in which procedural democracy is being tested. Thus art here has become an important civic strategy for expanding the substantive dimension of democracy, for pluralizing the public sphere in order to engender citizens' deliberations and negotiate differences.

SPACES OF DISSENT

The March–May 2003 "Architectures of Gender" exhibit at New York's SculptureCenter not only was the first presentation by Polish women artists in the city but was also the first U.S. group show in twenty-seven years (since 1976) by artists from Poland.[12] What is perhaps not immediately obvious to an American audience is that the exhibit provided both a stimulating experience for the American audience—judging from the reviews—and a testimony to the process of wide-ranging transformation taking place in Poland that goes beyond the foundations of a new political system and economy. Despite the fact that the exhibition was carefully envisioned for that specific site, with no plans for it to be re-created in the home country, it is difficult not to ask whether, and how, it engages with the usual context of the Polish cultural space in which the artists work and live.

The exhibit took place in Long Island City, across the East River from Manhattan, in a neighborhood of old factories, workshops, and warehouses. This physically "unattractive" part of Queens, but with a good deal of available space, a lot of light, and easy subway connections with Manhattan, has recently become a lively and colorful hub of contemporary art. Around the corner from SculptureCenter sits the P.S.1 Museum, which has for thirty years presented the latest in artistic experimentation. It is here that the Museum of Modern Art established a temporary home while its Manhattan location was undergoing a major expansion. Here, too, is the Isamu Noguchi Garden Museum. And it was here that SculptureCenter moved

from Manhattan to its own new, hip, place—one of the oldest New York
art institutions, dedicated to the stimulation and continuous redefinition
of sculpture and spatial art, hosting "Architectures of Gender" as the first
major show at its new site.

Maya Lin, creator of the Vietnam Veterans' Memorial in Washington, D.C., redesigned an old trolley repair shop as an exhibition space for
SculptureCenter by leaving exposed the original red bricks characteristic
of the old industrial buildings in the neighborhood, by strengthening and
revealing the steel construction, by utilizing the raw, labyrinthlike basement-
level spaces, and by redesigning a walled, rectangular outer courtyard with
a glass and steel gate.

Curated by Aneta Szylak, one of the best-known Polish curators of
the younger generation, the exhibition was designed in a tense interaction
with the extraordinary 6,000-square-foot space of SculptureCenter. Some
of the artworks were conceived for the space, and some were selected by the
curator with this particular space in mind, thus making the testing of the
space itself an essential task of the show. The presentations are themselves
space-oriented installations, exploiting specific raw features of the space in
Queens. The result was the creation of an intensely dialogical environment
forcing the visitor to explore the interactions not only between the private
and the public but also within the realms of the emotional, the sensual,
the sexual, the intimate, the personal, and, finally, the gendered, as these
were variously expressed in the heterogeneous installations. The exhibition
as a whole testified to an art scene in Poland whose dynamism arises in
substantial measure from the powers of observation, the mastery in crafting
objects and shaping space, the audacious imagination, and the intellectual
inquisitiveness and boldness of diverse women artists.

Aimed at exploring complex spatial relationships, the show could
be seen as an expression both of more global or cosmopolitan concerns
and issues not necessarily specific to Poles, and of a more local, internal
discourse on matters concerning Polish culture, society, and politics. The
works presented in New York were created in some cases decades apart
and had never had the opportunity in Poland of being seen in interaction
with each other in a single setting. The main spaces or "architectures" of
this setting that framed the works at SculptureCenter were the adjacent
walled courtyard leading to the entrance, the large main floor exhibition
space, and the basement, as well as an outdoor municipal plaza nearby.
That you may appreciate the role that women's art in Poland is playing in
the battle over the vanishing public sphere, I would like to invite you to
visit this exhibit with me, on the day of its opening.

Touring the Exhibit

Our first encounter with the show already takes place a couple of hundred
yards short of the actual edifice of the SculptureCenter, on the way from the

subway. Here, on a patch of green called Court Square, surrounded by the old building of the Town Hall, a very modern courthouse, and a wide street with heavy traffic, an artist from Gdansk, Julita Wojcik, in a gardener's apron and with garden tools, can be seen tending a small plot. It is early April, and in the middle of this public lawn, she has planted new pansies and petunias, and even some vegetables, and put up a small decorative green picket fence. She has worked there for several days, and both before and after the official opening she welcomes opportunities for conversation on gardening not only with us, arriving visitors to the SculptureCenter, but also with neighborhood lawyers and shop clerks during their lunch hour—turning *My Garden* into both a performative installation and a social space. A local daily has announced: "Special Garden Grows in Long Island City: Polish Artist Plants Her Work at Courthouse." Wojcik's work continued to draw onlookers long after the exhibition closed in July.

The next outdoor work is a wall installation by Jadwiga Sawicka entitled *Numbers*. Along the gray wall enclosing the long, gravel-filled courtyard at the entrance to SculptureCenter runs a narrow, computer-designed, delicate-looking pink tape with numerically increasing horrific statistics from recent events: "5 militiamen dead in Grozny," "75 Iraqis dead, 17 wounded," "100,000 demonstrate in Paris," "1,000,000 soldiers await orders to attack," "5,000,000 refugees." The narrow strip of pink tape testifies to endlessly mounting death and havoc everywhere, and for those of us who are attending the opening—a few days after the U.S. invasion of Iraq—it has a heightened impact.

Facing the gray wall and obscuring the actual door to the gallery, there is a large white boxy structure that looks like an entrance. This third outdoor work, *The Entrance*, was built by Monika Sosnowska especially for the New York exhibit. Upon opening a regular-sized white door, we discover behind it another, identical but a bit smaller, followed by a sequence of fully operating, gradually smaller, doors, until we reach the last one, the size of a cigarette box. This elusive entrance into a succession of mounting exclusions is a perfect commentary on an allegedly open world full of opportunities.

The intermediate reception area leading to the gallery—bright, modern, and sterile in feel—has been taken over by Anna Plotnicka and her installation *Livestories* (2001–2003), documenting on hundreds of postcardlike printouts assorted fragments of ordinary conversations she has had with her American women friends ("My son has caught an infection again, apparently nothing serious, but I am still a bit worried; Lynn"; "I hate washing my hair. It's disgusting to be wet all over, hair and skin; Elizabeth.") All the cards, displayed on the reception's counter, walls, and shelves, make the place appear to be filled with the voices one might hear in any hotel reception area. I feel like joining in on the familiar chatter. Copies of the cards available for visitors are signed "Anna Plotnicka and Volunteers."

Immediately beyond the reception area there opens up a strikingly different, cavernously expansive exhibition space, with its original concrete floors and timeworn walls in which the designer had left fragments of once functional metal structures and pieces. The space within this vast, high-ceilinged, rectangular, and dimly lit hall accommodates—and is broken up by—four very large artworks.

On the evening of the exhibit's gala opening, upon entering this main space we find along its longer wall to the right a row of gleaming tables with candles, food, and cooking gear, and a busy woman in a cocktail dress behind them continuously serving fresh appetizers. Each piece of cheese or vegetable has a small paper flag providing bold nutritional information ("1 piece of cheese = 46 calories; 10 minutes of brisk walking to burn it off"). The area smells of freshly baked pastry, and everybody wonders what the unfamiliar-looking round steel electric pots are for. It soon becomes clear that this is not a regular opening-night reception; rather, the guests are taking part in a theatricalization of ordinary reality, a cooking performance by artist Elzbieta Jablonska, and that the steel contraptions are the kind of baking pots that have been a fixture in every Polish kitchen since the 1960s. Once the opening night is over, this live performance, entitled *From the Stomach to the Heart* (1999, 2001, 2003), will be replaced by a continuous-loop video projection of Jablonska cutting carrots, cooking, and washing dishes in her own kitchen in the northern Polish city of Bydgoszcz.

On the opposite side of the hall we face a pair of full-sized replicas of Michelangelo's Moses, in a long-term project that originated in the 1970s and is presented here in its most recent version as *The World as War and Adornment* (2003). The two massive marblelike sculptures, positioned side by side, are exact duplicates in fabric and glue of the original, except that on one of them Moses's toga is made of a perfectly sculpted, brightly feminine patchwork fabric, while on the other it is army camouflage. The artist, Zofia Kulik, internationally known for her broad spectrum of feminist works, has here reduced a giant and otherwise impressive and domineering male figure into that of an uncomfortable, not very festive masquerader, a spectacle of deactivated power.

Nearer the entrance, in the middle of the hall, we are initially mystified by Isabella Gustowska's technologically elaborate sculptural video installation *Passions and Other Cases* (2000). From a distance we can identify three identical podlike plexiglass-and-metal structures on iron legs, glimmering with green light and exuding a low murmuring sound. Designed to open slowly when the approaching viewer triggers a motion censor attached to it, each oyster-shell-like pod reveals on its inner surface a video projection, a glowing, greenish, life-sized close-up image of a couple in affectionate embrace: in the first, one man tenderly kissing another, in the second, a woman hugging a woman, and then a man kissing a woman. On the back wall behind the pods, in their reflected green light, float enlarged and somewhat blurred continuous images of the couples facing each other and glancing at the viewers. With each couple given equal space and projecting an equally warm intimacy, the three models of love leave us sensing an uncanny commonality in diversity.

In the back of the main floor space, the curator has positioned the *Men's Bathhouse*, an already notorious video installation by Katarzyna Kozyra, awarded an Honorable Mention at the 1999 Venice Biennale when it was originally presented at the Polish Pavilion. Upon entering the octagonal structure we are surrounded by a nonstop four-screen projection of film material shot surreptitiously on male territory—inside the men's mineral baths at the Budapest Gellert hotel: unselfconscious, nude, often flirtatious men entering the pool, chatting, toweling off, lounging on the tiled benches—and among them a slight, bearded, and somewhat more anxious-looking male with a plastic shopping bag. The same images are visible on the external walls of the octagon. Outside of the structure, on a separate smaller monitor, we can watch the videotaped process of disguising the female body of the female artist, Kozyra, into that of a man we can recognize later as the anxious bather: individual hair painstakingly glued to her chest and face, eyebrows made bushier, and finally the attaching of prosthetic genitalia. With a camera hidden in a plastic bag and rolling, the artist along with two male friends entered the exclusively male space. I wonder to myself whether this speech act (of a sort) would have been considered by Austin an infelicitous, "unhappy performative," since Kozyra—in order to say "I am a man"—went through a process that only made her look like a man; she did not really mean it. The resulting video footage has become the basis for an installation that initially leaves me puzzled and concerned about the liberties the artist took in testing the limits of the cultural construction of gender.

Just beyond the opposite end wall of the main floor, a separate white room has been arranged by Paulina Olowska as an homage both to modernism in general and to one of the few women who was ever admitted to the male-dominated world of avant-garde architecture—Charlotte Perriand, a close associate of Le Corbusier. The center of this rationally designed, boxlike, gray-floored living room is a plain gray sofa, reminiscent of sleekly functional Bauhaus furniture, placed on a burgundy-colored plain carpet. On the wall the artist has hung a female outfit, constructivist-inspired, made out of blocks of beige and burgundy fabric, with two white strips running on one side from the top to the bottom of the dress. Viewers, when sitting on the sofa as we do, face four poster-sized photographs of architecturally positioned women wearing that very outfit, whose rectangular spots of blue are repeated on the faces and hands of the photographed women. I feel that experiencing *Fabricating Abstraction* (2003) is an ultimate immersion in modernism!

From the main hall a narrow staircase leads down to the basement, where arrows guide us to seven separate cavelike spaces. The first of these is filled at its far end with hundreds of tiny, meticulously constructed furniture models, built in 1988–1989 by Katarzyna Jozefowicz, and entitled *Habitat*. The clean, straight lines of the vertically rising wooden structures contrast with the rounded, concrete vault of the basement. A floor-to-ceiling universe of miniature dressers, drawers, shelves, cabinets, cupboards, closets, and other little containers is arranged to resemble an urban landscape with visibly compartmentalized, limited, but also limiting space.

These are also in stark contrast with the lush, flowing opulence of the second arched chamber, which offers in a dim, reddish light what looks like the aftermath of a big New Year's Eve party, with colorful streamers hanging in cascades from the ceiling and covering the floor. The impression is reinforced by the presence of an industrial-strength vacuum cleaner parked in the midst of this forest of streamers. Only after closer examination, while entering along a narrow path through the postparty clutter, do we notice that denser clusters of streamers on the floor are shaped like fallen bodies, as if exhausted, emptied of personality, discarded. Venturing through Agnieszka Kalinowska's initially cheerful-looking *Just a Little Bit More*, one finds that one has literally stumbled into an ironic contradiction.

Proceeding then from the nearer end of the basement to the rear through a long narrow corridor lined with the building's exposed heating ducts and water pipes, we maneuver past a somewhat daunting installation called *The Field*, by Dominika Szkutnik, who explores in her art optical and sensory perception. In this work, created after her arrival in New York, she worked with and built upon the character and function of this narrow underground passageway in SculptureCenter's basement. Midway down the dimly lit corridor she has wound many layers of thick copper wire around an existing pipe to create a large, egg-shaped, gently but ominously humming cocoon or beehive. A sign reads, "Attention: Strong Electromagnetic Field. Please enter one person at a time." Some slip quickly past, clearly ill at ease or nervously shielding cell phones, while others try to savor the subtly tingling impact that accompanies the hum.

The corridor leads to two more arched chambers at the far end of the basement. The first is filled with five identical, beige, normal-sized but inflated hammocks, suspended at regular intervals between the longer walls of the chamber. The artist, Hanna Nowicka-Grochal, is known for her works that resemble pieces of furniture made from a fleshlike material that she developed through much trial and error. Under the title, *Pleasure out of Reach*, the hammocks in this installation are begging to be reached and touched, and under the slightest touch they respond by swinging with an anxious movement suggestive of bodily desire. And then we notice the rear wall, behind the farthest hammock, filled with a vague photomural in a skin color that echoes the color of the hammocks. After more patient examination, the photo reveals the image of a male body wrapped in a rubbery fabric. The atmosphere of the space projects a yearning sensuality.

In the adjacent chamber, Natalia LL has used the narrow arched space to unfurl from the rear a cascade of black-and-white multiple photographic printouts, rhythmically repeated as if on wallpaper, of an erotically evocative image of an anthurium, a flower that has both phallic and vaginal aspects, reminiscent of Georgia O'Keeffe's paintings. The photographic installation is called *Allusive Space,* created by an artist known since the 1970s for her unapologetically feminist art.

Just outside a separate corner room leading back from the rear of the basement, one already hears loud booming sounds and human grunting from Dorota Nieznalska's installation entitled *Omnipotence: Gender Male.* We pass through a curtain of thick black rubber strips into a dark room dimly lit by red fluorescent lights, with mirrored walls, heavy rubber mats, and the now almost deafening sounds of male voices grunting in an ambiguous mixture of passion and agony and the boom of heavy weights being dropped to the floor. There's no mistaking that we are in a fitness center, a temple built for the perfection of the male body. And if we stay there for a while, we notice that the fitness machine supports overhead are capped with horizontal phallic protrusions.

On exiting from this dark red space we experience a striking change: a bright, white, extremely clean and quiet room, actually a long passageway back to the front of the basement. Since only one person is allowed to pass through at a time, I go first, and I enter a narrow aisle flanked on each side by a graceful row of fragile, clear glass poles connected by delicate ropes also made of glass—eight poles on each side. The rows of hand-blown glass poles, looking not much thicker than wineglass stems, look very delicate and unmistakably, almost naturalistically, phallic. The surprise comes—again, for observant visitors like us—when we take a closer look at the upper ends of the glass poles and notice that the ones on the left are subtly crowned with literal representations of individual penises, while on the right we find variations on the vulva. The male and female elements in this glass installation by Karolina Wysocka, called *Cautiously,* are presented as equals, in fact seem from a slight distance almost identical, and, being disengaged in their separate parallel rows, are connected only by the eyes of the slowly walking and curious visitor.

CHALLENGING CULTURALISM

There is a tacit agreement among Poles that the nineteenth century, which was marked by the loftiest *liberum conspiro* efforts on behalf of the struggle for national liberation, did not really end until the end of the twentieth, in 1989. But while it lasted, argues one of the most insightful thinkers on the subject, Maria Janion, a unified romantic-symbolic style of culture reigned supreme, serving a compensatory-therapeutic function for the nation.[13] This all-embracing romantic paradigm designated a very clear role for art and the artist throughout most of the past two centuries: Polish art was expected, and conditioned, to perform service on behalf of the captive nation torn between imperial powers. From the early nineteenth century, this hegemonic and highly functional cultural paradigm rallied around the task of regaining political nationhood, and for its sake appeared mostly unyielding, as all parties agreed on the historical, cultural, theological, and messianic legitimacy of the task.

What Maria Janion calls the romantic paradigm I would like to call—following Arjun Appadurai—*culturalism,* or *salvational cultural-ism,* as I am interested above all in the lingering power of this paradigm, the sole role of which is to mobilize cultural differences in the salvational service of Polish national politics.[14] Although Appadurai is examining the twentieth-century world of mass mediation, migration, and globalization,[15] his concept also captures very well the founding period of the movement that was developed by exiled and displaced Polish artists and thinkers from Chopin to Mickiewicz, who lobbied in Europe—mostly in France—for recognition, sympathy, and support for Poland's aspirations for political self-determination. Responding to the contexts of changing dominations that nourished it over many decades, the culturalist paradigm was continuously redigested and reappropriated for yet another new circumstance of subordination.

The most recent climax of culturalism was the Solidarity movement of 1980–1981 and its underground activities under martial law, which were supported by various diasporic communities in the West. This was a peculiar mixture of national and civic-oriented currents resembling earlier romantic-national efforts. The goals of a future democratic, self-governing, autonomous nation-state that respects the dignity of its citizens found a popular rationale in the narratives of historical suffering and injustice, and were dignified by works of the imagination provided by artists and—for the most part—embraced by the Catholic Church.

While mapping unexplored areas of concern that had long been silenced or neglected as having a lesser urgency for the national community, the artworks by women artists staged a major rejection of what Appadurai has called culturalism, or at least its Polish manifestation. Like any culturalism, its Polish version supplied, supported, and emphasized a spectrum of cultural differences that served a useful function in Poland for both the nineteenth-century movement toward national autonomy and the late twentieth-century movement of resistance against an authoritarian state imposed by "the others."

The key elements of the culturalist syndrome are the general preoccupation with history, above all the recounting of a heroic past, a prime builder of national consciousness; the cultural idea of a tortured nation, usually closely identified with the Catholic religion; and in the absence of a satisfying reality, a life within symbols and allegories, a community of the spirit, nurtured by family memories of the resistance experience and shared by each generation. Any effort to challenge Polish culturalism—shaped as it was by various culminations of the romantic national mission and heavily dotted with the graveyards of every Polish family—has been and still is considered a very controversial, if not sacrilegious, undertaking. A classic case of such a challenge aimed at breaking the shell of Polish patriotism to liberate it from its *form* is the work of the exiled writer Witold Gombrowicz. The "Architectures of Gender" exhibition in New York was the most recent major manifestation of such a challenge to Polish culturalism.

Space Versus Time

One of the first striking features of the exhibit is an almost complete disregard for the temporal sphere of human experience, seen in terms of a trajectory of events relating the present to the past. Ignoring the *temporal*, above all the past and the providential view of history, the artists explore the *spatial*, the horizontal rules of combination, the synchronies rather than diachronies. It manifests itself when Jadwiga Sawicka, in her *Numbers*, juxtaposes information and data from historically and geographically distant events/disasters, framing them by a horizontal expanse of pink ribbon. Space, more specifically the common space of an urban square with its diverse users, is an organizing principle of Julita Wojcik's *My Garden*. The vibrations of an electromagnetically charged space are experienced in a nonvisual way and are the product of the copper-wire structure built by Dominika Szkutnik in *The Field*.

Exploring space means escaping the authority of the past in general and the corset of responsibilities vis-à-vis the community of the dead in particular. In the New York exhibit the past appears only indirectly as the subject of a play in Olowska's modernist interior and in Kulik's replicas of Michelangelo's classic sculpture. Instead of the temporal—closely associated with the idea of national community—the artworks focus on the spatial, a key dimension for individual or personal relationships, in sites offering choices, such as Gustowska's three models of intimacy, Jozefowicz's modularized living space, or Kozyra's and Nieznalska's testing of masculine territory at a men's bath and gym, respectively.

The shift from time to space as the new organizing principle of societal life indicates a shift from the dominant discourse of national belonging to an identity that becomes gradually denationalized. Whereas the first is marked by a historical narrative, the second is liberated from it. Wysocka's glass installation, *Cautiously*, completely free of any pressure from time, history, tradition, or custom, leaves it to the viewer to "cautiously" negotiate the spaces of sexuality and gender constructed by her glass fences, starting anew with a fragile set of potentialities. Though space liberates us from time, a manmade space could be equally constraining. The subtle warning in *Cautiously* is more directly expressed in Sosnowska's *Entrance*, where gradually diminishing doors open up to increasingly restricted space; and in the *Habitat*, with its proliferation of containers assigning, dividing, and confining our life's breathing space.

Efforts to challenge salvational culturalism, undertaken by some twentieth-century Polish writers and artists[16]—especially efforts to contest the legitimizing power of time, as in the heroic historical narrative—have been consistently defeated, as they competed with a key priority: the unfinished project of national sovereignty.

Resisting the National

Resisting the dominant historical narrative meant resisting a past that had absolutized the nation and constructed culturalism as the protective garrison for an exclusive national identity. Early nineteenth-century romantic nationalism with its internationalism and progressive social ideas was replaced later in the century, everywhere in Europe, by a vision that highlighted the exclusive ethnic community as the only source of the good life. And this new concept of the nation required new imagery. In Poland it was increasingly framed by writers and artists in terms of a family that was kidnapped, abused, and torn into three parts by the neighboring empires, and whose survival—once political and military efforts were repressed—required a continuous cultural mobilization on the part of both those who lived in the partitioned lands and those in the diaspora and exile.

The familial imagery, which became a key source of patriotic agitation and which at the time was almost entirely generated by men, was dominated by female figures. Maria Janion's work[17] provides ample evidence of the mobilizing power of women's imagery at a time when preserving the nation had become a collective task. Women were used not only as an allegory of the nation (Polonia, like Germania and Italia in *risorgimento* nationalism, is a woman) but are portrayed in Polish literature and the arts as extraordinarily committed fighters, soldiers, conspirators, and leaders in national salvation. Closely connected to the topos of Mother Pole, well explored in Polish feminist literature, is that of Matka Polska (Mother Poland). It is through a woman, both Mother Pole and Mother Poland, that the nation develops its badly needed *differentia specifica*: Polonia, an obvious product of the male gaze, is always a heroic and suffering woman: chained, throwing herself into an abyss, following her exiled husband to Siberia, or poignant, with a single tear running down her face, as on the popular poster *Votre Solidarite,* printed by the French Trade Unions after the imposition of martial law in Poland in 1981. Thus Polish patriotic culture, heavily relying on a female representation of the national tragedy, appeared to be a strongly *matriotic* one.

As depicted by male artists in the latter part of the nineteenth century, women "naturally" lent themselves to a passionate, stormy relationship with the nation, especially when identity and belonging began to be defined on an ethnic, organic basis. The images of suffering but stunning-looking women, representing the nation and reproduced in thousands of copies, were disseminated through the period's most popular medium of personal communication: postcards. The matriotic culture provided an overwhelming foundation for national identification as it began to transcend the confines of the educated classes by utilizing the genres of popular culture: melodic songs, simple verses, and adoration of iconic representations of the Virgin Mary crowned as the queen of martyred Poland. Matriotism thus assigned women a significant role in societal culture from which they were able to derive a sense of exceptional respect and undeniable symbolic power, even though the power extended to the symbolic realm was only rarely translated into a relationship of partnership or equality.[18] Instead, the cult of women and their position on a national pedestal made it easy to discount all the other roles they played or could play in public life. And their empowerment was a work of the imagination, which led to real disempowerment once the goal of national self-determination was reached in 1989.[19]

Polish culturalism—with its dramatized fusion of nation and family, public and private, with dubiously empowered women, and upholding a sharp distinction between *us*—Poles—and *them*—non-Poles—is still a vibrant source of political mobilization, as in the case of the surprising parliamentary victory in 2001 of a populist-nationalist party, named, aptly enough, the League of Polish Families. The appeal of culturalism, especially in rural and provincial Poland, provides a considerable challenge for democratic transformation and also for the young feminist movement, as it does not conform to the crisper patterns of exclusion analyzed by Western scholars. There has emerged a consensus among leading feminist intellectuals in the country that the power of the imagery and the associated burden of responsibility vis-à-vis women has been overwhelming, making the task of liberating them from it both an urgent and an uneasy one.[20] The artists, independent of feminist authors and activists, took on the challenge of disarming Polish salvational culturalism along with its gendering idiom.

The women's artworks exhibited in New York and in Poland resist the pressure of the *national* and the expectations it imposes on members of the national community, both men and women. But above all they emancipate women from their symbolic subjection to the nation by denationalizing them. The required heroism and suffering on behalf of the group is replaced here by a relentless investigation of ordinary, unremarkable, unexceptional activities such as gardening, cooking, cuddling, or—as documented in Plotnicka's *Livestories*—chatting about sore muscles after aerobics class. Plotnicka's postcards, pasted in the reception space, authentic personal statements by individual women, stand in sharp contrast to the postcards displaying visual allegories of suffering Polonia. Artists reject art as a realm reserved for the heroic and symbolic, and the message it offers is consistently antiheroine, thus liberating women from a tradition that puts both artist and subject on a pedestal. The sounds of actual suffering, moaning, and groaning originate in a men's gym, penetrating almost the entire basement space of the exhibit. The imposing figures of Moses dressed in army camouflage and in dazzling patchwork are suddenly domesticated, losing their stern fatherly image. The numbers of fatalities of war, accidents, and natural disaster running along the pink tape turn suffering, death, and dying, all closely associated with the realm of the national,[21] into unexceptional events taking place all over the world, thereby disembedding them from the unique model of native salvational culturalism.

Denationalization also means dematriotization, often shifting from the feminine to an exploration of masculine images. It could be observed either as an inclusionary effort to dissolve the difference or as an effort to turn the tables in order to experience the other (Kozyra's *Men's Bathhouse*, Nieznalska's *Omnipotence: Gender Male*, or Gustowska's *Passion and Other Cases*). Hence there is a visible downplaying of women as the subject of the exhibit. If they are present at all, they are there to confront the romantic-symbolic culturalist strategy. Conceptual art is not hospitable to allegories; instead it presents women as real persons, representing themselves, and making others aware that the activity of gardening, preparing food, or documenting what appear to be insignificant conversations are practices oriented toward others, directly affecting our lives and therefore socially significant. Olowska's modernist living room, in contrast, a three-dimensional essay on Charlotte Perriand, is a concrete example of intellectual activity by a conceptual artist.

Despiritualization on Trial

The pervasiveness of spiritual suffering, mixed with messianic fervor and popular religiosity—all products of the romantic outlook and further strengthened by Communist repression of the Catholic Church—constitutes one of the key aspects of Polish culturalism. In a bold move to expose this culturalism's spent force, made irrelevant after the achievement of ultimate liberation in 1989, conceptual art initiated a shift from the symbolic/spiritual to the physical/sensual, and from the intuitive/passionate/emotional to the rational/discursive. This move away from a romantic fixation on the soul brought about various transgressions. Artists proposed new explorations of the body as the site of erotic love (Gustowska's *Passions and Other Cases*, Natalia LL's *Allusive Space*), the site of gender destabilization and construction when Kozyra's female body is being turned into a male one in preparation for entering the men's bath (*Men's Bathhouse*), the site of painful perfection in a gym (Nieznalska's *Omnipotence: Gender Male),* the paradox of living objects (bodylike hammocks) separating us from the lifeless "real" bodily image on the photograph (Nowicka-Grochal's *Out of Reach*), or the decomposed and disposable bodies in the after-party space (Kalinowska's *Just a Little Bit More*).

These installations all testify to the cultural construction of the body (including its nineteenth-century romantic-symbolic version), as well as to its inescapable physiology. The body constitutes a distinctly material site in *Olympia*, a series of striking works by Katarzyna Kozyra shown in

Poland in 1996. In the installations, referring to Manet's famous work that challenged in its day the canon of earlier nude paintings, Kozyra, naked, reclining on a chaise longue just like Manet's enticing courtesan with a flower pinned to her hair, displays her bald head and fatigued, pale body after chemotherapy. Kozyra chose Manet's *Olympia*—which in the second part of the nineteenth century had questioned the romantic tradition in portraying women—to challenge, almost 150 years later, the still very commanding tradition of Polish romanticism. The tradition of romantic iconography, in which the perfectly processed icon of a woman symbolized a suffering nation, is questioned here by the very physicality of the meticulously displayed truth of the usually excluded concrete, limited, individual body that dares to reveal a difference. One of the most consummate and radical body artists in Poland is Alicja Zebrowska, who, using photography and video technology, explores the generally obscured bodily processes of female sexual parts, as in her *Birth of the Barbie*, studying their functions, their physiological responses—all risky projects in the morally contentious climate and precarious legal context of post-1989 Poland.[22]

The challenging of the cultural paradigm by disclosing male sexuality and by despiritualizing the reasons for suffering in the installation *Passion,* exhibited in Gdansk,[23] brought an unprecedented lawsuit against its author, Dorota Nieznalska. The artwork, or rather two of the disassembled elements necessary for setting it up as an installation, were confiscated as crime evidence in early 2002. Following her return from the opening of the New York exhibit, Nieznalska faced a trial in Gdansk in July 2003. A group of individuals representing the nationalist League of Polish Families—including two parliamentarians who had never seen the exhibit except for some brief footage on television shot shortly before the show closed—filed a suit, and the artist was indicted on the basis of Article 196 of the Polish Penal Code concerning crimes against the freedom of conscience and religious belief.[24] The court pronounced Nieznalska guilty of offending the religious feelings of various persons and argued that in her *Passion* she publicly insulted an object of religious worship by juxtaposing the cross, the religious symbol of suffering, with male genitalia. The artist was sentenced to a limitation of her freedom, namely, "socially useful" work at twenty hours per month—monitored weekly—for a period of six months and was ordered to cover the entire cost of the trial herself.[25]

"An Open Letter Concerning the Conviction of a Polish Artist," disseminated widely via e-mail, quotes a description of the *Passion* work provided by Aneta Szylak:

> The installation consists of two following elements: an object in the form of a Greek cross made of metal, suspended from a ceiling, and, with a color photo of men's tights, hips, and genitals applied to its surface. The cross is displayed in front of a silent, single-channel video projection of a man lifting weights. Filmed from above, mostly his head and shoulders

are visible to the audience, and one can see the grimace of torment on his face.[26]

To anybody who saw the exhibit in New York, *Passion* has obvious affinities to Nieznalska's *Omnipotence. Gender: Male.* "In order to emphasize the ritual of the strenuous workout, to acquire proper bodily form combining masculinity with strength," writes Pawel Leszkowicz, "the artist inserts into the space a cross with a photographic close-up of male genitalia. Suffering, masculinity, nakedness, and the cross constitute a continuity of symbolic associations. Brought up in a Catholic culture, full of representations of the crucified Christ and naked martyrs, Nieznalska simply follows that trail."[27] He sees *Passion* as a portrait of masculine masochism, in which the path to strength leads through suffering. Nieznalska, called to the witness stand, was forced to spell out her intentions and the meaning of her work: "A fascination with masculine strength, of which I am also afraid, is a theme of many of my works. *Passion* belongs to those works in which I analyze the cultural stereotype of masculinity. It has, of course, a double meaning: doing something with passion, and suffering like Christ on the cross. I was thinking of the absurdity of elevating one's body, one's masculinity, to the status of the sacred."[28]

The court case provoked a flood of reactions. Articles in the liberal media called the sentence an assassination of free speech, the legalization of censorship, evidence of barbarity, an act more characteristic of theocratic regimes. "Do we want to live in a country where the most talented and most sensitive are penalized, and where artistic visions are divided between those which are permitted and those which are not permitted?" asked a writer in the major daily *Gazeta Wyborcza* in an article entitled "Sacrum and Genitalium."[29] The issue of the freedom of expression in Poland was raised in a press conference on the occasion of the trial by the spokesman of the European Union. A protest against "the restitution of censorship" was signed by a group of senior professors from various Polish universities. Leading artists, curators, and art critics stressed in one of several open letters the right to difference expressed by Nieznalska and referred to the stated position of the Human Rights Tribunal in Strasburg. An enlightened member of the clergy criticized the League of Polish Families, saying it uses the name of the church to defend religion but does it wrongly, as the matter should not ever have ended up in court.[30] A female philosopher published a sharp critique of populist culture and constructed a bold parallel with fascist Germany, referring to the exhibition of degenerate art.[31] A right-wing newspaper boasted about the public applauding after the sentence was read in court,[32] and the judge, asked by the media why the sentence was so severe, responded that, after all, the artist got plenty of publicity from the case.

Religious references in conceptual art, often applied to unsettle and to destabilize the native culturalism, have been routine targets of political and religious circles that are usually able to exert pressure on sponsors, gallery owners, or state cultural institutions. Made during the war in Kosovo, Kozyra's billboard installation *Blood Ties* (1999) came under attack for its "undignified" use of religious symbols. As a result the trademarks of two humanitarian organizations, the Red Cross (Christian) and the Red Crescent (Islam), next to the pained figures of naked women were obscured, and then—under pressure from political and religious circles—the company supporting public art that had sponsored the installation decided to dismantle the billboards.

The populist Radio Maryja called upon its listeners to boycott the Museum of Posters in Wilanow because the International Jury in the 2002 Poster Biennale had awarded two works having visual religious associations that the Radio deemed offensive (a poster-painting by Dominika Rozanska of a figure that appeared to be the Virgin Mary standing at a distance, who turns out to be a Coca-Cola bottle, holding a baby Coke; and Alain Le Quernec's homage to Toulouse-Lautrec, in a stance suggestive of crucifixion, a poster painting that was pulled from the exhibit despite its award). The presentation in Warsaw of Maurizio Cattelan's sculpture, *The Ninth Hour*, of the Pope crushed under a meteorite provoked another outcry in late 2000. Two Members of Parliament from the League of Polish Families damaged the sculpture when it was on display in Zacheta, the National Gallery in Warsaw. Pressure from the nationalist right on the Ministry of Culture forced Anda Rottenberg, an imaginative and very accomplished female director of Zacheta, to resign. Aneta Szylak, who in 1988 founded the vibrant Center for Contemporary Art "Laznia" (The Bathhouse) in Gdansk and was its director until spring 2001, had to leave the center because of political attacks that made her work at Laznia impossible. And the many letters defending her position from both Poland and abroad were of no help. Finally, after the eruption of the Nieznalska matter, the Academy of Arts in Gdansk refused to house the Wyspa gallery on its grounds.

In the summer of 2003, the grip of culturalist forces still appeared to be very firm, particularly when the efforts at despiritualization clearly indicated the presence of a defiant secular undercurrent originating from liberal segments in the society. Nieznalska's trial mobilized collective actions that supported the right to difference and assisted in the formation of a counterculturalist public concerned with the threatened state of democracy in Poland. The trial located the main source of the obstacles to a reasoned public discussion in a hegemonic culturalism that refused to accept the changed political circumstances requiring both dialogue and the accommodation of diversity.

DIVERSITY, INDIVIDUALITY, DELIBERATIONS

In an ethnically and religiously homogeneous country where diversity is an invisible—and for most people a disturbing—variable, and where xenophobic attitudes are nurtured by hate speech disseminated by right-wing media, it was conceptual art that uncovered and dramatized the condition of diversity and difference. The women's conceptual artworks exhibited throughout Poland furnished a space for an initial reasoned meeting with "the other." The juxtaposition of the gay, lesbian, and heterosexual couples in Gustowska's *Passion and Other Cases* provides such a space, as do other works exploring various dimensions of gender construction (Kozyra, Jablonska, Nieznalska, Plotnicka), sexuality (Natalia LL, Nowicka-Grochal, Wysocka), ethnicity and religion (Kozyra's *Blood Ties*), or unsightly illness as in Kozyra's *Olympia*.

The artists' projects constitute patient intellectual arguments, intentionally devoid of sentimentality and distanced from the emotional appeals found in salvational culturalism. They break the illusion of reality by studying and documenting the creative process itself: recording the disguising makeup session and pointing to the video camera in a plastic bag before entering the bathhouse, by engaging in conversation with onlookers at the gardening project, by preparing and labeling food in front of the guests, or by posting a printed text on the methodology of collecting the data for *Livestories*.

The preplanned rational procedures, the mastering of media and other technologies (Gustowska's pods reacting to movement, Nowicka-Grochal's invention of a skinlike rubber, Szkutnik's studies of the properties of copper wire, and Wysocka's tests and experiments in a glass factory), interpose an additional intellectual distance between the artwork and life itself. The result, just as Brecht intended with his *Verfremdungseffekt*, makes it possible to see such conceptual art as an extension of the discursive order, in which replacing faith with reason fosters critical thinking.

But unlike Brecht, who wanted his theater to educate and to speak on behalf of the proletariat, and unlike the Polish romantic artists who spoke on behalf of the nation, these Polish women artists do not speak on behalf of any particular collective, group, or community. And yet, whether understood as nation, class, church, or *volk*, the collective has dominated the culture and politics of modern Poland, from its romantic-national, through the proletarian-Communist, to its current exposure to populist-nationalist ideology.

In all their renditions, the rights of individuals—and above all, those of women—have been subordinated to an obligation to serve a variously defined collective. In all their renditions, different forms of dogmatism that limit the freedom of expression, discussion, and criticism have been invoked by the community, by the church, or by the state. Although the conceptual art of Polish women artists refutes the celebration of a group and argues for an autonomous individual, it nevertheless does not conform to the traditional position of western feminism, which is sharply critical of liberalism with its stress on a public-private divide, the key source of women's exclusion. Yet in the local context of salvational culturalism, the rise of cultural liberalism offers Polish women an indisputably liberating opportunity, as it weakens the national, the ethnic, the authoritarian, and finally the populist.

By putting the spotlight on the individual, the artists bring up the issue of difference: political preference, lifestyle, religion, sexual orientation, or ethnicity, thus opening up the possibility of wrestling with particularity and negotiating it. The spatial dimension of the installations and their conceptual objective—to revisit cultural certitudes—aims at unmasking reality and revealing the ambiguities of things cultural that usually carry more than a single sense. The galleries and exhibition halls then become public squares where the differences and commonalities can be recognized, thus leading to the formation of a diversified public. The art projects encourage the formation of an engaged, critical individual, a more fully realized citizen in a democracy.

In the situation of a transitional society, relying in its initial period on the rudiments of procedural democracy, these artworks stimulate the emergence of deliberations, customs, and mechanisms that promote public discussion on the substantive dimension of democracy.[33] In the course of such deliberations, citizen-viewers are presented with an opportunity to consider unsettling but socially pertinent issues from alternative, often multiple, points of view, and thus have an opportunity to expand their views and understandings.

The creative energies of civic-minded women artists brought about *deliberative art,* a mechanism opening up a possibility for the recognition and legitimization of difference and the institutionalization of tolerance. At a time of societal disillusionment with democratic institutions and procedures, and with a growing sense of helplessness in contesting the increasing marginalization of critical voices, deliberative art conceived by women has become a crucial vehicle of dialogue, which has recharged and expanded the public sphere. Institutions alone do not suffice, as they have to be populated and watched by a democratically disposed citizenry. Determined to bring long-silenced issues before the public, deliberative artists patiently instigate new *habits of the heart,* a long-term process but a necessary one in order for any democracy to take root. Striving to reconcile national identity and diversity, deliberative art brings to light the questions of equality and exclusion, which in post-Communist societies were relegated to the back burner, and which are of major importance for women. And last but not least, this significant emergence of women artists as shapers of the agenda for public discussion goes beyond performativity. It not only changes the gender of civil society, but indeed helps to enGender democracy itself.

8

Postscriptum on an Old Bridge

It is in times of crisis like ours, marked by the spread of violence and by mounting conflicts between cultural groups—whether living within the same state, next to each other, or oceans apart—that people sometimes try to conjure up or find hopeful images that can help them to envision possible solutions. The sources of such imagery are often in the arts, literature, and oral history. Poetry is known for having such a capacity, as it captures an otherwise inexpressible combination of historical and visual experience, of time and space, of insight and emotion. My own guide in difficult times has been the wise poetry of Czeslaw Milosz, a writer who lived under various systems, who spoke various languages, and who had more than one heart.

For some time already I have been thinking about the stimulating image of a *civil world* that I found in a novel that takes place not far from Sarajevo, written in the middle of the twentieth century by Ivo Andric and entitled *The Bridge on the Drina*.[1] The very imagery of a bridge and the effort to "bridge" is frequently used in discussions on social capital, networking, and the need to bring people together in an increasingly divided world. But the bridge in Andric's book is a very special one—not because it is so old and picturesque, and not even because it bridges a river between Bosnia and Serbia—but because of the unusual design by its fourteenth-century architect, as it doubles in the middle to allow for something more than just a crossing of the river on foot or on horse. And it is not so much the bridge itself that interests me but this additional physical space in the middle of it, called the *kapia*. The bridge's social, cultural, and political power lies in this extra space, the *kapia*, with its terraces and "sofas" on either side that can accommodate conversations, get-togethers, or the savoring of Turkish coffee by those who most frequently used the bridge:

Muslim Bosnians and Turks, Orthodox Christian Serbs, and later on also Catholic Croats and Jews.

The *kapia,* this square on the bridge, was a place where those who would otherwise not meet could look at each other, sit together, and get to know each other. Not a marketplace, not a temple, not a court, not a school, the *kapia* was a place that people did not have to stop at, or come to, but they did. With its "sofas" on both sides, a stand with a brass cof-feemaker, and a constant flow of people speaking different languages and worshipping different gods, the *kapia* was a space that people made really good use of. This neutral site, in the middle of the bridge, made it possible for people to get to feel at home with each other, to look through each other's lenses, and to plant the seeds of trust. If we could lift the image of the *kapia* from the novel and look at it as our new modern agora, this richly textured space, inhabited by diverse voices and faces—what would be, if any, its new features and principles?

In a way the *kapia* is a kind of borderland, except that the very notion of a border is here conspicuously absent. Still, a *kapia,* a place on a bridge, is a *threshold,* a turning point, a place of challenge and transformation. *Kapia* is about horizons, not borders, and in times of crisis it opens new prospects, new openings to the future. *Kapia* is a lookout, and I do not mean an outpost or a guard, but a place from which one can see much farther. Such lookouts used to be the harbor cities of Gdansk, Odessa, Lubeck, or Cape Town, full of different flavors and voices. This is where foreign sailors came, with their different languages, foods, costumes, and customs. A *kapia,* then, though a man-made construction, may indeed be called a "natural" site for dialogue. The *kapia* is not a ready-made possibility but rather something people have to work on, to envision, and then to build. The *kapia* is a "space of appearance" that makes performativity possible.

The Roman poet I mentioned earlier, Quintus Ennius, was the one who observed that he had more than one heart, as he spoke not one but three languages: Latin, Greek, and Oscan. He meant that this made him at home with three different ways of comprehending the world, as each language opened for him a new way of knowing. What I like about this observation is that it does not suggest that one has to lose one's own self in order to understand the other. Instead, it makes it easier to see oneself through the eyes of the other. (Or perhaps at least to try to see oneself in that way, as in reality this can never be fully achieved.) After living in the United States for a quarter of a century, I understand now that it is not possible to have my two hearts achieve a state of blissful harmony. Perhaps it would be easier to do some trading, and then to pretend that I am this completely changed new person, with no traces of my old self. Perhaps. But it is also possible to choose another—and I believe healthier, though not easier—route, and enter into a state of perpetual exchange, discussion, and dialogue that eventually leads to the achievement of a certain level of reciprocal understanding or mutual consideration between one's two hearts.

Such mixing-and-matching efforts are no less taxing than the never fully successful effort to switch hearts and to assimilate; and I believe—as I am a strong advocate of such practice—that this captures my vision of multiculturalism more fully than do the multicultural policies of a liberal state that are aimed at reinforcing the borders between cultural groups. I'd like to argue that "mixing and matching" reduces the fear of the different other—so easy to exploit for political gain—and helps to build trust.[2] I am talking now at the individual-personal level about meetings within one-self, but one can imagine ways in which these very much subject-centered answers could be transmitted into arrangements at the community level. On a far broader geopolitical level—not the individual/personal or local community level—such an effort has been undertaken by the construction of the European Community, a place with gradually dissolving borders, with strong local self-governments, and a thriving variety of local cultures and perspectives opened up—at least theoretically—to each other. And the project of building a new postapartheid society in South Africa, which has involved intense work on personal, community, and society-wide levels, is perhaps the most inspiring such project of our times.

One of the most imaginative and effective realizations of the *kapia* potential is a small group that calls itself the Borderlands Center, which works—primarily by means of the arts—in Sejny, a small, once predominantly Jewish shtetl in northeast Poland, near the Belarussian, Ukrainian, and Lithuanian borders. But it also works in the Balkans, the Caucasus, and Indonesia. While on their website I came across a lexicon of the builder of the famous bridge in Mostar, a man named Nejman, an amazing effort by the Borderlanders to understand the space between the two towers of the bridge that links the Bosnian and Croat populations. They think about the space between the two towers, the *Tara* and *Halebija,* as a very specific space expressing and embracing both diversity but also individuality; a space disclosing difference and at the same time a space suggestive of accord. I often think about the impossibility of translating terms conveying culture-specific categories, or about introducing to one's own language terms from other cultures in their original form. I have noticed that in the Polish version of Nejman's lexicon as listed on the website, the names of people and objects intimately linked to the place, like Czardak, Mostari, Usulija, Hajrudin, Czuprija, Kapija, and Jurodivy, are left as they were when used in their original context. This is why I believe that bridges, and above all *kapias,* help us to think in terms that—though initially alien, with their strange-sounding, unpronounceable names—make it possible for us to enter the space and have a sense of sharing in it.

The potential of *kapias*—like borderlands—lies in their dynamism and their constant flow of diverse peoples. I think of New York City as such a *borderland kapia,* with people on the move, a site of continuous repositionings, transfers, and transformations, mirroring the other, echoing others' voices, inserting foreign words, mixing languages, elevating remoteness, hardly noticing outlandish looks, discerning affinities and contradictions. Bakhtinian polyphony, multivoicedness, and heteroglossia are the ruling principle here, though it has nothing to do with losing one's capacity to maintain one's own voice, while communicating with and living next to the other, and celebrating the mix. Such *kapias* are sites that facilitate good *neighborhood,* help to develop neighborliness, lessen borders (real or virtual), and extend the sense of home. These are sites of diversity where recognition takes place, and where it is granted naturally. A space where work has to be done, and where it can be done. And this is the last point I want to return to: the principle of mixing.

I am not the only one who questions the lingering power of the two-century-old ethnonational romantic paradigm developed in various parts of Europe in the age of empires. The paradigm was to mobilize cultural differences in the salvational service of national politics, more specifically in the task of gaining, or regaining, the status of a sovereign nation-state. I know about this, of course, since I am a grateful Pole whose country in 1918 was awarded by the Western powers its own independent state; I know that the strategy of salvational culturalism, or *salvational monoculturalism* as I've already called it before, was one of the few available roads to modernity for the subjected peoples of colonized eastern and southern Europe. And I know that this strategy assigned prominence to the unifying ideological core of what were considered "unmistakably national" Polish, Lithuanian, Ukrainian, Hungarian, or Serbian traits and values. Yet the culture's core theme of past sufferings lends itself nicely to the always-resonant political imperative of mobilizing the population around the task of protecting the national and ethnic identity. To spread the fear of losing identity, to feed the phobias about "others" who are interested in weakening "us," to mount a new host of divisive politics, even within those nation-states that are ethnically homogeneous and have no minorities to speak of, is to bring about a period of democratic lent.

But even in the relatively homogeneous context of today's Poland, one can also observe the fairly recent emergence of a substantial—and to many, surprising—countermovement of active and creative exploration of a forgotten, multifaceted world, its erased diversity, silenced voices, vanished words, and dimly remembered music. It is an effort to reinsert these back into the world they once belonged to, an effort that for many critics seems hopeless, forced, or artificial. And though the movement is of little meaning to those who are gone, who are not there anymore, who cannot speak for themselves, it is of real significance to those who live there, as it opens up—and not just symbolically—their long-locked communities, it extends their horizons, it dynamizes them and helps them to become aware, to know.

Those efforts are virtual *kapias,* and I know them from Poland, with a master initiative already launched some time ago by the Borderlands Center, a work that not only spans and melts the immediate borders but also crosses the oceans. The peculiar thing about some of the recent efforts in my old country is that they force my compatriots to see the absence of the other, a potential participant in an encounter, and perhaps in a dialogue. One of the controversies surrounding the very popular annual Festival of Jewish Culture in Krakow is that the thousands of young people who come to Krakow to take part in its events—both joyous and solemn, designed in a participatory, interactive mode—are almost exclusively Poles. The Jewish Krakow is gone, and what is sharply articulated there is that tangible presence of its absence. And I want to stress that presence.

Another *kapia,* one that also actively brings back voices into the place they were once a part of and that challenges the romantic national paradigm, was established by the people of *The Gate* in Lublin. *The Gate* is a real space, a physical seventeenth-century building, a few stories high, which served as an elaborate entry to the Jewish part of town, at the foot of the Lublin castle. Once in a state of disrepair, it was given to a young theater group that worked on it, restored it, and saved it from being dismantled. It is this group that now, using various art-mediated forms, facilitates encounters of the people of Lublin with their absent Jewish citizens.

Bakhtin would have appreciated their efforts to return polyphony back to the town and to serve as the proxy host for those who were rounded up, taken away, and murdered in a nearby concentration camp, Majdanek. In this case (as in the case of the Krakow events) the idea of *hospitality* takes on an entirely new meaning. Though *The Gate* people cannot speak with the voices of those who are absent, or see themselves through the eyes of a modern Jewish population that was still thriving seventy years ago but no longer exists, their initiatives launched in Lublin are preparing the ground for a conversation. They are hospitable to a dialogue.

Still, the idea that one could launch a dialogue in which one party to the exchange is absent and is represented by somebody else (an idea that can be traced back to Socrates) strikes many as theatrical and artificial and therefore not honest. It strikes me—no matter how sentimental this may sound—that such a committed work, one involving the emotional, the ethical, and the cognitive, might also be an effective way of growing that second heart, pluralizing perspectives, and paving a pathway to transformation. But, again, there is nothing easy about building the conditions for a dialogue to take place and then entering into it. And as we already know, it often requires personal courage, as more often than not, knowing—which brings both shame and pain—creates a threshold for change.

Whether we call them borderlands, round tables, agoras, gates, or *kapias,* we know that they exist, and I recommend that we try to find them or build them. These often unassuming sites of encounters, with all their local distinctiveness, are also places where the superiority of cultural purity is challenged, and where mixing and matching can occur. They would help us to think in terms that are not just ours and to facilitate a gradual but meaningful transformation. And this should fill us with hope.

Notes

NOTES FOR CHAPTER I

1. Seweryn Blumsztajn on Solidarity period in Poland 1980–1981. Interview for the documentary film *Citizens* by R. W. Adams (1986), on which I collaborated.

2. Jeffrey Goldfarb, *The Politics of Small Things* (Chicago: University of Chicago Press, 2006).

3. It has been gratifying to realize that mine is not a voice in the wilderness, as there have recently been a new crop of publications in sociology that also bring to the study of social action the explanatory power of the concepts of performance and performativity. Two of the first were *Social Performance*, ed. Jeffrey C. Alexander, Bernhard Giesen, and Jason L. Mast (Cambridge: Cambridge University Press, 2006); and *The Civil Sphere*, by Jeffrey Alexander (Oxford: Oxford University Press, 2006), in which he considers the performative core of the U.S. civil rights movement. There are related books by Laura Desfor Edles, *Symbol and Ritual in the New Spain: The Transition to Democracy after Franco* (Cambridge: Cambridge University Press, 1998), and Tanya Goodman, *Staging Solidarity: Truth and Reconciliation in a New South Africa* (Boulder, CO: Paradigm Publishers, 2008), on the hearings in South Africa.

4. J. L. Austin, *How to Do Things with Words* (Cambridge, MA: Harvard University Press, 1975), p. 60.

5. The linguistic side is explored by Judith Butler in her book on hate speech, *Excitable Speech: A Politics of the Performative* (New York: Routledge, 1997).

6. Hannah Arendt, *The Human Condition* (Chicago: University of Chicago Press, 1958), p. 179.

7. Hannah Arendt, "Reflections on Violence," *New York Review of Books* 12, no. 14 (February 27, 1969): 65.

8. Nelson Mandela, Address to the Nation on the Assassination of Martin Thembisile (Chris) Hani, April 12, 1993, http://www.anc.org.za/ancdocs/history/mandela/1993.

9. Leszek Kolakowski's *Hope and Hopelessness* was written in 1971 (*Survey* 17, no. 3 [Summer]); Adam Michnik's *The New Evolutionism* was written in

1976 (in English *Letters from Prison* [Berkeley: University of California Press, 1985]); and Vaclav Havel's "The Power of the Powerless" was published in 1978 (in English in *Living in Truth* [London: Faber and Faber, 1987]).

10. This emphasis on the key function of citizens in democracy is given also by Philippe C. Schmitter and Terry Lynn Karl in their seminal piece, "What Democracy Is ... and Is Not," in *The Global Resurgence of Democracy,* ed. Larry Diamond and Marc F. Plattner (Baltimore: Johns Hopkins University Press, 1996).

11. M. Bakhtin, *Rabelais and His World* (Bloomington: Indiana University Press, 1984), pp. 123, 280.

12. It has been pointed out to me recently that a similar—though, I admit, more succinctly stated—position has been presented by Dipesh Chakrabarty in his article "Museums in Late Democracies," *Humanities Research* 9, no. 1 (2001).

13. The changing of the legal status of speech is identified and discussed at length by Kim Lane Scheppele in her forthcoming book, *The International State of Emergency: Challenges of Constitutionalism After September 11.*

NOTES FOR CHAPTER 2

1. Miklos Haraszti, *The Velvet Prison: Artists Under State Socialism* (New York: Basic Books, 1987). The original version was published in French as *L'Artiste d'Etat* (Paris: Fayard, 1983); the first Hungarian edition was published as *Samizdat* (Budapest: A. B. Fuggetlen Kiado, 1986).

2. The most dramatic were the bloody invasion of Red Army tanks in Budapest in October 1956; the beatings, imprisonment, and repression against the students and faculty protesting against censorship in March 1968 in Poland; the invasion of Czechoslovakia by the "brotherly" armies of the Warsaw Pact, crushing the reformist aspirations of the Prague Spring; and the "state of war" imposed by the Polish military government on December 13, 1981, to outlaw the Solidarity Union.

3. Stanislaw Baranczak, *Breathing Under Water and Other East European Essays* (Cambridge, MA: Harvard University Press, 1996).

4. One of the best and early works on the topic is a sociological study by Jeffrey Goldfarb, *The Persistence of Freedom* (Boulder, CO: Westview Press, 1980). Another was written by Polish sociologist Aldona Jawlowska, *Wiecej niz Teatr* (Warsaw, 1988). Those interested in the Czech scene of "authorial theaters" should refer to Dennis C. Beck's essay, "Divadlo na Provasku and the 'Absence' of Czech Community," *Theatre Journal* 48, no. 4 (1996). The current chapter is a follow-up on an essay, "Poland: Living Through Theatre," that I wrote in late 1979, published by the UN University in a volume called *Alternative Ways of Life in Contemporary Europe,* ed. A. Sicinski and Monica Wemegah.

5. Antonin Liehm, *The New Social Contract and the Parallel Polity: Dissent in Eastern Europe,* ed. J. Leftwich Curry (New York: Praeger, 1983), pp. 173–181.

6. Hannah Arendt, "Power and the Space of Appearance," in *The Human Condition* (Chicago: University of Chicago Press, 1958), pp. 199–207.

7. One of the best accounts can be found in the book by Jerzy Szacki, *Liberalism After Communism* (Budapest: Central European University Press, 1995).

8. A collection of interesting, and inspiring, sociological studies analyzing Polish society at a time of crisis was published (in 100 copies!) by the Institute of Sociology at Warsaw University: *Spoleczenstwo Polskie Czasu Kryzysu,* Stefan Nowak, ed. (Warszawa: Uniwersytet Warszawski, Instytut Socjologii, 1984).

9. That function of student theater was noticed by many, but had already been pointed out in 1965 by Konstanty Puzyna, the respected theater and cultural critic, in his article "The Social Role of the Student Theatres," later published in his book *Syntezy za Trzy Grosze* (Warszawa, 1974), p. 169.

10. The Students Association, which was a member organization of students with no declared political agenda, was renamed in 1974 the Socialist Students Association. The change provoked a strong protest among students and led to serious repercussions against those who signed a letter protesting it.

11. H. Arendt, "Reflection on Violence," *New York Review of Books* (February 27, 1969).

12. This is a discovery that Mikhail Bakhtin made while analyzing Dostoyevsky's novels. See also M. Bakhtin, *Dialogical Imagination* (Austin: University of Texas Press, 1981), p. 427.

13. The Eighth Day Theater, Jednym Tchem (collective creation: script and directing, Lech Raczak). Text based on the volume of poetry by Stanislaw Baranczak, *Jednym Tchem* ("Without Stopping for Breath") (Warszawa: Orientacje, 1970).

14. The Eighth Day Theater, which was in fact a theatrical commune, always emphasized the process of collectively creating the performances. In the period I am interested in, their leader was Lech Raczak, who directed the performances and served as spokesperson for the group.

15. "Our theater so tightly adheres to events outside the stage, to the personal life of each of us," Z. Gluza, *Teatr Osmego Dnia* (Warszawa: Karta, 1994), p. 6. Author's translation.

16. Zdzislaw Hejduk, the leader of Theater 77, said the group's axiom was "Towards Non-Theatre," *Sztuka Otwarta: Wspolnota, Kreacja, Teatr* (Wroclaw: Akademicki Osrodek Teatralny Kalambur, 1977).

17. I owe to Konstanty Puzyna this very vivid and sensitive review of the performance, which I had the privilege of seeing with him. Konstanty Puzyna, *Polmrok* (Warszawa, 1982), pp. 54–61.

18. Jawlowska, *Wiecej niz Teatr,* p. 66.

19. Nowak, *Spoleczenstwo Polskie Czasu Kryzysu,* p. 416.

20. "Stawanie sie wypowiedzi" (Making of a Statement), *Sztuka Otwarta.*

21. Civic friendship is a category examined by Tom Bridges in *The Culture of Citizenship: Inventing Postmodern Civic Culture* (Albany, NY: State University of New York Press, 1994).

22. In the western town of Olesnica they chose three shabby buildings in the rear of the Market Square. Small teams of actors knocked at the doors of different apartments: "We are from a theater. We are interested in houses and their residents. We may be shooting a film here. Is it all right with you?" In Olesnica they received a welcoming response. They asked whether in case they'd be building decorations they could count on their help. While actors entered the courtyard with long white bands of linen sheets, the residents were asked to perform some simple daily tasks (supposedly rehearsing them for the film): taking trash to the bin in the courtyard, getting a child on a stroller out of the apartment. Several

days later, people from the neighborhood, attracted by the sound of an accordion played by one of the residents, came to see a magical house, colorfully lit as never before.

"Resident-actors" appear in the windows to perform their tasks: a man shaves, a woman combs her hair. An older man in his best suit takes the trash to the bin. On the wall of the house the silent footage of the family supper filmed in one of the apartments is screened. A sudden change of mood: the filters are demonstratively removed from the lights, and the house is shown in all its scruffiness and deterioration. The magic is gone, but the residents in their Sunday best will stay to share their impressions. The crowd of 150 people is slowly dispersing. The group ends up having family supper in several apartments, invited by the residents.

23. Krzysztof Wodiczko, "Sztuka Publiczna," *Centrum Sztuki Wspolczesnej* (Warszawa, 1995), p. 35.

24. Arendt, "Power and the Space of Appearance," pp. 199–207.

25. Ibid.

26. Nancy Fraser, "Rethinking the Public Sphere: A Contribution to the Critique of Actually Existing Democracy," in *Habermas and the Public Sphere,* ed. C. Calhoun (Cambridge: Massachusetts Institute of Technology Press, 1992).

27. The only exception to this process of political standardization under instructions from the USSR was the Yugoslav Party, which retained a measure of independence from Moscow through most of the four decades (1948–1989).

NOTES FOR CHAPTER 3

1. Kuron, a historian, educator, and political prisoner, was the founder of KOR, the Committee in Defense of the Workers, in 1976.

2. As a result of strikes and demonstrations against the drastic food price increase, just before the Christmas holidays more than 1,000 people were injured, 41 killed, and more than 3,000 arrested.

3. The strike in the shipyard began on August 14 and was concluded on August 31. The governor of the Gdansk region, Jerzy Kolodziejski, is quoted here in the historical quarterly *Karta* 30 (2000): 33.

4. The full set of thirteen strike bulletins entitled *Solidarity* has been published in English in *The Polish August: Documents from the Beginnings of the Polish Workers' Rebellion—Gdansk, August 1980,* ed. Oliver MacDonald (Seattle: Left Bank Books, 1981).

5. Jürgen Habermas, *The Structural Transformation of the Public Sphere* (Cambridge: Massachusetts Institute of Technology Press, 1991), p. 235.

6. K. Nowak, "Kryzys legitimizacyjny systemu w perspektywie doswiadczenia zycia codziennego," in *Spoleczenstwo Polskie Czasu Kryzysu* (Warszawa: Wydawnictwo Uniwersytetu Warszawskiego, 1983), p. 356.

7. Victor Perez-Diaz, *Spain at the Crossroads* (Cambridge, MA: Harvard University Press, 1999).

8. A. Michnik, *New Evolutionism (Letters from Prison)* (Berkeley: University of California Press, 1985), p. 147.

9. On different uses of language, and on the three kinds of speech acts (locutionary, illocutionary, and perlocutionary), see J. L. Austin, *How to Do Things with Words* (Cambridge, MA: Harvard University Press, 1962), pp. 105–120.

10. "The Letter of 59 Intellectuals to the Speaker of the Diet of the Polish People's Republic" was issued in Warsaw on December 5, 1975; for an English version see *Polish Review* 51, no. 1 (2006): 95–98.

11. Ibid.

12. Stefan Nowak, "Values and Attitudes of Polish People," *Scientific American* 245, no. 1 (July 1981): 45–53.

13. The film *Workers '80* was shot during the strike by the group of Polish documentary filmmakers and in early fall screened in the movie theaters.

14. Jürgen Habermas, Sara Lennox, and Frank Lennox, "The Public Sphere: An Encyclopedia Article," *New German Critique* 3 (Autumn 1974): 49.

15. H. Arendt, *The Human Condition* (Chicago: University of Chicago Press, 1958), p. 179.

16. Point four of the Gdansk agreement specified such a possibility of transforming ISC into ICEISTU.

17. MacDonald, *The Polish August,* p. 102.

18. The poet is Stanislaw Baranczak. This and his subsequent remarks are from an interview I did with him in the early 1980s for the documentary film *Citizens,* produced and directed by Richard W. Adams. Baranczak is speaking here about "Without Stopping for Breath," the poem used by the Eighth Day Theater as the basis for its performance discussed in the previous chapter.

19. Robert Putnam, *Making Democracy Work: Civic Traditions in Modern Italy* (Princeton, NJ: Princeton University Press, 1992).

20. M. Bakhtin, *Rabelais and His World* (Cambridge: Massachusetts Institute of Technology Press, 1968), p. 10.

21. See Adam Michnik, "W poszukiwaniu utraconego sensu," *Gazeta Wyborcza* (September 13, 2005).

22. Michael Walzer, "The Concept of Civil Society," in Walzer, ed., *Toward a Global Civil Society* (Oxford, UK: Berghahn Books, 1998), p. 16. See also Walzer's article "Loyalty" in the *Stanford Encyclopedia of Philosophy,* available at http://www.seop.leeds.ac.uk/entries/loyalty.

23. Michnik, *New Evolutionism,* p. 144.

24. The shipbuilding engineer is Andrzej Gwiazda, member of the Interfactory Strike Committee, in a statement from the documentary film, *Workers '80,* shot during the strike in Gdansk by a crew from the Documentary Film Studio, Warsaw, and directed by Andrzej Zajaczkowski.

25. The women were Alina Pienkowska, a nurse, Henryka Krzywonos, a tramway conductor, Anna Walentynowicz, a crane operator, and Ewa Ossowska, who sold newspapers at a newsstand. Interview with a key organizer of the strike, Bogdan Borusewicz, *Gazeta Wyborcza,* August 18, 2000; also "Powstanie Gdanskie," *Wprost* 1185 (August 21, 2005).

26. The writer was Lech Badkowski, member of the Interfactory Strike Committee, as recorded in the documentary *Workers '80.*

27. Baranczak, interview for *Citizens.*

28. The prime minister was Mieczyslaw Jagielski, head of the government's negotiating team, as recorded in the documentary *Workers '80.*

29. The priest is Father Hilary Jastak, and the excerpt from his homily is quoted from *Karta* 30 (2000): 23.

30. The person who presented this postulate at the negotiating table was Bogdan Lis, a worker from ELMOR, another Baltic enterprise, member of the

Interfactory Strike Committee, and later a well-known Solidarity activist, in an exchange recorded in the documentary *Workers '80.*

31. Baranczak, interview for *Citizens.*

32. The worker is Rudolf Ogrodzki from the Ursus Tractor Factory near Warsaw, in an interview I did with him for the documentary film *Citizens.*

33. Hannah Arendt, "The Revolutionary Tradition and Its Lost Treasure," in *On Revolution* (New York: Penguin, 1990), p. 280.

34. Czeslaw Milosz, *You Who Wronged,* trans. Richard Lourie, in *New and Collected Poems* (New York: HarperCollins, 2001), p. 103.

35. Milosz, "A Task," in *New and Collected Poems,* p. 259.

36. Jozef Tischner, *Etyka Solidarnosci* (Krakow: Znak, 2000), p. 17.

37. Jerzy Olbrychtowicz, a graphic artist from Nowy Targ who was in charge of printing the regional bulletin "Solidarnosc Podhala," whom I interviewed for the documentary film *Citizens.*

38. Nowak, *Values and Attitudes of the Polish People,* pp. 45–53.

39. I remember a discussion we had at a meeting of the Cultural Commission of Solidarity, and our immediate decision that we should not allow the Party to steal the holiday from us; after all, it was supposed to be the workers' day. We agreed that the poster prepared by Solidarity artists for that occasion would display a simple line: *May First—The Day of Workers' Solidarity.* Of course, "Solidarity" was to be printed in the famous logo's familiar script, affectionately called *"solidaric,"* in a pun on *Cyrillic.*

40. Adam Michnik, "I Am a Polish Intellectual," in *Letters from Freedom,* ed. Irena Grudzinska-Gross (Berkeley: University of California Press, 1998), p. 302.

41. Perhaps a Briton, Timothy Garton Ash, could be seen as a contemporary Tocqueville, providing a very lively image of the Solidarity period and the subsequent 1989 "refolutions," as he calls them, in Central Europe.

42. Alexis de Tocqueville, *Democracy in America,* vol. 1 (New York: Vintage Books, 1990), pp. 187–188.

43. Sergiusz Kowalski, *Krytyka Solidarnosciowego Rozumu* (Warszawa: PEN, 1990), p. 63.

44. Stefan Nowak, "Postawy, wartosci, i aspiracje spoleczenstwa polskiego. Przeslanki do prognozy na tle przemian dotychczasowych," in *Spoleczenstwo Polskie Czasu Kryzysu,* ed. S. Nowak (Warszawa: Wydawnictwo Uniwersytetu Warszawskiego, 1983).

45. *Reinventing Civil Society: Poland's Quiet Revolution, 1981–1986* (New York: U.S. Helsinki Watch Committee, 1986).

46. Bakhtin, *Rabelais and His World,* pp. 7–11.

47. Ibid., p. 6; Tischner, *Etyka Solidarnosci,* p. 9.

48. Marcin Kula, ed., *Solidarnosc w Ruchu* (Warszawa: 2000), p. 143.

NOTES FOR CHAPTER 4

1. One of the most emblematic discussions was launched by Tony Judt, "Radical Politics in a New Key," *Northwestern University Law Review* 81 (Summer 1987); see also Jonathan Schell, "Introduction," in Adam Michnik, *Letters from Prison and Other Essays,* ed. Irena Grudzinska Gross, trans. Maya Latynski (Berkeley: University of California Press, 1985). A thoughtful discussion on a

possibility of utilizing political thought of democratic opposition in Eastern Europe for articulation of a viable project of liberal socialism was initiated by Ira Katznelson in his book *Liberalism's Crooked Circle: Letters to Adam Michnik* (Princeton, NJ: Princeton University Press, 1996). Jonathan Schell discusses Michnik's philosophy and practice of nonviolence as a precious dimension of his thought in *The Unconquerable World* (New York: Metropolitan Books, 2003).

2. Adam Michnik, "The New Evolutionism" (which was written in 1976), in *Letters from Prison*. The role of the text as opening a new vista for the dissidents in Eastern Europe is acknowledged by all key thinkers of democratic opposition from this part of Europe.

3. Adam Michnik, "Czego potrzebuje demokracja," *Wscieklosc i Wstyd* (Warszawa: Zeszyty Literackie, 2005), p. 285.

4. Jan Strzelecki, "Moj Nauczyciel" (My Teacher), *Kontynuacje* (Warszawa: PIW, 1969), p. 158. Author's translation.

5. Adam Michnik, *Letters from Freedom: Postwar Realities and Perspectives,* ed. Irena Grudzinska Gross (Berkeley: University of California Press, 1998).

6. Adam Michnik, *Z Dziejow Honoru w Polsce: Wypisy Wiezienne (From the History of Honor in Poland: A Prison Reader)* (Paris: Instytut Literacki, 1985), p. 59. Author's translation.

7. Michnik, "Shadows of Forgotten Ancestors," in *Letters from Prison,* p. 207.

8. Adam Michnik, *Takie czasy ... Rzecz o Kompromisie* (Such Are Times ... A Word on Compromise) (London: Aneks, 1985), p. 13.

9. Michnik, "Conversation in the Citadel," in *Letters from Prison,* p. 303.

10. Vladimir Tismaneanu, *Reinventing Politics: Eastern Europe from Stalin to Havel* (New York: Free Press, 1992).

11. Especially Anthony Giddens, *Central Problems in Social Theory: Action, Structure, and Contradiction in Social Analysis* (Berkeley: University of California Press, 1979).

12. See Adam Michnik, *Szanse Polskiej Demokracji* (London: Aneks, 1984), p. 250. See also Michnik, "Conversation in the Citadel," in *Letters from Prison,* at the very end of the essay. Author's translation.

13. Jozef Tischner, "Po co Bog Stworzyl Michnika" (Why God Created Michnik), an afterword in Michnik, *Kosciol Lewica, Dialog* (Warszawa: Swiat Ksiazki, 1998), p. 345.

14. Jaroslaw Marek Rymkiewicz, *Rozmowy Polskie Latem Roku 1983* (Polish Conversations: Summer of 1983) (Warszawa: Niezalezna Oficyna Wydawnicza, 1984). Author's translation.

14. Ibid., p. 5.

15. The phrase "our Pinochet" refers here to General Jaruzelski, whose military government introduced martial law in Poland on December 13, 1981.

16. Rymkiewicz, *Rozmowy Polskie Latem Roku 1983,* p. 5.

17. The enlarged edition of the book was translated into English by David Ost and titled *The Church and the Left* (Chicago: University of Chicago Press, 1993).

18. Michnik, "Shadows of Forgotten Ancestors," in *Letters from Prison.*

19. I am discussing here works written by Michnik before 1989, many published in *Letters from Prison.*

20. Michnik, "Shadows of Forgotten Ancestors," p. 205.

21. Michnik, "Conversation in the Citadel."
22. Michnik, "Powstanie Listopadowe—Polskie Pytania," in *Polskie pytania* (*The Polish Questions*) (Warszawa: NOWA, 1993) p. 209. Author's translation.
23. Michnik, "Z Dziejow Honoru w Polsce," p. 59.
24. Michnik, "Niezlomny z Londynu i Inne Eseje," in *Polskie Pytania*.
25. Ibid., p. 83.
26. Ibid. See also Michnik, "Maggots and Angels" (written in 1979), in *Letters from Prison*.
27. Michnik, "New Evolutionism," in *Letters from Prison*, p. 139.
28. "Some Remarks on the Opposition and the General Situation in Poland" (written jointly with J. J. Lipski in 1979), in *Letters from Prison*, p. 150.
29. Michnik, "Nadzieja i zagrozenie," in *Szanse polskiej Demokracji*, p. 62. Author's translation.
30. He discussed this question in "Maggots and Angels," which was circulated through the underground press.
31. Michnik, "The New Evolutionism," in *Letters from Prison*.
32. Michnik, *Powstanie Listopadowe—Polskie Pytania*.
33. Michnik, *Takie czasy ... Rzecz o Kompromisie*. Author's translation.
34. Ibid., p. 31.
35. "Antitotalitarian Revolt: A Conversation with Daniel Cohn-Bendit," in *Letters from Freedom*.
36. Michnik, *Z Dziejow Honoru w Polsce: Wypisy Wiezienne*.
37. Ibid., p. 135.
38. Adam Michnik, "We, the People of Solidarity," a talk given on the occasion of receiving an honorary degree awarded by the New School for Social Research in April and given to him in Warsaw on December 10, 1984. The entire text is published in Michnik, *Polskie Pytania* (Warszawa: NOWA, 1993).
39. Adam Michnik, "Niezgoda na Uklon" (Refusing to Bow), *Gazeta Wyborcza* (August 12, 2002).
40. Hannah Arendt, *Korzenie totalitaryzmu*, vols. 1–2 (Warszawa: NOWA, 1989).
41. For a more detailed description of the seminars see the introduction and prologue to *Grappling with Democracy: Deliberations on Post-Communist Societies, 1990–1995*, ed. Elzbieta Matynia (Prague: SLON, 1995).
42. Michnik, "Niezgoda na Uklon."
43. "Your President, Our Prime Minister," *Gazeta Wyborcza* (July 3, 1989), in *Letters from Freedom*, pp. 129–131.
44. Austin, *How to Do Things with Words*, pp. 108–120.
45. "Adam Michnik: Sisyphus of Democracy," interview by Philippe Demenet, *UNESCO Courier*, available at http://www.unesco.org/courier/2001_09/uk/dires .htm.
46. Adam Michnik, "Polska na zakrecie, Gazeta na zakrecie" (Poland at a Turning Point, *Gazeta* at a Turning Point"), *Gazeta Wyborcza* (May 8, 2004).
47. The World Voices, panel discussion organized by the New York PEN, April 26–29, 2006.
48. Wlodzimierz Cimoszewicz and Adam Michnik, "O Prawde i Pojednanie" (For Truth and Reconciliation), *Gazeta Wyborcza* (September 19, 1995).
49. Dawid Warszawski (Konstanty Gebert), "Beton ze styropianem," *Gazeta Wyborcza* (September 19, 1995).

50. Adam Michnik, "Rana na czole Adama Mickiewicza" (The Wound on the Forehead of Adam Mickiewicz), *Gazeta Wyborcza* (November 4, 11, 18, 25, 2006).

51. Michnik, "Three Kinds of Fundamentalism," p. 181; "Gray Is Beautiful: A Letter to Ira Katznelson," both in *Letters from Freedom*; Michnik, "Niezgoda na Uklon"; Arendt, *The Human Condition*, p. 237.

52. Adam Michnik, "Smutek Rynsztokow" ("Sadness of the Gutter"), *Gazeta Wyborcza* (September 9, 2006).

53. Adam Michnik, "Ultrasi Rewolucji Moralnej," *Gazeta Wyborcza* (April 15, 2005); English trans., "The Ultras of Moral Revolution," *Daedalus* 136, no. 1 (Winter 2007): 67–83.

54. Michnik, *Polskie Pytania*, p. 252.

55. Michnik, "Antitotalitarian Revolt," p. 30.

56. Especially Edward Abramowski; see Michnik, "Conversation in the Citadel."

57. Michnik, "Gray Is Beautiful," p. 320; see also response by Ira Katznelson in *Dissent* (Winter 1997).

58. Michnik, *The Church and the Left*, p. 33.

59. Katznelson, *Liberalism's Crooked Circle*.

60. He expressed the conviction that the conflict between right and left in Poland belongs to the past in one of his 1982 prison essays; see Michnik, "Letter from the Gdansk Prison," in *Letters from Prison*, p. 91.

61. Adam Michnik, "Czego potrzebuje demokracja" ("What Does Democracy Need?"), lecture at Warsaw University delivered on September 20, 2002, and published in *Gazeta Wyborcza* (October 5, 2002).

62. Slawomir Sierakowski, editor in chief of the quarterly *Krytyka Polityczna*, has published a large probing essay on Michnik titled "Polska do Nietzschego?" *Krytyka Polityczna* 6 (2004). The text was reprinted in a weekend edition of *Gazeta Wyborcza* (July 10–11, 2004), p. 19.

63. Michnik, "Niezgoda na Uklon" (Refusing to Bow).

64. Lew Rywin, a well-known film producer (*Schindler's List, The Pianist*), proposed to Michnik a deal for passing through the Polish Parliament a media law that would be favorable for *Gazeta Wyborcza*, which was interested in buying a TV station. *Gazeta*, or more specifically its company AGORA, was to pay 5 percent ($17.5 million) of the overall cost of the eventual transaction. Rywin indicated that he is a messenger of a group in power. Michnik taped the conversation with Rywin and a few months later made it available along with other materials through *Gazeta's* website, www.Gazeta.pl.

65. Maciej Zaremba, "A Good Editor Is a Prophet with an Eye on a Profit," *Axess 2004* 7, available at http://www.axess.se/english/2007/index.htm.

66. Michnik, "Polska na zakrecie."

67. Adam Michnik, "My Zdrajcy" (We, the Traitors), *Gazeta Wyborcza* (March 28, 2003), available at http://www.worldpress.org/Europe/1086.cfm. Some of his Western friends wondered how he could reconcile his unwavering anti-imperial stand and the conviction that democracy is a domestic growth that cannot be imposed from abroad with his support for the invasion of Iraq. Jonathan Schell asked Michnik this question at the panel discussion organized by the Institute for Human Sciences, "'New Europe' and the United States: The End of the Affair?" Boston University, April 2004.

68. Janos Kis and Adam Michnik, "After Five Years," *New York Review of Books* 55, no. 12 (July 17, 2008).

69. Michnik, "Maggots and Angels," p. 197.

Notes for Chapter 5

1. Hannah Arendt, *The Human Condition* (Chicago: University of Chicago Press, 1958), p. 178.

2. J. L. Austin, *How to Do Things with Words* (Cambridge, MA: Harvard University Press, 1962), p. 116.

3. "Great change without the great utopia" is Adam Michnik's expression.

4. Laurence Whitehead, *Democracy: Theory and Experience* (New York: Oxford University Press, 2002), p. 17.

5. Mikhail Bakhtin, "Discourse in the Novel," in *Dialogical Imagination* (Austin: University of Texas Press, 1981), p. 263.

6. CODESA included delegations from nineteen governmental and political organizations, which began planning the creation of a transitional government and a parliament that would represent the entire society. The structure is comparable to that of the Polish Round Table, which was composed of three main issues-oriented tables and some additional subtables. CODESA instituted five working groups, each made up of thirty-eight delegates and thirty-eight advisers and concerned with (1) setting up a context for free political activity, (2) agreeing on key constitutional principles, (3) establishing transitional procedures for the four so-called independent homelands, (4) setting and supervising timetables for the transition, and (5) dealing with any problems that may arise during the transition process.

7. Adam Michnik, lecture delivered at the annual Democracy and Diversity Institute organized by the New School University in Krakow, Poland, July 1999.

8. Joe Slovo, "Negotiations: What Room for Compromise?" available at http://www.sapc.org.za/people/SLOVO/negotiations.html. This is also why Mandela and de Klerk, despite continuous threats to the fragile process of negotiations coming from all sides, kept resuming the talks. The image, sometimes translated as "mutual siege" (or mutual dependence), was brought up by Jeremy Cronin at his lecture in Cape Town in January 17, 2006, at the annual Democracy and Diversity Institute organized by the New School for Social Research in collaboration with IDASA. Cronin, who took part in the CODESA talks as a representative of the newly unbanned Communist Party of South Africa (SACP), was at the time of the lecture in Cape Town the deputy secretary of SACP and a Member of Parliament representing the ANC.

9. Krzysztof Wolicki, "Cos," in Krzysztof Leski, *Rzecz o okraglym stole* (Warszawa: Plus 1989, mimeographed publication).

10. Address to CODESA by Nelson Mandela, president of the African National Congress, December 1991, available at http://www.anc.org.za/ancdocs/history/transition/codesa/anc.

11. On July 17, 1992, a massacre of more than forty people occurred in Boipatong. The event, inspired by those opposing the negotiations with the Inkatha

Freedom Party, involved bloody intervention by the police and brought about a general outrage among the black population. Mandela and ANC accused the regime of complicity and requested that the UN Security Council discuss the killings. The United Nations sent to South Africa its special representative, Cyrus Vance, who recommended a deployment of international observers to monitor the situation in the country.

12. Michnik, lecture delivered at the annual Democracy and Diversity Institute organized by the New School University in Krakow, Poland, July 1999.

13. Sadly, the assassin was a Polish emigrant, Janusz Walus, connected to the far-right Conservative Party and its leader Clive Derby-Lewis.

14. Allister Sparks, *Tomorrow Is Another Day: The Inside Story of South Africa's Negotiated Settlement* (Johannesburg: J. Ball, 1995), p. 147.

15. I was cautioned by Professor André du Toit, one of the *verligte* himself, who took part in the 1987 meeting with ANC in Dakar, not to overemphasize the one *verligte*-related narrative.

16. Sparks, *Tomorrow Is Another Day*, p. 75.

17. Bronislaw Geremek and Jacek Zakowski, *Rok 1989: Geremek odpowiada, Zakowski pyta* (Plejada, 1990).

18. Available at http://www.sahistory.org.za/pages/main-chronology-1990s .html.

19. The negotiations on how to introduce some form of democracy and how to dismantle the structures of apartheid in South Africa were similarly lengthy, as they began at the end of 1991 and concluded with the new constitution approved by twenty-one parties in November 1993, and the first democratic elections took place in April 1994.

20. A. Michnik, *Takie czasy ... Rzecz o Kompromisie* (London: Aneks, 1985).

21. Ibid., p. 138.

22. Lech Walesa, *Droga do Wolnosci* (Warszawa: Spotkania, 1991), p. 95.

23. Sparks, *Tomorrow Is Another Day*, pp. 62–65.

24. Van Zyl Slabbert, *Tough Choices: Reflection of an Afrikaner African* (Cape Town: Tafelberg, 2000).

25. Discussion paper, "The Issue of Negotiations," June 16, 1989, available at http://www.anc.org.za/ancdocs/pr/1989.

26. Sparks, *Tomorrow Is Another Day*, pp. 16–17.

27. Joe Slovo discussing the future of negotiations. Report on the interview with general secretary of SACP Joe Slovo by Gaye Davis, available at http://www .liberation.org.za/collections/sacp/slovo/republic.php.

28. Groote Schuur Minutes, available at http://www.anc.org.za/ancdocs/ history/transition/minutes.html.

29. Pretoria Minutes, available at http://www.anc.org.za/ancdocs/history/ transition/minutes.html.

30. Konstanty Gebert, *Mebel* (London: Aneks, 1990), p. 35.

31. Memo from the meeting in Magdalenka, March 2, 1989, prepared by Jacek Ambroziak, in Peter Raina, *Droga do Okraglego Stolu* (Warszawa, 1999), p. 352. See also Geremek and Zakowski, *Rok 1989*, p. 113.

32. CODESA I, December 20–21, 1991; CODESA II, May 15–16, 1992.

33. Shireen Hassim, "A Conspiracy of Women": The Women's Movement in South Africa's Transition to Democracy," *Social Research* 69, no. 3 (Fall 2002).

34.   Catherine Barnes and Eldred de Klerk, "South Africa's Multiparty Constitutional Negotiation Process," available at http://www.c-r.org/accord/peace/accord13/samul.shtml.

35.   The number of participants mentioned is, depending on sources, either 228 (Sparks, *Tomorrow Is Another Day*) or 238 (Barnes and de Klerk, "South Africa's Multiparty Constitutional Negotiation Process").

36.   Gebert, *Mebel,* p. 14.

37.   Sparks, *Tomorrow Is Another Day,* p. 102.

38.   Available at http://www.anc.org.za/anc/newsnrief/1992/news9205.16.

39.   Available at http://www.anc.org.za/anc/newsnrief/1992/news9205.15 (May 17, 1992).

40.   Slovo, "Negotiations: What Room for Compromise?"

41.   Hugh Corder, "Towards a South African Constitution," *Modern Law Review* 57, no. 4 (July 1994). See also Patti Waldmeir, *The Anatomy of the Miracle* (New York: Viking, 1997).

42.   Hugh Corder, "Negotiated Transition in South Africa: The Process and Its Promises," lecture at the Democracy and Diversity Institute, January 10, 2006, Cape Town, South Africa. Hugh Corder, who in 2006 was the professor of public law and the dean of the school of law at the University of Cape Town, in the refurbished round table was a member of the Technical Committee on Fundamental Rights during the Transition, which served the negotiating process from May to November 1993. See also his article "Towards a South African Constitution."

43.   Sparks, *Tomorrow Is Another Day,* p. 145.

44.   Statement of the president of ANC, Nelson Mandela, on the assassination of Martin Thembisile Chris Hani, available at http://www.anc.org.za/ancdocs/pr/1993/pr9304.html.

45.   COSAG was established in 1992 as an alliance of the Inkatha Freedom Party, the territorial governments of KwaZulu, Ciskei, and Bophuthatswana, and two Africaner parties, the Conservative Party and the Afrikaanse Volksunie.

46.   Austin, *How to Do Things with Words,* p. 121.

47.   Gebert, *Mebel,* p. 15.

48.   Ibid., p. 16.

49.   Walesa, *Droga do Wolnosci,* p. 114.

50.   Gebert, *Mebel,* p. 24.

51.   Geremek and Zakowski, *Rok 1989.*

52.   Gebert, *Mebel,* p. 23.

53.   Ibid.

54.   Walesa, *Droga do Wolnosci,* p. 114.

55.   Ibid.

56.   Ibid.

57.   Joe Slovo in an interview with Gaye Davis, February 11, 1990.

58.   Available at http://www.anc.org.za/anc/newsnrief/1992/news9205.15 (May 17, 1992).

59.   Intervention of the president of the African National Congress, Nelson Mandela, at the Second Session of the Convention for a Democratic South Africa (CODESA), available at http://www.anc.org.za/ancdocs/history/mandela/1992.

60.   Waldmeier, *The Anatomy of the Miracle,* p. 41.

61. Roelf Mayer, "Paradigm Shift: An Essence of Successful Change—A Personal Experience," available at http://www.ciaonet.org/wps.

62. Walesa, *Droga do Wolnosci*, p. 111.

63. *General Kiszczak mowi ... prawie wszystko* (Warszawa: BGW, 1991), p. 266.

64. For a thorough description of the outcome of negotiations, see Frederik Van Zyl Slabbert, Heribert Adam, and Kogila Moodley Adam, *Comrades in Business: Postliberation Politics in South Africa* (Cape Town: Tafelberg, 1997), pp. 69–71; and Sparks, *Tomorrow Is Another Day*, pp. 151–152.

65. Available at http://www.anc.org.za/anc/newsbrief/1993/news1119.

66. Address by Nelson R. Mandela to the plenary session of the Multi-Party Negotiation Process held at the World Trade Center in Kempton Park, November 17, 1993, available at http://www.anc.org.za/anc/newsbrief/1993/news1118.

67. Adam Michnik, "Your President, Our Prime Minister," *Gazeta Wyborcza*, July 3, 1989; Michnik, *Letters from Freedom*, pp. 129–131; Tadeusz Mazowiecki, "Spiesz sie Powoli," *Tygodnik Solidarnosc*, July 14, 1989.

68. Those two parties created in the 1950s to give the impression of party pluralism were the United Peasant Party (ZSL) and the Democratic Party (SD).

69. Michnik, lecture delivered at the annual Democracy and Diversity Institute organized by the New School University in Krakow, Poland, July 1999; Nelson Mandela, Nobel Prize Lecture, 1993.

NOTES FOR CHAPTER 6

1. Hannah Arendt, *The Human Condition* (Chicago: University of Chicago Press, 1958), p. 32.

2. The poster was designed by Polish graphic artist Tomasz Sarnecki.

3. I analyze these paradoxes in the essay "Finding a Voice: Women in Postcommunist Central Europe," in Amrita Basu, ed., *The Challenge of Local Feminism: Women's Movements in Global Perspective* (Boulder, CO: Westview Press, 1995).

4. A. Metelska and E. Nowakowska, eds., *Gdzie Diabel nie moze* (Warszawa: BGW, 1992), p. 145.

5. Ann Philips, "Does Feminism Need a Conception of Civil Society?" in Simone Chambers and Will Kimlicka, eds., *Alternative Conceptions of Civil Society* (Princeton, NJ: Princeton University Press, 2002).

6. Nancy Fraser, "Rethinking Recognition: Overcoming Displacement and Reification Politics," in Barbara Hobson, ed., *Recognition Struggles and Social Movements: Contested Identities, Agency, and Power* (Cambridge: Cambridge University Press, 2003).

7. Transparency International, *Global Corruption Report 2001,* available at www.globalcorruptionreport.org.

8. Saskia Sassen links the trafficking in women more specifically to the hyperindebtedness of many countries.

9. UN Office on Drug and Crime (UNODC). Available at http://www.unodc.org/unodc/en/human-trafficking/index.html.

10. Ibid.

11. J. Regulska, quoting Barbel Butteweck from La Strada's Prague office. "W poszukiwaniu przestrzeni dla kobiet: Integracja Europy a Rownosc Plci," *Biuletyn OSKA* 12.

12. "Finding Women's Security in the Twenty-first Century: A Gendered Perspective," panel presentation and discussion organized by the National Council for Research on Women, New York City, February 21, 2002.

13. The others are the Czech Republic, Estonia, Hungary, Latvia, Lithuania, Poland, Slovakia, and Slovenia.

14. For more details see the very informative website www.unc.edu/depts/europe/conferences/eu/cfsp/enlarge.

15. The concept, brought up for the first time at the UN Third World Conference on Women in Nairobi "in 1985, launched a vigorous debate, especially in western Europe, was adopted as part of the Platform for Action, and was eventually further highlighted as a key strategy at the 1995 Beijing Conference." See also Council of Europe, *Gender Mainstreaming: Conceptual Framework, Methodology, and Presentation of Good Practices,* EG-S (9) 2 rev, available at www.nrights.coe.int/equality/Eng/word.docs.

16. Ibid., p. 15.

17. J. Regulska, "W poszukiwaniu przestrzeni dla kobiet"; and Stephane Portet, "Integracja Polski z Unia Europejska a Relacje Plci," *Biuletyn OSKA* 12.

18. M. Fuszara, "The New Gender Contract in Poland," SOCO/IWM working papers, Vienna, 2000.

19. Joanna Regulska was one of the first to point out the major difference of employment status between women from Western and Eastern Europe, in "W poszukiwaniu przestrzeni dla kobiet." See also Fuszara, "The New Gender Contract in Poland."

20. Agnieszka Graff, "Patriarchat po seksmisji," *Gazeta Wyborcza,* June 19–20, 1999.

21. "Minister Jaruga-Nowacka o Swoich Planach," *Gazeta Wyborcza,* January 24, 2002.

22. Bishop Tadeusz Pieronek.

23. The "Letter of One Hundred" was published in *Gazeta Wyborcza* on March 7, 2002, one day before International Women's Day, and opened a flood of polemics in Polish media.

24. CBOS, October 2001.

25. A. Brzeziecki and M. Flak, "Zagwarantowac zagwarantowane," *Tygodnik Powszechny* 2795 (February 2, 2003).

26. E. Matynia, "Reluctant Feminism, or Are We Listening?" paper presented at a conference in Ann Arbor, Michigan, April 1998. The reasons for that situation were many: a still not yet fully developed appreciation of the representative role of elected officials, a tendency toward a certain disdain for the general public, and a rather widely ingrained indifference to women's issues on the part of traditionally male-dominated governments.

27. For full analysis of this phenomenon see Chapter 7.

28. Graff, "Patriarchat po seksmisji."

29. Shana Penn, "The Great Debate: When Feminism Hit the Headlines, Poland Hit the Roof," *Ms. Magazine* (January 2001).

30. Agnieszka Graff, *Swiat bez Kobiet* (Warszawa: W.A.B., 2001); K. Szczuka, *Cinderella, Frankenstein, i inne* (Krakow: efka, 2001); E. H. Oleksy, *Wrobelek ze zlamanym skrzydlem […] i kieliszek czystej;* S. Walczewska, *Damy, Rycerze, i Feministki* (Cracow: efka, 1999); K. Klosinska, *Cialo, pozadanie, ubranie;* E. Kondratowicz, *Szminka na Sztandarze* (Warszawa: Sic!, 2001); and K. Szczuka, *Milczenie Owieczek: Rzecz o Aborcji* (Warszawa: W.A.B., 2004).

31. Fuszara, "The New Gender Contract in Poland," p. 4.

32. There have been many articles in the West featuring Wanda Rapaczynska and Helena Luczywo, the two women behind the media giant AGORA. One of them was Peggy Simpson, "In Poland, Women Run the Largest News Organizations," *Nieman Reports* (Winter 2001).

33. The percentage of those who support the role of woman as homemaker decreased from 86 percent in 1992 to 76 percent in 1998. Those of the opinion that women ought to sacrifice their professional careers for the sake of their husbands decreased from 46 percent in 1992 to 32.9 percent in 1992. See H. Domanski, "Nagie Oko i Fakty," *Res Publica* (January 2002).

34. CBOS, February 2002.

35. A very interesting and subtle argument concerning the durability of the romantic paradigm in Poland was developed by the brilliant Polish scholar Maria Janion in her recent book, *Do Europy, Tak—ale razem z naszymi umarlymi* (To Europe, Yes—But Only with Our Dead) (Warsaw: Sic!, 2000), p. 37.

36. The wisdom of the two major Polish insurrections, led by noble but not very responsible people and having tragic long-term consequences, is still hotly debated in Poland. Some try to imagine what Poland would be like if the uprisings had not happened. "Whole generations of young people were wasted. How many were killed? How many were banished to Siberia, how many escaped to the West, how many were lost to Polish thought and culture? How very badly we used our intelligentsia class!" J. Jedlicki, "Swiat na peryferiach Ameryki," *Nowe Ksiazki* (July 2000). The brief intermission from 1918 to 1939 in the Poles' struggles for national sovereignty was followed by the Nazi invasion and occupation (1939–1945) and then four decades of Communist rule, of which the worst period—the Stalinist—was again littered with executions and imprisonments. The more liberalized periods, however, allowed for the sprouting of an alternative culture, one very much inspired by the repertoire of resistance strategies developed a century earlier, with the illegal publication and circulation of censored literature, the revival of "flying universities," the establishment of self-help initiatives, and so on.

37. Walczewska, *Damy, Rycerze, i Feministki*, p. 187.

38. *Matka Polka,* suspended, as it were, between knights and peasants as one of the first representatives in literature of an emerging new nineteenth-century social stratum, the intelligentsia, is a figure from Polish romantic-patriotic poetry whose fundamental qualities are motherhood, duty, and the spirit of sacrifice. Like Maryja, she is the mother of a son, and as she sacrifices herself for him, so he must then sacrifice himself for the *mother*land.

39. Interestingly, "they"—perhaps because of successful efforts of the state propaganda—were always envisioned as Germans.

40. M. Fuszara, "Udzial Kobiet we wladzy," *Babiniec,* available at www .babiniec.multinet.com.pl.

41. E. Matynia, "Women After Communism: A Bitter Freedom," *Social Research* (Summer 1994).

42. Among the writings on the subject is Shana Penn, *Solidarity's Secret: The Women Who Defeated Communism in Poland* (Ann Arbor: University of Michigan Press, 2005). See also Kondratowicz, *Szminka na Sztandarze;* and Graff, *Swiat po seksmisji.*

43. Shana Penn describes the most drastic case in "The National Secret," *Journal of Women's History* (Winter 1994): 55–69; and also in *Solidarity's Secret.*

44. Myra Marx Ferree and William A. Gamson write of abortion politics in Germany and the United States as *governance of gender and gendering of governance.* See their study in Barbara Hobson, ed., *Recognition Struggles and Social Movements: Contested Identities, Agency, and Power,* pp. 35–62.

45. Manifa, which is a carnavalesque event that attracts the media and demands equal rights for women, is organized annually by the younger generation of Polish feminists, among them the already mentioned author Agnieszka Graff.

46. Examples of populist manifestations are Radio Maryja and Samoobrona (a political party led by Andrzej Lepper, who in 2006 was stripped of his position as a deputy speaker of the Parliament and his immunity as a member of Parliament). The ultra-right-wing political party Liga Rodzin Polskich exhibits a fundamentalist mentality.

47. J. L. Austin, *How to Do Things with Words* (Cambridge, MA: Harvard University Press, 1962).

48. Ibid.; felicitous, or happy, performatives do not just act as though they are doing what they are saying, but actually have a real immediate (illocutionary acts) or delayed (perlocutionary acts) effect.

49. Nanette Funk and Magda Mueller, eds., *Gender Politics and Post-Communism* (New York, Routledge, 1993); Ann Snitow, "The Church Wins, Women Lose: Poland's Abortion Law," *Nation* (April 26, 1993); Jirina Siklová, "Different Region, Different Women: Why Feminism Isn't Successful in the Czech Republic," in Margit Feischmidt, Enikő Magyari-Vincze, and Violetta Zentai, eds., *Women and Men in East European Transition* (Cluj-Napocaj, Romania: EFES, 1997); Jirina Smejkalová, "On the Road: Smuggling Feminism Across the Post–Iron Curtain," in Feischmidt, Magyari-Víncze, and Zentai, eds., *Women and Men in East European Transition;* Maria Nemenyi, "The Social Construction of Women's Roles in Hungary," *Replika* (1996 special issue); Siklová, "Why Western Feminism Isn't Working in the Czech Republic" (1999), available at http://www.cddc.vt.edu/feminism/cz4.html.

50. Jerzy Szacki, *Liberalism After Communism* (Budapest: CEU Press, 1995).

51. J. Habermas, *The Structural Transformation of the Public Sphere* (Cambridge: Massachusetts Institute of Technology Press, 1996), p. 235.

52. E. Matynia, *Reluctant Feminism,* pp. 16–17.

53. E. Matynia, "The Lost Treasure of Solidarity," *Social Research* 68 (Winter 2001).

54. A. Phillips, *Engendering Democracy* (Philadelphia: University of Pennsylvania Press, 1991), p. 149.

55. A. Snitow, "Response," in J. Scott et al., eds., *Transitions, Environments, Translations: Feminism in International Politics* (New York: Routledge, 1997).

56. See the interesting book by Dipesh Chakrabarty, *Provincializing Europe: Postcolonial Thought and Historical Difference* (Princeton, NJ: Princeton University Press, 2000).

57. Saskia Sassen, "Finding Women's Security in the Twenty-First Century: A Gendered Perspective," panel presentation and discussion organized by the National Council for Research on Women, New York City, February 21, 2002.

NOTES FOR CHAPTER 7

1. H. Arendt, *The Human Condition* (Chicago: University of Chicago Press, 1958), p. 169.

2. Jirina Siklová, "Different Region, Different Women: Why Feminism Isn't Successful in the Czech Republic," in Margit Feischmidt, Enikō Magyari-Vincze, and Violetta Zentai, eds., *Women and Men in East European Transition* (Cluj-Napocaj, Romania: EFES, 1997); Jirina Smejkalová, "On the Road: Smuggling Feminism Across the Post–Iron Curtain," in Feischmidt, Magyari-Víncze, and Zentai, eds., *Women and Men in East European Transition;* Jeffrey Goldfarb, "Why There Is No Feminism After Communism," in *Civility and Subversion: The Intellectual in Democratic Society* (Cambridge: Cambridge University Press, 1998).

3. Among the artists was one who began her career in the 1960s (Natalia LL), two who entered the scene in the 1970s (Izabella Gustowska and Zofia Kulik), three whose debuts took place in the 1980s (Katarzyna Jozefowicz, Hanna Nowicka-Grochal, and Anna Plotnicka), four who began exhibiting in the 1990s, and six who only started to become known in the twenty-first century (Julita Wojcik, Dorota Nieznalska, Dominika Szkutnik, Karolina Wysocka, Paulina Olowska, and Monika Sosnowska). All of these artists are graduates of various art academies in Poland.

4. The art that I am discussing here, which is visual, physical, and material, is referred to, following the curator of the New York exhibit, as conceptual art. Since, as noticed by Pawel Leszkowicz, conceptual art is generally associated with the art of the 1970s, it may in fact be more appropriate to refer to the phenomenon I describe here as postconceptual art.

5. My discussion is informed by Habermassian discursive theory of the public sphere in which civil society (private agents) creates a sphere of criticism of public authority. See Jürgen Habermas, *The Structural Transformation of the Public Sphere* (Cambridge: Massachusetts Institute of Technology Press, 1991), p. 51. Thus the public sphere represents the discursive aspect of civil society. I will later argue that just as his definition of public sphere, based on an analysis of a bourgeois society, did not capture the phenomenon of alternative culture developed by citizens under, and against, a Communist system, his theory has to be similarly modified if it is to explain the transitional societies. Hence my introduction of the category of "alternative discursive space."

6. Ewa Toniak, "Pani Bond z siatka albo o zmianach plci polskiej w latach dziewiedziesiatych," *Res Publica Nowa* (June 2001): 39.

7. For an excellent insight into this problem, see Shana Penn, *Solidarity's Secret: The Women Who Defeated Communism in Poland* (Ann Arbor: University of Michigan Press, 2005).

8. For more on different types of activity vis-à-vis the authoritarian regime, see Chapter 3; see also Elzbieta Matynia, "The Lost Treasures of Solidarity," *Social Research* 68, no. 4 (Winter 2001).

9. Pawel Leszkowicz, "Szczesliwy Powrot Polskiego Modernizmu?" *Magazyn Sztuki* 26 (February 2001).

10. A similar point was brought up by Aneta Szylak, the curator of the exhibit, during her lecture-video presentation at the New School for Social Research, on April 17, 2003. The presentation was one of the events that accompanied the opening at SculptureCenter.

11. Matynia, "The Lost Treasures."

12. The exhibit at SculptureCenter took place April 11–June 8, 2003. It was coproduced by the Polish Cultural Institute in New York and accompanied by public lectures, panel discussions, and screenings of experimental films by Polish women filmmakers. A sizable catalogue of the exhibit, *Architectures of Gender: Contemporary Women's Art in Poland,* with essays on the subject, pictures of the artworks, and information on the artists, was published by the National Museum in Warsaw, 2003.

13. Maria Janion, *Kobiety i Duch Innosci* (Warsawa: Sic!, 1996), pp. 22–27.

14. Arjun Appadurai, *Modernity at Large* (Minneapolis: University of Minnesota Press, 1996), p. 15.

15. Ibid., p. 16.

16. See the writings of Polish authors Gombrowicz, Milosz, and Mrozek.

17. Janion, *Kobiety i Duch Innosci.*

18. Notable exceptions to this rule characterized the role of—and regard for—women during the underground struggles of World War II and following the December 1981 imposition of martial law.

19. Elzbieta Matynia, "Finding a Voice: Women in Postcommunist Central Europe," in Amrita Basu, ed., *The Challenge of Local Feminism: Women's Movements in Global Perspective* (Boulder, CO: Westview Press, 1995).

20. A feminist philosopher, Jolanta Brach-Czaina, writes about the urgency of such a task in "Przewodnik po polskiej literaturze feministycznej," *Res Publica Nowa* (November 2001).

21. Benedict Anderson writes at length about the problem of fatality in his *Imagined Communities* (London: Verso, 1983), p. 43.

22. The most exhaustive work on the subject, illustrated by a set of photographs, is the book by Izabella Kowalczyk, *Cialo i Wladza: Polska Sztuka Krytyczna lat 90* (Warsaw: Sic!, 2002). Pawel Leszkowicz, an art critic of the younger generation, authored several illuminating essays on the relationship between body, politics, and sexuality. One of his English language works, titled "Poland: The Shock of the Homoerotic," is published in *The Gay and Lesbian Review Worldwide* 10, no. 3 (May–June 2003).

23. The installation was exhibited from December 14, 2001, to January 20, 2002, in the Gdansk gallery Wyspa, located on the grounds of the Academy of Arts. On January 21, when the installation was taken down, packed into boxes, and the gallery was closed to the public, around thirty members of the League of Polish Families Party (LPR) entered the gallery. Among them were two ministers of the coalition government. The group, accompanied by representatives of the media, ignored the doorman's reminder that the exhibit was closed and demanded

to see it, or at least one of its elements, a massive steel cross. The artist, who was present in the gallery at the time, refused to unpack the boxes, as a new show was already in the process of being installed. The media recorded the aggressive behavior of the group. On March 2, 2002, Nieznalska was summoned to report to the local police precinct to inform the police about the whereabouts of the artwork, which had been requested by the court as criminal evidence. On March 14 she was summoned again to view the indictment records. The documentation revealed that thirteen indictment files had been filed by three private individuals and ten members of LPR, including the two holding ministerial positions. The basis of the indictment was the television footage of the exhibit. On April 12, 2002, the artist received a notice from the regional court in Gdansk, with the indictment citing chapter 24, article 196 of the Polish Penal Code on crimes against the freedom of conscience and religious belief. On July 18, 2003, the regional court in Gdansk, after seven sessions held on separate days in 2002 and 2003, pronounced Nieznalska guilty (see www.spam.art.pl).

24. Article 196 states, "Who offends religious feelings of other people, by publicly insulting objects of religious worship or places designated for public performance of religious rituals is liable to a fine or to penalty of limitation of freedom up to 2 years," *Dziennik Ustaw* 97.88.553.

25. www.spam.art.pl.

26. "Open Letter Concerning the Conviction of Polish Artist Dorota Nieznalska," http:lists.partners-intl.net/pipermail/women-east-west/2003-July.

27. Pawel Leszkowicz and Tomek Kitliński, *Love and Democracy: Reflections on the Homosexual Question in Poland* (Kraków: Aureus, 2005; in Polish with English, German, and French summaries).

28. "Instrukcja obslugi sadu nad Nieznalska," *Przekroj* (August 31, 2001).

29. Tomasz Piatek, "Sacrum czy Genitalium," *Gazeta Wyborcza*, July 22, 2003, p. 10.

30. "Nieszczesna Pasja: Dorota Miklaszewicz Talks with Rev. Krzysztof Niedaltowski of the Gdansk Archdiocese," *Gazeta Wyborcza*, July 21, 2003.

31. Jolanta Brach-Czaina, "Boze skrusz miecz, co siecze kraj" (God, Crush a Sword That Slashes the Country), *Krytyka Polityczna* 4 (2003): 114–119.

32. "Kara za Profanacje Krzyza," *Nasz Dziennik,* July 19, 2003.

33. Unlike most theories of deliberative democracy (Jon Elster, Joshua Cohen), which argue that democratic theory ought to focus on deliberative procedure alone and stay away from substantive principles (such as individual liberty or equal opportunity), I am following here the dissenting position proposed by Amy Gutmann and Dennis Thompson in "Deliberative Democracy Beyond Process," *Journal of Political Philosophy* 10 (2002): 153–174. See also a contribution calling for the reconstitution of place-based deliberative democracy by David Peritz, "Social Space for Deliberative Democracy," *Good Society* 10, no. 2 (2001).

NOTES FOR CHAPTER 8

1. Ivo Andric, *The Bridge on the Drina* (Chicago: University of Chicago Press, 1977).

2. I come very close here to the view represented by Anthony Appiah in his *Cosmopolitanism* (New York: W. W. Norton, 2006).

Index

Authoritarian rule, 4, 8, 147
AWB. *See* Afrikaner Resistance Movement
Azanian Peoples Organization (AZAPO), 103, 105

Badkowski, Lech, 175n26
Baka, Wladyslaw, 96
Bakhtin, Mikhail, 6, 169, 173n12; authoritative word and, 12; carnival and, 42, 51, 52; human relations and, 52; performative democracy and, 9
Baranczak, Stanislaw, 21, 40, 56, 175nn18, 27, 31; on *Velvet Prison*, 16
Baszkiewicz, Jan: on capitalist Poland, 106
Beckett, Samuel, 132
Beijing Conference (1995), 184n15
Berlin Wall, 4, 79, 87, 117
Beszelo, 64, 66
Bill of Rights (South Africa), 103, 112
Birth of the Barbie (Zebrowska), 159
Black Madonna of Czestochowa, 42, 130
Blood Ties (Kozyra), 161, 162
Blumsztajn, Seweryn, 3, 4
Boipatong, massacre in, 85, 181n11
Borderlands Center of Arts, Culture, and Nations, 167, 168
Borusewicz, Bogdan, 175n25
Bosberaad, 102
Botha, P. W., 81, 90
Botha, Roelof Frederik "Pik," 101
Brach-Czaina, Jolanta, 188n20
Brecht, Bertolt, 162
Breytenbach, Breyten, 93
Bridge on the Drina, The (Andric), 13, 165
Bujak, Zbigniew, 96, 106, 111
Buthelezi, Mangosuthu, 98, 104, 113

Captive Mind, The (Milosz), 15, 64
Carnival, 9–10, 12, 29, 42, 51, 52
Catholic Church, 35, 85, 125, 131, 134, 154; Communist regime and, 42; icons of, 129–130; intelligentsia and, 77

Cattelan, Maurizio, 161
Cautiously (Wysocka), 153, 155
CEDAW, 126
Cegielski Factory, 45
Censored, 138
Censorship, 2, 9, 16, 39, 43, 45; outsmarting, 41; preventive, 30, 44; restitution of, 160
Center for Contemporary Art "Laznia," 161
Central Committee, 18, 93, 96, 99, 106
Chagall, Marc, 119
Chakrabarty, Dipesh, 172n12
Charter 77: 9, 64
Chopin, Frederic, 129, 154
Church, the Left, and Dialogue, The (Michnik), 60
Cimoszewicz, Wlodzimierz, 70, 71
Ciosek, Stanislaw, 89, 91, 96, 111; on *Gazeta Wyborcza,* 106; Solidarity and, 92
Circle, or Triptych, 23
Citizens, 40, 68–77; through theater, 25–30
Citizens (film), 175n18, 176nn32, 37
Citizens Committee, Walesa and, 91, 93
Citizenship, 133, 142, 144, 146
Civic actions, 25, 31, 41, 66, 68, 132, 147
Civic force, 69–70
Civic knowledge, 11, 58, 81, 118
Civic movements, 29, 118, 135
Civilizing mission, 76
Civil liberties, 68
Civil society, 39, 41–42, 58, 135, 139, 156; concept of, 118; consensus-based, 136; discursive aspect of, 187n5; gender and, 144–147, 163; growth/vitality of, 126; police state and, 106; public sphere and, 144; regime and, 4; self-determination and, 65; stability and, 105; women's, 119, 124, 128, 146
Civil Society Initiative, 114
Civil war, 8, 86, 104, 105; cold, 83
Club 77 (Lodz), 23–24

Democracy, 49, 122; art and, 163;
building, 6, 8, 10, 40, 70, 74,
108, 116; change for, 64; citizens
in, 172n10; compromise and, 70;
consolidated, 12, 147; deliberative, 189n33; destabilization and,
105; direct, 5; domestic growth
and, 180n67; education about, 69;
globalization and, 119; gray, 12, 75;
institutionalized, 13, 54, 146; liberal,
6, 53; nonracial, 83; parliamentary,
66; performative, 5–12, 39, 42, 64,
80; procedural, 133, 145; representative, 6, 12; speech and, 7, 13;
substantive, 145, 147, 163; theater of,
50; transformation to, 10, 11, 79, 82,
141; women and, 135, 136
Democracy and Diversity Institute,
180nn7, 8, 180n12
Democracy Party (SD), 183n68
Democracy Seminars, 65–68, 69
Democratic opposition, 36, 66, 139
Democratic Party, 112
Democratic theory, 65, 189n33
Democratization, 8, 65, 96, 145
Derby-Lewis, Clive, 181n13
Derrida, Jacques, 69
Despiritualization, 158–161
Dewey, John, 74
Dialogue, 2, 6, 47, 71, 95; institu-
tionalizing of, 80; launching of, 81;
negotiation as, 83; vanishing of, 55
Diamantopoulou, Anna, 125
Dictatorship: collapse of, 68; negotia-
tions and, 84; transformation from,
11, 70, 79, 82
Dignity, 25, 48, 57, 61, 64; hope and,
13; humiliation and, 5; intellectual,
76; rights and, 5; self-respect and, 3
*Directives of the VII Congress of the Pol-
ish United Workers Party, The*, 36
Directly, 46
Discourse, 74; feminist, 135, 137; liberal, 129; patriarchal, 142; political,
134; public, 4, 13, 40, 69, 71, 141;
socialist, 129

Discrimination: gender, 99, 123,
129–130; race, 99
Dissent: culture of, 147; popular, 134;
spaces of, 147–153
Dissidents, 56–65
Diversity, 80, 151, 161–163, 168
Dostoyevsky, Fyodor, 173n12
Du Toit, André, 181n15

"Eastern Europe and Southern Africa:
Supporting Democracy and Devel-
opment" (conference), 87
Economic crisis, 18, 44, 121
Economic growth, 120, 129
Economic reforms, 129, 131; globaliza-
tion and, 119–121
Eighth Day Theater, 20, 21, 22, 23, 26,
30, 137, 173nn13, 14, 175n18
Electoral Act, 109
ELMOR, 175n30
Elster, Jon, 189n33
Elzenberg, Henryk, 64
EnGendering, 13, 141, 163
Entrance, The (Sosnowska), 149, 155
Equality, 80, 145, 157; gender, 118,
122, 123, 124, 128, 131–134, 139;
socialist, 2
Esterhuyse, Willie, 93
Ethnicity, 156, 162, 168
European Commission on Security and
Cooperation, 111
European Community (EC), 167
Europeanization, politics of, 121–126
European Union (EU), 74, 76, 77, 111,
135, 138, 146, 160; enlargement of,
119, 120, 121; negotiations, 123–
124; Poland and, 121, 122, 124, 125,
126, 133, 142
European Union (EU) Parliament, 111,
125
Evening Assembly, 27–28
*Everyday Life after the French Revolu-
tion*, 27
Evolution, 100; conciliation and, 62
Executive Committee (ANC), 113
Experience and the Future, 137

About the Author

Born and educated in Poland, **Elzbieta Matynia** is Associate Professor of Sociology and Liberal Studies at the New School for Social Research and Director of the New School's Transregional Center for Democratic Studies, through which she has developed innovative modes of learning and research grounded in international academic collaboration.